God, the Mind's Desire

This book reconfigures the basic problem of Christian thinking or theological cognition as a twofold demand for integrity: integrity of reason and integrity of transcendence. Centring around a provocative yet penetratingly faithful re-reading of Kant's empirical realism, and drawing on an impelling confluence of contemporary thinkers, Paul D. Janz argues that theology's 'referent' must be located within present empirical reality. Rigorously reasoned yet refreshingly accessible throughout, this book provides an important, attentively informed alternative to the growing trends toward obscurantism, radicalization, and anti-reason in many recent assessments of theological cognition, while remaining equally alert to the hazards of traditional metaphysics. In the book's culmination, epistemology and Christology converge around problems of noetic authority and orthodoxy with a kind of innovation, depth and straightforwardness that readers of theology at all levels of philosophical acquaintance will find illuminating.

PAUL D. JANZ is Assistant Professor of Philosophy and Religious Studies, Trinity Western University, Canada.

Cambridge Studies in Christian Doctrine

Edited by
Professor COLIN GUNTON, *King's College London*
Professor DANIEL W. HARDY, *University of Cambridge*

Cambridge Studies in Christian Doctrine is an important series which aims
to engage critically with the traditional doctrines of Christianity, and
at the same time to locate and make sense of them within a secular
context. Without losing sight of the authority of scripture and the
traditions of the church, the books in this series subject pertinent
dogmas and credal statements to careful scrutiny, analysing them in
light of the insights of both church and society, and thereby practise
theology in the fullest sense of the word.

Titles published in the series

God, the Mind's Desire
Reference, Reason and
Christian Thinking

PAUL D. JANZ

CAMBRIDGE
UNIVERSITY PRESS

PUBLISHED BY THE PRESS SYNDICATE OF THE UNIVERSITY OF CAMBRIDGE
The Pitt Building, Trumpington Street, Cambridge, United Kingdom

CAMBRIDGE UNIVERSITY PRESS
The Edinburgh Building, Cambridge, CB2 2RU, UK
40 West 20th Street, New York, NY 10011-4211, USA
477 Williamstown Road, Port Melbourne, VIC 3207, Australia
Ruiz de Alarcón 13, 28014 Madrid, Spain
Dock House, The Waterfront, Cape Town 8001, South Africa

http://www.cambridge.org

First published 2004

Printed in the United Kingdom at the University Press, Cambridge

Typefaces Lexicon No. 2 9/13 pt. and Lexicon No. 1   *System* LATEX 2$_\varepsilon$ [TB]

A catalog record for this book is available from the British Library

Library of Congress Cataloging in Publication data

Janz, Paul D.
God, the mind's desire : reference, reason and Christian thinking / Paul D. Janz.
    p.   cm. – (Cambridge studies in Christian doctrine ; 11)
Includes bibliographical references and index.
ISBN 0-521-82241-6 –
1. Philosophical theology.   2. Knowledge, Theory of.   3. Metaphysics.
4. Kant, Immanuel, 1724-1804.   I. Title.   II. Series.
BT40.J36   2004
230′.01 – dc22   2003065449

ISBN 0 521 82241 6 hardback

For *Beth*

Contents

Acknowledgements

I am grateful to all who have contributed in many important ways to the writing and successful completion of this book. First of all I am immensely indebted to Daniel Hardy, who from the very outset not only shared my basic vision for the book, but who often understood it, and grasped what I perceived as its promise, in deeper and richer ways than I myself had initially been able to see. His critical wisdom and incisive intellection has served as a vital source of focus and inspiration throughout the writing process. I am equally grateful to David Ford, my doctoral supervisor at Cambridge from 1998 to 2000, under whose creative and motivating guidance many of the leading ideas in this volume began to converge and take shape. I would also like to acknowledge the kind help of Kevin Taylor and Katharina Brett at Cambridge University Press who have been most supportive during the book's preparation. I thank Trinity Western University, where I now teach, for its support not only materially, by way of providing course-relief during the last year of writing, but also personally and professionally, by way of stimulating intellectual exchange and generous encouragement from faculty, students and administration alike. I am grateful to the Social Sciences and Humanities Research Council of Canada for making available a research grant in the final year of writing. Finally, I owe the deepest gratitude of all to my wife Beth, without whose patience, forbearance and loving encouragement over my many months of intense mental preoccupation 'elsewhere', this book would most certainly not have been written.

1

A reconnaissance of theology and epistemology

1 Theological integrity between reductionism and positivism

The idiomatic phrase 'Christian thinking' in the sense of theological cognition means to identify something specific. Its fundamental problem has traditionally been stated something like this: 'How can human discourse refer meaningfully to a transcendent, incomprehensible and hidden God?' Theologians of up to a generation ago often called this the most basic 'formal' question of theology, and by this they meant to designate the possibility of an introductory theological exercise, in some sense logically prior to the study of specific Christian doctrines per se, in which the question just stated, or the even more concise formulation 'How is Christian theology possible?', is given serious consideration as a problem in its own right. As a preliminary or 'formal' exercise it was often referred to more technically as a 'propaedeutic' or a 'prolegomenon' to Christian doctrine. Yet this was not meant in any temporally linear sense as an *actual* condition or prerequisite for the possibility of engaging meaningfully in theological endeavours. (After all, theology is often practised very fruitfully without a great deal of attention to the question of how the theological enterprise itself is possible.) It was meant, rather, simply to identify, on a level more general than the specific doctrines, certain fundamental parameters or indispensable conditions of thinking within which those doctrines come meaningfully to be engaged. In other words, although this exercise is not an actual methodological prerequisite through which proper theological engagement must always pass, it is nonetheless an indispensable orientation to which theology must again and again return in order to test its orthodoxy and assure its meaningfulness.

However, as indispensable as this kind of orientation is, it is clearly evident that the formal question per se has fallen into disuse in the last several decades. There are several reasons for this, two among which are most
prominent. The first has to do with the by now tedious and standardly
intransigent stand-off between 'natural theology' and 'revelational theology', to which this formal kind of questioning has invariably seemed to
lead in the past century.[1] This of course has been most prominently manifest in what many would today agree have become the rather unimaginative and stereotypical polarizations between Thomism and Barthianism
as the main exemplars of each. (Recent scholarship suggests increasingly
that Aquinas and Barth may share a great deal more in common on these
formal questions than the traditional scholarly consensus has been able or
willing to acknowledge.) At any rate, few today would deny the tiresome
predictability and present stagnancy of that stand-off. The second reason
for the abandonment of this kind of questioning has to do with the growing tendency, in an array of disciplines including theology, simply to deflate any questions that appear to lead to irresolvable conflict (the deeper
'post-modern' worry here is that irresolvable conflict tends to yield 'dualistic' answers) and to declare those questions themselves, by very reason
of their intractability, to be misstated or 'un-genuine'. If one adds to this
the prevalent perception that these 'formal' questions *must* be anachronis-
tic by virtue of their being framed in the dualistic language of 'form' and
'content', it is easy to see how the prospects of any such propaedeutic theological enterprise have come to be viewed as doubly foredoomed.

There is a third reason, I think, for the current avoidance of this kind of
questioning: namely, that in a theological environment where the most
visible theological-philosophical exchange often takes place amid such
qualifiers as radical, startling, subversive, erotic or profound, the character
of what I am outlining here as an enquiry into Christian thinking or theological reasoning may initially appear to be somewhat drier fare. Yet I hope
to show that although the present focus, at least initially, will be around
the rather less seductive terminology of epistemology and consciousness,
reference and intention, anti-realism and realism, act and being, it need
by no means signify any less important or less relevant, nor certainly for
that matter any less interesting or stimulating a study. Indeed there is a

---

1. Roughly, natural theology has typically been seen as operating on the basis of a continuum
between reason (or nature) and revelation, and revelational theology on the basis of a
humanly unbridgeable break between the two.

growing group of thinkers today, even, or perhaps especially, those proceeding from continental influences, who demonstrate forcefully that a reclamation of the more traditional if currently less fashionable philosophical concerns of modesty, attentiveness, clarity, logical consistency and integrity, and so on, need by no means suggest merely unimaginative 'incremental adjustments to a work already in place or positions already established'.[2] On the contrary, approaches that seek robustly to revive attention to these kinds of virtues can be strong arguments against 'the assumption – one that is virtually constitutive of the modern conception of what it means to be a philosopher on the continent – that originality and, yes, truth are always and only the result of a rush to extremes or a radicalization of thought'.[3] There are similar and equally compelling trends currently underway in analytical philosophy.

Whatever the reasons for its having fallen out of favour, I want to argue for a return to this kind of questioning on the grounds that we ignore it or deflate it at great peril, more specifically at the very imperilling of orthodoxy itself. Yet with a view to avoiding the standard polarizations and stalemates, as just described, I want to ask the question in a somewhat different way. I propose to reframe the 'formal' question of Christian thinking – 'How can human discourse refer meaningfully to a transcendent God?' – as a twofold demand for integrity: a demand for the integrity of reason, or rational integrity, and a demand for the integrity of transcendence, or revelational integrity. More specifically, instead of pegging the varying approaches to theological reasoning in the typical conflicting manner at opposing poles (natural/revelational, Thomist/Barthian etc.), I plan rather to speak in terms of two polarities or extremes between which orthodox theology properly seeks to navigate its way. I shall designate these extremes by the terms 'reductionism' and 'positivism', which correspond exactly to the emphasis of one kind of integrity at the expense or to the exclusion of the other.

Reductionism in its most basic definition is simply the explanation of one thing in terms of another. It can occur in any number of ways and contexts. So, for example, in the cognitive sciences reductionism occurs when it is claimed that the success of psychological theories can be fully accounted for by neuroscientific theories, or more basically that

2. Stephen Adam Schwartz in the introduction to an important new book by Vincent Descombes, *The Mind's Provisions* (Princeton: Princeton University Press, 2001), p. xiv.
3. Schwartz in Descombes, *The Mind's Provisions*, p. xiv.

psychological states *just are* bodily states. The same sort of claim is made by radically reductive materialist philosophers of mind (and some functionalists), who maintain that the mind *just is* the brain or that consciousness itself can be fully accounted for by physical functions inside the head. Another form of reductionism is logicism, which explains mathematics as a sub-discipline of logic, and so on. But, for philosophical realists at least, the broadest and most pervasive kind of philosophical reductionism is *idealism*. Idealism is deemed to be reductive because, in any of its historically varying degrees and guises, it at bottom does not want to allow for the full perceiver-independent integrity of a world outside the mind, but rather always demands to make the explanation of the world in some way necessarily dependent on the perceiver. Idealism thus reduces what the realist maintains is a world that exists in certain ways, whether it is perceived as such or not, to something the explanation of which is, in one way or another, necessarily dependent on the sensory and mental perceptions ('ideas') of the perceiver. In this light then, when we come to the analysis of religion or religious discourse, we find that the most common form of reductionism occurs precisely in this idealistic way: that is, in the explanation of religious phenomena or the content of theological statements in terms of 'projection theories', whether of psychological or sociological origin, for example as wish-fulfilment or fear-coping mechanisms along, say, Freudian, Feuerbachian or Weberian lines, and so on. All of these remain essentially forms of idealism inasmuch as they make religious experience and the subject matter of theological statements at bottom a product of mental or psycho-social processes or ideas.

However, it is important to recognize that for theology, unlike philosophy, it is not only idealism that can be reductionist in this sense. Philosophical realism or realist treatments of religion and theology can also qualify as forms of reductionism, even when they seek fastidiously to avoid the charge of naturalism. One sees this, for example, in different ways in the work Paul Tillich or John Hick, where religious transcendence, characterized as the 'ground of being' or as 'ultimate reality', is indeed given a kind of 'real' or perceiver-independent supremacy and autonomy. But even though they thus manage to avoid idealism (mind-dependence), what both of these approaches finally leave us with is a view of religious transcendence that in the end is still explainable in terms of something like a 'world enigma'. This effectively commits the same reductionist error as the idealistic projection theories, if in a somewhat different way, for it reduces transcendence merely to something mysterious within immanence (e.g., ground of being, ultimate reality) and thus violates the integrity of transcendence. In more current language, the error made in this 'realist' sense is that of construing the reality of God merely in terms of 'ontological difference', as if God's transcendent otherness were expressible as just another higher and more mysterious version of immanentist otherness or difference; or in other words as if God's otherness could be understood in terms of the same ontological difference that exists between me and you. At bottom then, the first kind of error or extreme that orthodox theology seeks to avoid is the reduction of theological subject matter to any kind of natural explanation, even if that for which explanation is sought remains insolubly mysterious (world enigma). The point is that reductionism by definition, whether in the form of idealism or realism, compromises the integrity of transcendence, in the endeavour to make theological discourse about transcendence genuinely meaningful or referential.

The error at the other extreme is positivism. Positivism gives theological subject matter a positive autonomy and authority that is set totally apart from any sort of natural (roughly, rational or empirical) scrutiny. Or in other words, it is to 'posit' transcendence or revelation in such a way that it remains fully authoritative over matters of reason and sense and yet also fully immune from the justificatory demands or jurisdictions of these. It is precisely in this sense that the logical positivism of twentieth-century analytical philosophy was 'positivistic': it posited the inviolability of its two principles of cognitive meaningfulness – that is, statements are meaningful or intelligible if they are either empirically verifiable or analytically true (true by definition) – even though these principles themselves are neither empirically verifiable nor analytically true. It is this same tendency within theology that Bonhoeffer claims to detect in Karl Barth, when he accuses Barth of engaging in a 'positivism of revelation'. Again, it is debatable to what extent Barth is really guilty of this (perhaps any more than Aquinas is of reductionism) even if he may tend in that direction.[4] But the preliminary point has been made sufficiently clearly: positivism in theology is any position that seeks to uphold the integrity of transcendence (or revelation) by giving up the integrity of reason or of natural enquiry. Against this backdrop, the aim of the present study is to preserve integrity

---

4. A more obvious example of this extreme can be seen in what has come to be known as the Radical Orthodoxy project. Barth at least accords reason an authority in its own sphere whereas Radical Orthodoxy (at least in John Milbank) sees reason as self-destructive when it is not rooted in revelation or transcendence. (I have actually argued elsewhere that Radical Orthodoxy tends, relatedly, more toward a kind of gnosticism than positivism.)

on both levels: that is, without being drawn to the extremes at either end, to which emphasis of one kind of integrity at the expense of the other will inevitably lead.

One further introductory point must be made here with regard to the term 'meaningful' or 'meaningful reference' (which has already occurred several times in these opening paragraphs) with respect to the way I will be employing it in this book, especially within the context of speaking meaningfully of God. The point, most concisely, is that the word 'meaningful' can be used intelligibly in the present context without requiring a prior full-fledged exposition of a theory of meaning. For all that the term purports to designate here is the possibility of 'aboutness' or intentional reference in human discourse, and this is something entirely different from the more technical and abstract metalinguistic concerns about the 'meaning of meaning' as explored within the philosophy of language and linguistic theory. These questions are indeed important, perhaps especially so for theology where nowadays scant work is being done in that field. But insofar as they seek to approach the problem of meaning on a more general and abstract level, detached from human discourse (even if somehow claiming to be inclusive of it), those kinds of questions aim at something fundamentally different from the focus of the present study. In fact, the sense in which I am equating 'meaningfulness' with 'aboutness' or 'intentional reference' here, or making these terms univocal or identical, is not really asking about the 'meaning of meaning' in any interesting sense at all. The equation rather expresses something merely trivially true or tautological: that is, something that is true simply by the definition of these terms themselves as they pertain to human discourse. For example, when I ask you what you *mean* by a certain statement I am simply asking you to explain or to give a further account of what you *intend* to *refer* to by that statement, or what you intend that statement to express or to be about; and we do not need to come to a prior theoretical agreement on the 'meaning of meaning' for our discursive exchange to be successful or for there to be a genuinely communicative meeting of minds around a particular subject matter, whether agreeing or disagreeing.[5]

In fact we may engage successfully or intelligibly in discourse even if we disagree on virtually all the standard aspects of a theory of meaning.

---

5. It is important to note in the same vein that by asking about the meaningfulness of a statement in this trivial or tautological sense, I am not so much concerned with its truth or falsity but rather only with its intelligibility as an assertion of reference.

Thus, for example, we may disagree, in what is perhaps the most traditional sense, on whether the meanings of statements are to be defined at bottom by their 'truth conditions' (i.e., by correspondence to 'what is the case' in the world) or in terms of their 'use' (i.e., by the coherence of a statement within a certain context or worldview): in other words, I may be a realist and you an idealist about the theory of meaning. We may disagree further, and even more metalinguistically, about whether meaning is centred in some universal structure of language or in a universal structure of innate learning capacities, or in neither of these; or on whether meaning is to be assessed according to the 'intension' or the 'extension' of an expression; or on whether sentence-meaning or word-meaning should have priority in a theory of meaning, and so on.[6] We may have opposing views on any or all of these legitimate theoretical questions. But none of these differences will in the least affect the tautological or trivially true nature of the claim that when you ask me what I mean by a certain statement you are concerned *by definition* with what I understand that statement to be about; nor will our theoretical differences affect my ability to understand the question as such. Indeed, our very ability to disagree in theory on these matters, and to express ourselves accordingly, already presupposes a shared understanding of discursive meaningfulness as intentional reference.[7]

In other words, the claim I am making here is really only a very minimal one, one that serves merely to emphasize that it will be entirely from within this tautological or true-by-definition sense of aboutness or intentional reference that the question of meaningfulness in theological discourse will come to be posed in this book. Nevertheless, far from this 'trivial truth' making the theological task any easier, the very clarification of it as such only serves to set our initial problem into even sharper relief. For *transcendence, by definition*, can never be a 'referent' of reasoning in the way that *meaningful* discourse, *by definition* ('trivially'), demands that it must be. (Or conversely anything that could be a referent of thought would by that

6. See, e.g., Donald Davidson, 'Truth and Meaning' in *Inquiries into Truth and Interpretation* (Oxford: Oxford University Press 1984), pp. 17–36. See also Hilary Putnam, 'The Meaning of "Meaning"', in, *Language, Mind and Knowledge*, Minnesota Studies in the Philosophy of Science Vol. VII (Minneapolis: University of Minnesota Press, 1975), pp. 131–2. 'Intension' roughly defines meaning around the idea that sets of things have associated 'concepts' that they actually instantiate individually. 'Extension' roughly associates meaning with the set of objects in the world that a term seeks to identify.

7. It is of course true that a currently very prominent anti-rationalist sector of 'post-modern' thought will declare this whole philosophical enterprise to be a 'ruse', or to be fabricated and self-serving in the first place. But that is another story, with its own set of problems, and we shall discuss it extensively as a separate matter in chapter 2.

very possibility relinquish its claim to transcendence.) The 'trivial' or tautological question of meaningfulness on the epistemological level thus becomes precisely the intractable 'formal' problem of theological thinking stated at the outset of this chapter.

2   Theology and rational obligation within the basic structure of this book

With the foregoing distinctions and goals in mind, I want now to step laterally and make some parallel observations that will serve as a guide into an overview of the book's basic structure and main sections.

Few scholars today would dispute the assessment that over the past several decades we have been witnessing something like an epistemological revolution. However disparately aligned and irreconcilable the several sides may otherwise seem, on the *fact* of the 'revolution' itself, at least, there will be agreement on all fronts: from the anti-rational 'end of epistemology' advocates, through the varying shades of anti-realism, to the group of stalwarts still remaining in the realist camp. Now I want to suggest that at the heart of this revolution there is a very simple question which not only captures, perhaps better than any other, what this revolution is essentially about, but on the basis of which the current intellectual landscape can be mapped out in a particularly helpful way. The question is this: Are there any *intrinsic obligations* to thinking or reason per se? Or more fully, are there are any *inherent* features of thinking or discourse by which particular instances of it could be deemed to be 'proper' or 'improper', genuine or specious? This is not any new question. It has been asked in various ways and at various times by a wide array of prominent thinkers. For example, a persistently relevant essay by Kant entitled 'What is Orientation in Thinking?'[8] was trying to address precisely this question from within an epistemological context equally as volatile or revolutionary as the present one. And what I am claiming here, with this in mind, is that by laying out the present epistemological revolution against this question of intrinsic obligations or orientation in thinking, we will see unfolding a spectrum of responses to it, a spectrum that divides naturally and heuristically into three broad sectors.

---

8. This was written in 1786. It currently appears most prominently in English in Immanuel Kant, *Kant: Political Writings* (second edition), H. S. Reiss (ed.), (Cambridge: Cambridge University Press, 1991), pp. 237–49.

2.1 A spectrum of obligation in thinking

If we now imagine this spectrum mapped out before us, we see at the one end of it a group of outlooks that simply answers the question at hand negatively. These are the self-described anti-rational or anti-epistemological outlooks; and what makes them anti-rational, at bottom, is precisely the denial that thinking or reason contains any intrinsic obligations or that there is any *inherent* normativity to rational discourse or processes. Because of their current popularity and present influence across broad sectors of the human sciences and theology, they are often taken to be a novel (i.e., 'post-modern' in the straightforward sense of the term) development, but they are not really anything new as such. In fact, they are, in basic respects, the same thing as what Kant was trying to describe two centuries ago in the forementioned essay when he used the term 'rational unbelief' to identify a group of intellectual outlooks that were then operating, in his words, according to 'the maxim of the independence of reason from its *own need*'[9] (original emphasis).

Expanding on this for the contemporary context, we could say that the current anti-rational trend involves precisely something like a shift away from the view of rationality arising *naturally* as 'need' (and thus normatively, orientatingly) and toward the view of rationality arising unnaturally or *artificially* as 'power' (and thus 'hegemonically' and 'self-legitimizingly'). More specifically, in ways that will be made clear below, the rejection of such a 'need-oriented' view of reason involves at bottom the rejection of the traditional consciousness-centred or semantic language of intention, reference and aboutness. The embrace of a 'power-oriented' view of reason involves the adoption in its place of the tactic-centred or syntactical language of 'coping mechanisms', or 'performativity', or non-purposive tactics in writing or in speech acts, and so on. We will discuss these anti-rational or negative responses to the question of rational obligation in some detail in chapter 2, but the real focus of the book thereafter will be on the different kinds of responses occurring on the positive side of the spectrum. The reason for this will be obvious enough: Any approach that rejects the idea of intrinsic obligations in discourse

9. Kant, *Political Writings*, p. 248. Kant's target at that point was a particular group of anti-rationalist outlooks, prominent among which was the radically fideistic pietism of Jacobi. The group of anti-rationalists today tend, to the contrary, to be from more atheistic quarters. But this is not always the case. For example, the Radical Orthodoxy project, cited above, is anti-rational in the sense I am describing here; indeed the radical pietism of Jacobi is among its formative influences.

will thereby also be unable to accommodate any talk of integrity, which orthodox theology with its intrinsic claim to authority must by definition be able to do, and which this book wants to make central. The summary contention of chapter 2 then, will be that, despite the good prospects they may initially seem to offer on several levels, nevertheless, because these anti-rational approaches cannot respond to the demands of integrity implicit in the claim to orthodoxy, their promise proves to be hollow and their strategies unworkable for theology.

It is at this point that the hard task of articulating a positive theory of theological reasoning begins. The task is made difficult in part because even as we move away from anti-epistemological responses at the far negative end of our spectrum and back into affirming the legitimacy of genuine philosophical or intentional-referential questioning for theological purposes,[10] we find that we are still, within contemporary theories of knowledge, confronted with the complex task of evaluating a widely disparate array of possible *positive* responses to the question of intrinsic obligations or orientation in thinking. As a way of gaining some mentally visual perspective on this, we can, by returning to our spectrum image, configure the affirmative responses to this question as taking place broadly between the two opposing poles of classical foundationalism and holism. But it is important as such to reiterate the proviso that, even though I speak here in terms of 'opposing poles', we are now dealing only with the positive 'subsection', so to speak, of the more complete spectrum of all possible responses to the question of rational orientation or obligation (from positive to negative), such that both foundationalism and holism, in the sense that I am speaking of them here, seek to offer different kinds of *affirmative* answers to the question at hand.[11]

With this in mind, we can now lay out a general comparison between foundationalism and holism in the following way. Foundationalism is the well-known (and currently highly polemicized) view that seeks to justify

---

10. I will explain the significance of philosophical questioning as intentional-referential questioning in the next chapter.

11. One of the reasons that this proviso is so important to bear in mind is that 'holism' in current usage has itself become a highly ambiguous term that is employed in confusing ways. It is used not only in the positive epistemological context in which I am employing it here, but also in a decidedly anti-epistemological vein, and the term comes to signify something importantly different in each case. In the former, rational sense, holism appeals to a kind of coherence theory which reflects certain basic commitments to normative stability. In the latter, anti-rational sense, it constitutes a radically free-floating kind of coherence. We shall discuss this distinction in detail in the following chapter, but it is in the former, normative epistemological sense that I use the term at this juncture.

intrinsic rational obligation in discourse based on certain 'foundational' assertions: that is, assertions that cannot themselves be called into question, or that are 'indubitable'. (Traditionally 'indubitability' has meant either rational incorrigibility or empirical self-evidence.) It is of course undeniable that the centre of gravity has in recent decades shifted decisively away from foundationalism, and this to such an extent that it is now decidedly a minority view. But there remain, as we shall see, prominent advocates of newer versions of it, versions that are articulated in more temperate, self-critical and less self-assured ways than the stereotypical understanding of foundationalism. Holism by contrast (with the crucial distinction in the foregoing footnote borne firmly in mind) will seek to justify rational normativity or assess rational obligation for discourse, not based on indubitable or incorrigible foundational principles, but rather based on how an assertion contributes to the overall coherence or reflective equilibrium of the entire context from which or into which it is spoken. In sum, as different kinds of affirmative responses to the question of intrinsic rational obligation or orientation in thinking, foundationalism would construe these obligations as stable and fixed, and holism (in the *epistemological* sense of the term) as in some way stable but not fixed.

2.2 Philosophy's perpetual polarities: anti-realism and realism

Now the reader who is somewhat familiar with recent developments in epistemology will recognize that all of this maps generally onto another, currently more visible and prominent intellectual dispute. I refer to what has come to be known as the anti-realism/realism debate, where realism sits roughly at the foundationalist end of the positive spectrum and anti-realism at the holist end. At the risk of being overly repetitive it must be reiterated as such that anti-realism in this dispute does not signify anything like the negative anti-rationalist responses discussed briefly above, and which will be the main focus of chapter 2. Anti-realism is not anti-rationalism, despite the fact that in many current discussions the two are routinely conflated. The main point of differentiation between the two in our context is once again that anti-realism responds positively to the question of intrinsic obligations or orientation in thinking whereas anti-rationalism denies any such intrinsic authoritative orientation. Richard Rorty, for example, a self-described anti-rationalist, is fully aware of this and is continually at pains to distance himself from the anti-realism with which others frequently and erroneously try to associate him.[12]

The best way to understand the current anti-realism/realism debate is to see it as just the latest manifestation of the perennial idealism/realism conflict, a dispute that has been at the centre of philosophical debate in different guises ever since the time of the Greeks, and that continues to re-emerge in new forms. In current discussion, for example, this perennial conflict is also often described as reflective of the two most basic and op-posing temperaments of philosophical enquiry: one 'internalist', espous-ing a perceiver-dependent view of reality (idealism or anti-realism), the other 'externalist', espousing a perceiver-independent view of reality (re-alism). But there is another, arguably more helpful and less fractious way of configuring the perennial dispute; and this is in its even more venera-ble formulation as a disagreement about whether human *sensation* or *intel-lect* should be given priority in philosophical questioning.[13] This disagree-ment is seen perhaps most formatively in the ancient conflict between *ais-thesis* and *noiesis*. (The atomism of Democritus, which privileges sensation, is often contrasted with Platonism and neo-Platonism here, which privi-leges thinking. Aristotle, like Kant after him in a different way, sought a harmonization of the two, even though Aristotle is often somewhat mis-leadingly contrasted with Plato here, as privileging the former.) The same distinction underlies the conflict between empiricism and rationalism, between scepticism and dogmatism, albeit here with a more negative em-phasis (we shall discuss this extensively in chapter 6), and of course, com-ing full circle, it has been very prominently visible within British and American philosophy in the debate between idealism and realism.

It is in connection with this long and highly visible history then, that anti-realism and realism will in chapter 3 become something like a spring-board for an extended enquiry into rational integrity for theological pur-poses. We will initially focus on Hilary Putnam and Thomas Nagel as contemporary exemplifications of the respective sides of the traditional

12. See, e.g., Richard Rorty, 'Realism, Anti-realism, and Pragmatism', in Christopher Kulp (ed.), *Realism/Antirealism and Epistemology* (Oxford: Rowman and Littlefield 1997), pp. 149–71; and Kulp (ed.), *Realism/Antirealism and Epistemology*, pp. 7, 11.
13. We may set aside for the time being the suspicions of dualism that anti-rationalists may see lurking in this distinction between sensory and noetic faculties. This will be addressed in chapter 2. However, it can already be said at this juncture that these suspicions often (but not always) reflect a bias against dualism that is applied so undiscriminatingly and uncritically that it borders on a kind of obsession, and thus is itself 'irrational', in the 'unconsidered' sense of that term.

debate, before moving on in chapter 4 to Donald MacKinnon, whose simple but highly illuminating reconfiguration of idealism and realism as a problem of learning – specifically, the question of whether learning is at bottom to be understood as 'invention' (idealism or anti-realism) or 'discovery' (realism) – opens up the debate in important new ways. In MacKinnon, for the first time, we will begin to see the fruitfulness of framing the traditional debate in terms of different approaches to *finality*. We will also for the first time see the theological question of transcendence come to be posed from within the anti-realism/realism framework straightforwardly as a question of *reference* (meaningfulness). Nevertheless, at the end of chapter 4, all three broad types of approaches on our spectrum – anti-rationalism, anti-realism and realism – will be found in varying degrees to be incapable of yielding satisfactory answers to the problem of how reference to the transcendent is possible; this, however, with the proviso that realism will have been shown to be preferable among the three in one particular sense: namely in its capability of providing at least a suitable preliminary disposition for theological questioning.

2.3 Philosophy's perpetual polarities: act and being

In hopes of making progress beyond these modest but important results, the book now moves outside of the stricter anti-realism/realism debate to what is probably the most basic or most broad of all philosophical polarities: the question of act and being. The guide in exploring this will not be Hegel or Heidegger, as might be expected, but rather Dietrich Bonhoeffer, whose early work, *Akt und Sein* (*Act and Being*),[14] approaches the philosophical question specifically with theological purposes in mind. One of the most important contributions that the consideration of act and being brings to our overall focus is that it problematizes the very subjectivity or anthropocentricity out of which all the other polar outlooks proceed, yet which they all either ignore or trivialize. The act and being configuration will thus yield important new insights with regard to the theological demand for rational integrity in the face of transcendence or revelation. But here too the final result will be that human beings are not capable of placing themselves into the truth about themselves.

As we come to the end of chapter 5 then, we find that, although we have made a certain amount of progress negatively (i.e., where *not* to begin in

---

14. Dietrich Bonhoeffer, *Akt und Sein*, Hans-Richard Reuther (ed.), Dietrich Bonhoeffer Werke, 16 vols. (Munich: Christian Kaiser Verlag, 1988), vol. II.

trying to build a contemporary theory of theological reasoning), we appear nonetheless to have arrived at a rather inauspicious intermediate destination with respect to making any positive progress in our enquiry into Christian thinking. The problem, specifically, is that at every turn in attempting to speak *meaningfully* about *God* – that is, in a way that preserves both the integrity of reason (i.e., discourse that is genuinely *meaningful*) and the integrity of transcendence (i.e., discourse that is genuinely *about God*) – at every turn, we find ourselves thrown back onto some configuration or other of philosophy's perpetual polarizations, and thus relatedly to unacceptable answers in the theological enterprise as well, since these polarities will always demand to treat transcendence inadmissibly either as invention or discovery or as some combination of the two. It seems at this point then, having all but exhausted the standardly diverging philosophical ways of approaching intentional reference or meaningfulness – *aisthesis/noiesis*, idealism/realism, empiricism/rationalism, antirealism/realism, act/being and so on – it seems then, if we are to have any hope at all of making further progress on the theological question, that we will have to find some other way of asking that question. It will have to be a way that is different from any of the standard philosophical approaches, all of which lead back into philosophy's perpetual polarities, yet which nevertheless, unlike the anti-rational responses, leaves the possibility of rational integrity intact while preserving the integrity of transcendence.

2.4   The Kantian inversion of all of these polarities

In fact, what I have just been describing is (in its philosophical aspect) not only the most basic initial premise of Kant's *Critique of Pure Reason*, but it is also the driving impetus for his undertaking what he calls a 'Copernican revolution' in philosophy more broadly, a revolution in which all of these standard philosophical questions are turned radically on their heads. Unfortunately, this 'revolutionary' core of Kant's philosophy has been largely overlooked in recent Anglo-American discussion,[15] even though it

---

15. I will discuss this and the reasons for it in chapter 6. Putnam's professed 'indebtedness' to Kant is really an indebtedness to only half of Kant and as such still reflects clear vestiges of a strong Strawsonian bias (I will explain this below), and accordingly constitutes a fundamental misconstrual of integral elements of Kantian epistemology. In other words, despite the value of Putnam's work on Kant in important ways, it is in equally important ways very far from what Kant himself is attempting to do, as we shall see in chapters 3 and 6.

is pervasive and pivotal in the *Critique*'s own development, to say nothing of its obvious and important relevance to contemporary anti-realism/realism issues. The book thus turns in chapter 6 to an examination of this revolutionary character of Kant's epistemology with a view to determining how this might help us forward in the problem of theological reasoning. Again, Kant seems especially relevant and promising for this endeavour because the polarizations with which until now we have found ourselves confronted at every turn (*aisthesis/noiesis*, idealism/realism, act/being etc.) are precisely the polarizations against which the *Critique* builds its own starting point. More specifically, Kant actually opens the *Critique of Pure Reason* by deploring philosophy's perennial stand-offs, especially lamenting the fact that these perpetual conflicts have throughout philosophical history invariably led to some form or other of the opposing intellectual stalemates of scepticism and dogmatism, both of which breed philosophical 'stagnancy'.

It is in hopes of renewing the possibility of progress in philosophy in the face of these prevailing deadlocks that Kant then proposes his Copernican inversion of the traditional approaches, in which many of the most basic questions of philosophy come to be asked in a fundamentally different way. It is vitally important to be clear about how central the *revolutionary* character of the *Critique of Pure Reason* really is to its proper comprehension.[16] The fundamental philosophical inversions that it proposes are to be understood quite literally; and I ask the reader to bear with me in the following few sentences in which a rather cumbersome use of qualifiers, parentheses and caveats must unavoidably be resorted to in order to explain in a brief summary form the basic sense of what Kant is trying to achieve in his 'Copernican revolution' vis-à-vis 'all previous philosophy'. Two inversions are most central. First, the traditional 'empirical idealism' (this is idealism in the standard sense addressed thus far, as reflected in *aisthesis* or empirical approaches; i.e., outlooks that privilege sensation in philosophical enquiry, and which invariably – because of the fallibility of sensory phenomena – end up placing the reality of the material world in doubt, leading to *scepticism*): this traditional 'empirical idealism' is now to be inverted to yield what Kant calls 'empirical realism', which avoids the scepticism of its opposite. Second, the traditional 'metaphysical

16. When approached ignoring this revolutionary character, the *Critique of Pure Reason* can indeed be seen, as anti-Kantian polemicists like Strawson and Pritchard have claimed, as 'perverse', 'disastrous' and 'incoherent'.

realism', or in Kant's terms, 'transcendental realism'[17] (this is realism in the standard sense addressed thus far, as reflected in *noiesis* or rationalist approaches; i.e., outlooks that privilege intellect over sensibility in philosophical enquiry and that have invariably led to *dogmatism*, a term Kant uses polemically to denote the unjustifiable rational positing of a 'more ultimate' supra-sensible reality beyond the sensible world): this traditional 'transcendental realism' (metaphysical realism) is also inverted to yield what Kant calls 'transcendental idealism', which avoids the dogmatism of its opposite, and yet which, despite its name, is utterly different (actually the opposite) of any kind of idealism or anti-realism we have encountered thus far.[18] These are the two most fundamental inversions of the *Critique* and both will be explored in detail.

But for present purposes it must be noted further that this latter inversion (transcendental idealism) includes Kant's famous doctrine of noumena or things-in-themselves, a doctrine that, as the scholarly consensus today would broadly allow, has 'in the past been the victim of more various misinterpretation . . . and of more shamelessly ill-informed criticism' than virtually any particular doctrine put forward by any other prominent historical thinker.[19] As we shall discuss in chapter 6, there are thankfully important 'corrections' currently taking place in Kant studies after several decades of what is now acknowledged as having been a particularly unfortunate period of Kant interpretation in Anglo-American philosophy in the second half of the twentieth century. Again, what this means will be addressed more fully below, but for now I will only say that these 'corrections' are driven by a renewed concern to allow Kant *to speak for himself* rather than, as had become almost standard procedure, utilizing

---

17. I grant that the terms 'metaphysical realism' and 'transcendental realism' are not entirely equivalent, but the rough alignment of them here helps to convey, appropriately and without any great distortion, what Kant is attempting to accomplish in this particular 'inversion'.

18. When one looks closely at the way Kant has set this up, it becomes clear that his two 'pillars' of inversion, so to speak (empirical realism and transcendental idealism) each generate, not one, but two opposites with regard to traditional theories of realism and idealism. If we look at these terms carefully, it is easy to see how this is so. 'Empirical realism' is initially set up as opposed to traditional 'empirical *idealism*', but it also turns out to be the opposite of '*metaphysical* realism'. Likewise, 'transcendental idealism' is initially set up as opposed to 'transcendental *realism*' (metaphysical realism) but it also turns out to be the opposite of '*empirical* idealism'. Thus Kant's empirical realism and transcendental idealism actually share opposites and are shown to be, unlike any other configurations of realism and idealism, not contraries but complementaries.

19. Actually this particular quote by G. R. G. Mure is in reference to Hegel's philosophy, but the force of it aptly expresses a common scholarly assessment today with respect to this aspect of Kant's philosophy. See G. R. G. Mure, *The Philosophy of Hegel* (London: Oxford University Press, 1965), p viii.

simplistic caricatures of Kant to serve all manner of specialized agendas, or co-opting him for particular purposes. Permitting the genuinely 'Copernican' or 'revolutionary' Kant to speak for himself, moreover, will reveal Kantian perspectives that are often fundamentally at odds with what have become the stereotypical misrepresentations of him, perspectives that are capable of speaking with surprising depth and freshness to an array of present concerns in both philosophy and theology.

Kant will offer a great deal that impacts our study, but with regard specifically to the central theological question of how reference to or characterization of the transcendent is possible he will enable an important reconfiguration of the question of aboutness or reference itself. More precisely, he will allow us to reformulate the requirement for theological reference as a new kind of demand for *finality*[20] and no longer as the seemingly impossible demand for an *'ontology* of transcendence' for which Bonhoeffer initially sought in vain. The particular benefit of this, again to use more current terminology, is that by paying attention to central developments in the *Critique* we will be able to map the beginnings of a way for theology to remain genuinely *realist* (or genuinely referential) without becoming onto-theological, that is, without construing the real otherness or over-againstness of God merely in terms of ontological difference. Yet just as importantly, Kant's avoidance as such of ontological presumption with regard to transcendence (i.e., transcendence understood as 'discovery') will not point us back in the direction of idealism ('invention') either.

However, despite thus making an enormous contribution to the formal theological endeavour by fundamentally altering our questioning with regard to it, Kant himself will in the end not bring us far enough for what theology requires. For what the *Critique of Pure Reason* ultimately leaves us with is a finality of the transcendent, purely as an *als ob* ('as if') in which God is encountered merely as a 'hypothetical transcendent' or as a purely 'provisional' transcendence. We will thus need to explore ways of re-fashioning Kant's otherwise dispositionally appropriate finality into something more robust in order to pave the way for genuine reference in the way that meaningful discourse about God requires. And in order to broach that task we will turn in chapter 7 to an extended discussion of tragedy as a kind of finality.

20. 'New', that is, compared to the finality of realism versus anti-realism discussed in chapter 3.

But before outlining that in broad introductory strokes here, we must first mention briefly a vital, related point in Kant's treatment of transcendental ideas or noumena, a point that, again, has been routinely misconstrued because the essentially revolutionary character of what Kant is doing has been ignored. I speak of Kant's insistence that his 'transcendental ideas' or 'noumena' – despite the fact that he describes these ideas as 'things-in-themselves' – are always to be treated in the same *als ob* vein as all Kantian transcendentals, that is, only *as if* they were things-in-themselves, and never as *real things*-in-themselves. (Indeed, as we shall see, Kant would be the first to agree with his would-be detractors that any talk of a *real* thing-in-itself is entirely incoherent, or 'sheer illusion' as Kant himself puts it.) This is why Kant names his doctrine of noumena 'transcendental *idealism*' and *not* its opposite 'transcendental realism', which falsely construes noumena or things-in-themselves as real, or in some sense 'ultimate', entities. (To Kant this is dogmatism.) All of this will be amply demonstrated in chapter 6. But just granting that for now, there is a further crucial result following from it that is the real focus of my concern here. The point is that, just as noumena, according to Kant, are always to be treated only *as if* they were things-in-themselves, so by extension they are never to be treated as anything like *ends*-in-themselves either.

To the contrary, Kant clearly stipulates that things-in-themselves or noumena are instead merely ideas that are posited *by* the understanding for another *specific purpose outside of themselves*. In other words, the *purpose* (or end) of the transcendental ideas is not self-referential. They are not posited to serve themselves or to serve 'pure reason'. (It should not be forgotten in this light that the *Critique of Pure Reason* is a *critique* of pure reason and not merely a *defence* of it.) Rather, and here we come to the pivotal point, the specific purpose outside of themselves for which things-in-themselves or noumena are posited is, in Kant's own words, to preserve 'the greatest systematic unity of *the empirical use of our reason*'.[21] In other words, things-in-themselves are never self-sustaining or self-referential, or anything ultimate on their own, but rather always point beyond themselves back to the real, empirical, spatio-temporal object. The fact is that, from beginning to end, from the first page virtually and quite literally to the last, the *Critique*'s 'transcendental idealism' is always portrayed in this way as operating in the service of 'empirical realism'. This, as I shall demonstrate

---

21. Immanuel Kant, *Critique of Pure Reason*, Paul Guyer and Allen W. Wood (tr. and eds.) (Cambridge: Cambridge University Press, 1998), A679/B707, emphasis added.

fully in chapter 6, will be unmistakably clear when Kant is permitted to speak for himself on these matters. But the further important point, which will later be so pivotal for theological purposes, is that the real *finality* put forward in the *Critique of Pure Reason* is therefore not to be looked for or located in abstract noumena or things-in-themselves at all (for these again are all merely *als ob* ideas[22]), but rather in the contingencies of spatio-temporal *empirical reality*, in relation to which these noumena will then in turn provide a kind of universal a priori orientation (and by extension, obligation) for thinking. It is unavoidable that all of this will appear rather cryptic at this juncture but I am confident that even the reader without a great deal of prior familiarity with Kant will be able to follow what he is attempting to do here as these ideas are presented in a way that is carefully attentive to Kant's own explications of them.

But now, what all of this is leading to more ultimately is the suggestion that if we look at the kind of thinking per se that Kant proposes in the *Critique of Pure Reason* – that is, thinking that is grounded in *empirical reality*, and whose primary concern at all stages along the way, even at its most thoroughly abstract (noumena), is the redirection of the understanding back to its *empirical use* – then we will find here a kind of thinking, a kind of intellectual or epistemological disposition, that is capable of being uniquely responsive to theological demands and open especially to Christological promptings. In other words, the direction in which all of this is moving is ultimately toward Christology. But the ground must be further prepared in order to show how Christology can respond to these newly formulated epistemological questions without resorting to positivism or succumbing to reductionism.

Consider then, with these goals in mind, the following pivotal twofold result of our discussion thus far.[23] The most essential, important and unique feature of Kant's doctrine of noumena, or transcendental idealism, is its ability to supply a genuinely *rational justification* for the kind of *empirical finality* that we encounter in the real, spatio-temporal world of human

---

22. And I am not forgetting that finality is developed subsequently by Kant in a somewhat different, yet by no means contradictory but complementary, way in the *Critique of Practical Reason*. But even here the *als ob* stipulation is still clearly apparent: 'So act *as if* your maxims were to serve at the same time a universal law'; Immanuel Kant, *Grounding for the Metaphysics of Morals*, tr. James W. Ellington (Indianapolis: Hackett, 1981), p. 43.

23. The reader should not be overly concerned if this particular paragraph is not entirely clear at this early juncture. Its content will be clarified in chapter 6. I only need to state these results here preliminarily in order to give some introductory indication of how our Kant enquiry will connect to the last two chapters.

experience (empirical realism).[24] Yet the equally important point is that it is also able to do so without speaking of this finality ontologically, that is, without resorting to the kind of rational presumption that treats the sensible, spatio-temporal object as a kind of mental possession (via conceptual classification), thus violating the empirical integrity of that finality.[25] If, then, we are to use this mutually inter-working relation of Kant's empirical realism and transcendental idealism as something of a preliminary model for theological reasoning, we will have to be able to respond to two separate but inseparable kinds of requirements. In the first place we will have to show how the finality of the transcendent can be encountered, not merely as a hypothetical 'as if', but with the same kind of robust tangibility as the finality encountered in empirical experience. Secondly, we will have to be able to locate a conceptual or rational account of this finality which does not seek to bring it into any standard ontological framework, yet which nonetheless preserves rational integrity with regard to it.

2.5   Tragedy and finality

It is toward these ends then, and especially in anticipation of the convergence of the concept of penultimacy and Christology in chapter 8, that we move in chapter 7 beyond the more strictly epistemological concerns, with which we have been dealing thus far, into the domain of ethics, and specifically to an investigation of the kind of finality that we encounter in tragedy. The question here will be whether the finality of tragedy can in any way help us to understand how the finality of the transcendent might be encountered as something more tangible and robust than a merely hypothetical 'as if'. The initiating impetus as such will be MacKinnon's claim that in tragedy we encounter a kind of finality or authority that enables us to project our questioning in reference to the transcendent in entirely unique ways. The depth and brilliance of MacKinnon's work in this area often remains enigmatic and critically undeveloped (and perhaps for this reason under-appreciated), in part because of the kind of literary style he often adopts, but also quite evidently because of an underlying conviction that too much 'clarity' would threaten the very integrity of what he is trying to bring to our attention in tragedy. As such, an important

---

24. Transcendental idealism is thus how Kant's empirical realism will avoid the scepticism that naturally results from what he calls 'mere empiricism'. It is also what most fundamentally distinguishes Kant's empirical realism from mere empiricism.
25. Transcendental idealism is thus also how Kant will avoid the dogmatism naturally resulting from mere rationalism.

part of what chapter 7 seeks to accomplish is to provide certain mechanisms that will illuminate the darker aspects of MacKinnon's brilliance on these issues without undoing what tragedy uniquely brings to the whole problematic.

The first of these mechanisms unfolds around a new kind of distinction between what I will portray as *two senses* of finality: a 'finality of resolution' and a 'finality of non-resolution'. For the most part, when we speak of finality (in the sense of authority) we mean something like a 'finality of resolution' or a finality of justification; that is, a finality that derives its authority from a certain capacity for settling disputes or problems by resolving the queries involved. For example, the kinds of finality we grant to a mathematical theorem or to a scientific theory or, in theology, to an apologetic strategy or a theodicy, these are always at bottom finalities of resolution inasmuch as their authority rests on the way they can be shown to resolve into proofs (deductively), or on their explanatory capacity (inductively), or even just in some way on their plausibility (e.g. through abduction or perhaps holistic evaluation etc.).

Tragedy, by contrast, in its very definition admits of no such resolution; *and yet* its tangible empirical finality is as unquestionable as the most conclusive finality of resolution. Tragedy confronts us with what we might call a kind of mind-stopping finality, a kind of finality we encounter, for example, in certain unspeakable episodes of human history such as the Jewish holocaust at the hands of Nazi Germany. What we are confronted with here can only be spoken of as a 'finality of non-resolution', in the sense that any attempt to 'account' for this evil in a broader apologetic strategy or theodicy utterly breaks apart and shatters against the actual, individual and collective, tangible experiences of ineluctable human demise, violation and undoing that comprise these events. Tragedy here means the end of every kind of design or *telos* or system of explanation. Dietrich Ritschl gives powerful expression to this conviction: 'Anyone who wants to say that Auschwitz – as a paradigm of evil and suffering in our time – is willed by God or good, even if we only realize it later, has to shut up, because such statements mark the end of both theology and humanity.'[26] In this light, and as insensitive as the application here may initially appear, this mind-stopping or epistemologically final feature of tragedy can actually help us forward with regard to the question of how reference to or characterization of the transcendent is possible.

26. Dietrich Ritschl, *The Logic of Theology* (Philadelphia: Fortress Press, 1987), p. 38.

The initial point is that the finality or authority that we encounter in the transcendent can be seen as somehow related to what I am calling the 'finality of non-resolution' which we encounter so tangibly in tragedy. Of course this is not to say that tragedy per se will somehow 'open up' a way of gaining reference to the transcendent. It is not as if tragedy and transcendence are 'similar', or as if the former becomes a model of some sort for the latter, for this would be precisely to participate in the kind of presumptuous and thoughtless reasoning that Ritschl and others condemn as both ethically and theologically bankrupt. To do so would be a violation of the finality of non-resolution of tragedy by orienting it to some more ultimate end. And so our attention in chapter 7 will rather be turned to something else. And here we come to a second mechanism for illuminating what remains rather cryptic in MacKinnon. Our concern will not be with any sort of analogical similarity between tragedy and transcendence. Rather it will be the particular *relation* that will be found to obtain between what I will distinguish as *two senses* of tragedy – tragedy-as-discourse[27] and real tragedy in history – that will help us further with the question of tangible reference to the transcendent. At bottom, tragedy-as-discourse will be found to be able to give expression to real tragedy in history in a way that no other form of discourse can, precisely because it alone, by definition, never allows resolution into any broader system of explanation or 'moral' or rationale; tragedy-as-discourse remains utterly unredemptive, so to speak. It is on the basis of these kinds of distinctions that we begin to see the promise and power of MacKinnon's initial statement that tragedy as a form of discourse is able to represent the relation of the familiar to the transcendent like no other form of discourse.

Yet MacKinnon himself always leaves us in purely negative territory on these matters, again arguably out of concern that any sort of positive development might violate the intrinsic character of tragedy. Nevertheless, we remain in search of an affirmative result. And so it will be on the basis of these essentially negative parameters that we will then in the second half of the chapter broach, via Bultmann, Bonhoeffer and Marion, some existing approaches offered by others for locating a suitable *positive* referent for theology – that is, a referent that is both fully tangible (empirical) yet that does not admit of resolution into any broader system of explanation (i.e., which remains a finality of non-resolution). More exactly, we will first explore the basic problems involved in epistemological reference for

27. As seen in different ways, for example, in Sophocles, Shakespeare or Racine.

theology in general, before turning to one specific and compelling current account of this in Jean-Luc Marion's treatment of empirical reference and the Eucharist. All of these explorations, however, will for various reasons ultimately fail to provide for the requirements of theological discourse but most decisively because of their invariable susceptibility to enigma and positivism.

2.6   Penultimacy and Christology

As an alternative to these, chapter 8 then offers a new way forward for meaningful theological reasoning, based on the clarifications in the previous chapters of what the 'formal' question of Christian thinking must involve. This 'new way forward' begins from a theological deployment of the logical or analytical relation between ultimacy and penultimacy, an idea that comes to powerful, if somewhat enigmatic expression in Bonhoeffer's *Ethics*, and that allows for application in our context in ways that he himself perhaps did not initially envision. The theological appropriation of penultimacy then builds toward Christology, and the provision of a 'counter-ontology' for meaningful discourse about God. In an oblique way, penultimacy and Christology will be seen as belonging together on a theological level in much the same way that Kant describes empirical realism and transcendental idealism as separate but inseparable descriptions of the same thing. Yet this indirect likeness will not be treated as anything formulaic or general, especially not in the sense of an attempt to find any sort of continuum between reason and revelation. It will rather offer a new, hitherto virtually unexplored way of understanding the convergence of (or the confrontation between) epistemology and Christology, which preserves the integrity of both of them. In short, it will outline a way in which theological subject matter can become the focus of rational scrutiny without succumbing to reductionism or resorting to positivism; that is, in a way that preserves the demands of orthodoxy.

2

Theology and the lure of obscurity

The widening rift perceivable between philosophy and the increasingly anti-philosophical outlook in large sectors of the human and social sciences in Britain, North America and France confronts theology with a peculiar set of challenges.[1] The rift is becoming more clearly visible and distinct within the university setting itself, with the increasing emergence of departments and institutes for comparative literature, critical theory, and ethnography, as well as 'hermeneutically' predisposed approaches to the humanities and interdisciplinary studies. These disciplines can appear to be deeply philosophically rooted insofar as they engage heavily with philosophers, especially from Descartes onward. But they are most often resolutely anti-philosophical and even radically anti-rational in outlook. I will discuss presently what I mean to identify precisely by the terms anti-philosophical or anti-rational, but first I want to address generally the peculiar kind of pressure that these new developments exert on theology, whose relationship to philosophy has never been straightforward or univocal. On the one hand, theology has always engaged with the philosophical traditions of the day (or indeed helped to form them), appealing to the public authority of philosophy for the defence of its own intellectual and doctrinal integrity, especially to certain general principles of right thinking (logic, epistemology) or to the idea that things have 'natures' that are in some way scrutable (ontology, metaphysics). But theology also struggles heavily against the very philosophy to which it appeals for rational and doctrinal integrity. This is especially obvious where philosophy

---

1. Since I can not express it any better, these first three paragraphs replicate roughly the opening of my article 'Radical Orthodoxy and the New Culture of Obscurantism', (Oxford: Blackwell, 2004) in *Modern Theology*. Two other brief paragraphs of this chapter borrow from that essay as well.

marginalizes or rejects theology as unintelligible and incoherent, or as something merely superstitious. But the conflict arises equally, if more subtly, where philosophy is willing to grant to theology a kind of respectability, for example as that which seeks to give expression to the most 'noble' aspirations of humanity, yet where, precisely by granting this respectability, philosophy wants also to claim for itself a kind of ultimate jurisdiction over theological subject matter and endeavour. The point here is that theology's allegiances for or against philosophy have hitherto been held broadly in a kind of tension. However, with the emergence of the anti-philosophical temperament as a bona fide intellectual outlook, legitimized by the universities with the creation of departments where this outlook is advanced, there is strong empirical evidence to suggest that the traditional theological ambivalence is now also beginning to shift more decisively away from philosophy and rational normativity. Even theologies that aspire to be orthodox show signs of becoming increasingly 'radical' in this anti-philosophical and anti-rational sense.

But what exactly do we mean when we describe these noetic outlooks in the human sciences and theology as anti-philosophical, anti-epistemological or anti-rational? It is difficult to capture under a single qualification all the various manifestations of what I am trying to describe here – for example various strains of post-structuralism arising out of widely divergent influences, ultra-pragmatism (post-structuralism and ultra-pragmatism will be discussed in more detail shortly), critical theory or other forms of textualism, hermeneutics-based human sciences and so on. But the most defining characteristic which all of these noetic dispositions share in common is best described in terms of *a move away from the human subject*, or more specifically, as a move *away* from any sort of thinking that puts *human consciousness, intention and reference at the centre of discourse* and meaningfulness.

Let me explain this a bit further. These anti-rational or anti-subject approaches are often (misleadingly) referred to simply as 'post-modern'; and the reason for this common practice is that most of them operate on an understanding that somewhere around the time of Descartes there occurred in philosophy a 'turn to the subject', and that this 'turn' identifies something peculiar and specific about 'modern' philosophy since that time. The Cartesian 'turn to the subject', it is claimed, marks the inception of a fundamentally misbegotten intellectual enterprise that culminates roughly in Kant (or, for some, in the German idealism that followed Kant). But in truth, even though it may be more accentuated in certain ways after Descartes, virtually all traditional philosophies ever since the pre-Socratics are 'philosophies-of-the-subject' inasmuch as they, almost without exception, put consciousness, intention and reference at the centre of discourse and human meaning. This is why the present anti-rational move *away* from the subject (i.e., purporting to 'undo' the putative turn *to* the subject in modern philosophy) is best described not merely as anti-modern (or post-modern) but as thoroughly anti-philosophical or anti-intentional-referential. (Another reason for avoiding the common label here is that there are many writers who are often referred to, rightly or wrongly, as 'post-modern' but who are by no means anti-philosophical or anti-rational in the way that I am addressing here.[2]) As such, for purposes of overall clarity and economy, I will in this book simply group all of these anti-rational, anti-philosophical approaches together under the qualification *'post-subject'* or anti-subject outlooks. But in order to ensure that this important point has been made with sufficient clarity and care, let us look more closely at the two most prominent broad strains of what I am calling post-subject thinking: French post-structuralism and American ultra-pragmatism.[3]

1 'Post-subject' thinking: post-structuralism and ultra-pragmatism

In the 1950s, Ferdinand de Saussure's earlier, turn-of-the-century linguistic structuralism[4] began to exert considerable influence within French universities, most prominently in the anthropology of Lévi-Strauss, the psychoanalysis of Lacan and the literary theoretics of Barthes. My present interest is not to delve into the complex array of philosophico-political reasons for this rise[5] but merely to note its emergence as a considerable

2. Levinas, Ricoeur or Marion are examples.
3. To be completely clear about this, the term 'post-subject' thinking is used as a broader category than either post-structuralism or ultra-pragmatism in order to identify the main common feature that unites them *as* anti-philosophical or anti-rational outlooks. This main common feature, as just explained, is a turn *away* from the human subject (specifically, a turn away from matters of human consciousness, intention and reference in discourse), a move that is undertaken ostensibly in order to 'correct' or undo what is claimed to be a misdirected turn *to* the subject which *putatively* occurred in 'modern' philosophy (even though virtually all philosophies since the Greeks are philosophies-of-the-subject).
4. The definitive work here is Ferdinand de Saussure's *Course in General Linguistics*, tr. Wade Baskin (New York: McGraw Hill, 1966).
5. For an illuminating account of this, see, e.g., Vincent Descombes, *Modern French Philosophy* (Cambridge: Cambridge University Press, 1980), chs. 1–2.

force in the French academy beginning in the latter half of the twentieth century, as a predecessor to post-structuralism.

Structuralism provides what might be called the 'other side' to a distinction that is a commonplace in French philosophy but is rarely made in Anglo-American circles. I speak of the distinction between philosophies of consciousness and philosophies of structure. The former of course are the traditional philosophies-of-the-subject I have just been describing, which begin from questions of consciousness, intention and reference. Structuralism, by contrast, begins with questions concerning the status of cultural and social phenomena (husband, wife, sister, brother, magistrate, vagrant, cleric, criminal, prime minister, diplomat and so on). It reasons that while these are not physical objects, they are nevertheless undeniably 'entities of meaning' and seem to admit of some sort of analysis as such. Having already implicitly rejected the possibility of any causal or material analysis (in virtue of their non-physicality) Saussure suggested instead that these cultural and social entities are somehow 'intrinsically relational' and proposed that their meaning or significance arises solely with reference to the structure they share or presuppose and does not depend on anything intrinsic to them. A simple but helpful analogy to Morse code is sometimes made here. A novice's dot may be longer than an expert's dash, but what really matters, or where the dot really acquires its significance or meaning, is in the structural relation or the distinction between dot and dash. What makes structuralism so fundamentally different than philosophies-of-the-subject, in this light, is that it wants to treat distinctively *human* domains in this way: that is, as abstract structures in which meanings do not inhere in conscious subjects but which rather are constituted solely by relations among the elements comprising formal structures or systems. In other words, what we might call the 'constituent elements' (including human, self-conscious constituents) which form the 'raw material' of any cultural or social system: these raw elements themselves do not contribute anything to their own meaningfulness or significance. Instead, their meaning or significance arises entirely out of the differences between them as *relata*, differences ascertained on the basis of qualitative phenomenological oppositions and fundamental dichotomies: small/large, male/female, odd/even, appearance/reality, false/true, opinion/knowledge and so on. Absolutely vital here is the recognition that Saussurean structuralism began in *human* domains and reduced or absorbed these entirely into linguistic relations in hopes of raising or promoting the study of human and social affairs to a genuinely objective scientific level. Structuralism's two basic character-istics, as such, are (i) the elimination of the meaningful subject or con-stituent within any structure, and yet (ii) the concomitant affirmation of a sort of 'internal objectivity' or authority of the structural system itself.

Once this is understood, a definition of 'post'-structuralism is straightforward: at its most basic, post-structuralism involves quite sim-ply an embracing of the first characteristic and a rejection of the second. That is, post-structuralism wants to retain structuralism's 'anti-subject' or 'post-subject' component (which has here been shown to mean the full *elimination* of the subject or constituent as anything significant), but sees structuralism's continuing claim to be able to hold on to some sort of system-theoretical objectivity as an 'unacceptable remnant of a "totalizing" philosophical tradition'.[6] In other words, although struc-turalism is indeed itself already an anti-subject or post-subject outlook as described above, it is not yet strictly speaking anti-philosophical or anti-rational in the way that post-structuralism or ultra-pragmatism are. For it retains an element of normative stability in the structure itself, within which meaning can still be assessed (even if purely contextually) and against which the propriety or impropriety of reasoning processes, or rational obligation, can be measured. It is precisely these vestiges of semantic orientation and rational authority that post-structuralism sees as imposed or arbitrary and hence rejects.

Having said this, however, it is important to note that even though I have traced it here through its Saussurean roots, post-structuralism need not be the cognitive offspring of any *particular* chronology or genealogy of ideas. In other words, in its different manifestations, post-structuralism need not reflect any sort of common historical origin to qualify *as* post-structuralism. (Indeed, this would prove its undoing for it would give it a kind of normativity or stability which it cannot tolerate.) Instead, post-structuralism is identifiable purely as a set of broadly negative discursive commitments, commitments that can arise in any number of intellectual

---

6. Fredric Jameson in Jean-Francois Lyotard, *The Postmodern Condition: A Report on Knowledge,* Geoff Bennington and Brian Massumi (tr.) (Manchester: Manchester University Press 1984). This means a rejection of *both* Hegel and Sartre (since both are 'philosophies-of-the-subject' proceeding from matters of consciousness, intention and reference) and corresponds to the anti-totalitarian intellectual/political climate in which post-structuralism initially took root historically. That is, even though Sartrean Marxism itself involved yet another rejection of Hegelian idealism, nevertheless both remain, each in its own way, cross-cultural, trans-historical – even on some grand cosmic scale teleological or eschatological – metanarratives of history and human development. Sartre becomes as 'totalizing' as Hegel and is rejected largely for that reason (cf., e.g., Descombes, *Modern French Philosophy*, chs. 1–2).

contexts or 'histories'. Thus Foucault credits Nietzsche and not Saussure or Lévi-Strauss for initially causing him to break with the totalizing traditions of 'historicism and Hegelianism';[7] and Derrida's post-structuralism, as we shall see, was always in opposition to structuralism in a way that even Foucault's was not. As such, whether post-structuralism is best viewed as a *reaction* to structuralism or simply an *extension* of it is debatable; in fact, many caution against any sort of chronological designation of the terms at all, claiming that on certain readings (notably Deleuze's *Nietzsche and Philosophy*) post-structuralism can be shown to be 'older' than structuralism.[8] As such, even Rorty's ultra-pragmatism – the other main strain of post-subject thinking we are considering here – turns out on this account to be no less 'post-structuralist' than Foucault, Lyotard, Derrida, Bourdieu or Latour. For even though his ultra-pragmatism takes its anti-philosophy or anti-rationality cues from his readings of Dewey and James (although also importantly from Heidegger), it remains at bottom the same double rejection as that advocated by post-structuralism: (i) the rejection of the conscious subject along with intention and reference as the centre of meaningful discourse, and (ii) the rejection of the possibility of any sort of objectively authoritative framework of meaning even if this is purely contextual.[9]

1.1 Ideological historiography and the problem of authentication

But the obvious question now confronting any of these self-proclaimed anti-rational enterprises is how they can conceivably authenticate or justify themselves *as* 'outlooks', that is, as anything coherently unified, or as advocating any kind of viewpoint, in the absence of any possible appeal to reason. Their first response to this challenge will typically be to attempt, in one way or another, to deny that they are seeking to justify or authenticate themselves at all, and that even the expectation that they should seek to do so is just another remnant of the hegemonic philosophical regime that they are seeking to overturn. In short, the initial response to the challenge of authentication will be to try to deflate the expectation

---

7. Michel Foucault, 'Structuralism and Post-Structuralism: An Interview with Michel Foucault', *Telos* 55 (spring 1983), pp. 203–4.

8. See, e.g., Peter Dews, *Logics of Disintegration: Post-structuralist Thought and the Claims of Critical Theory* (London: Verso 1987), pp. 1–4; and also Jameson and Lyotard in *The Postmodern Condition*, who likewise affirm the basic ahistorical nature of post-structuralism.

9. Richard Rorty, *Philosophy and the Mirror of Nature* (Oxford: Blackwell 1980), e.g., pp. 3, 6, 9, 11, 371, 392 and also especially chs. 1, 2 and 8.

for authority or justification itself. Rorty, for example, not only *doesn't* see the absence of any broader authority as a loss for discourse but celebrates it as something 'freeing'. He models his approach partly on his reading of Heidegger, whose methods of challenging traditional philosophical authority are, according to Rorty, 'beautifully designed to make one feel foolish when one tries to find a bit of common ground on which to start an argument'.[10] He acknowledges that there will be those who will 'feel exasperated [maintaining that] there ought . . . to be *some* standard' by which such anti-rational outlooks can be authenticated or compared to others, or that there ought to be '*some* competitor running in the *same* race'.[11] But even 'our sense of exasperation' here, he continues, 'is just one more product of the notion that philosophy is supposed to be a competition between arguments'.[12] The first traces of a kind of elitism (an almost inevitable result of anti-rationalism) begin to manifest themselves here, as further evidenced in Rorty's claim that the anti-rationalist or anti-epistemologist 'wants not to have to argue with his fellow philosophers and wants also to say that he is doing something much more difficult than they are trying to do'.[13] We are thus encouraged to divest ourselves of any requirement for authentication or authority in the usual sense, even if this means abandoning our most deeply rooted common-sense intuitions.

But no matter how much such approaches seek to deflate questions of authority, or no matter how much they may try to project themselves in 'non-competitive' terms, they cannot, as Putnam points out in one of his frequent jousts with Rorty, help but present their outlooks as in some sense *better* than that which they are seeking to annul or dissolve. Thus, despite the initial rejection of the legitimacy of the stipulation that a justification should be required of them in the first place, such outlooks almost invariably *do* seek to provide authentications for their views after all. And thus we return to the question of how they can conceivably achieve this in the absence of any possible appeal to reason.

---

10. Richard Rorty, *Consequences of Pragmatism* (Minneapolis: University of Minnesota Press, 1982), p. 38.
11. Rorty, *Consequences of Pragmatism*, p. 38 emphasis altered.
12. Rorty, *Consequences of Pragmatism*, pp. 38–9.
13. Rorty, *Consequences of Pragmatism*, p. 38. Of course I do not, by saying this, mean to identify difficulty with elitism. (See, e.g., Thomas Nagel, *The View from Nowhere* (Oxford: Oxford University Press 1986), pp. 11–12 on the subject of difficulty in philosophy.) Nor do I overlook a different kind of elitism that can be seen within certain sectors of analytical philosophy and the natural sciences.

It is at this juncture that we encounter one of the most pervasive and prominent features of post-subject outlooks, the one that most characteristically draws them together as a group: this is their distinctively peculiar attitude to intellectual history. In other words, as a result of their marginalization of consciousness, intention and reference, almost all such outlooks will seek to justify their views, or authenticate themselves, on the basis of highly specialized and arbitrary 'alternative' *ideological historiographies*. Let me explain what I mean by this more exactly, especially with reference to historical texts or writings. It will be obvious, even from our brief discussion of structuralism, post-structuralism and ultra-pragmatism above, that none of these post-subject outlooks can really allow for the intelligibility of anything like a persisting original authorial *intention* in any writing or text, since whatever significance or describable character the text may have is determined *entirely* by its context (or its relations within a given structure) and not from anything inherent in it. In other words, there is nothing intrinsic to the text or no stable 'presence' within the text per se that could serve as an authoritative guide for determining whether any particular construal or interpretation of that text qualifies as a *legitimate* or *proper* interpretation. Another way of stating this would be to say that these outlooks cannot allow original authors *to speak for themselves* (or they cannot be genuinely 'attentive') since this would be to admit a persisting 'presence' in the text which could be attended *to*, and this is precisely what their post-subject ('non-significant') commitments by definition disallow. Now this creates a particularly fortuitous set of circumstances for post-subject outlooks which, having lost the possibility of authenticating or justifying their views on any sort of rational basis, are otherwise hard pressed to find any authenticating mechanism. The point is that, because any sort of original persisting authorial intent (or, for that matter, any other kind of intrinsic content or 'presence') in a writing can now be overlooked, historical texts can be remoulded virtually at will (and without great pangs of intellectual conscience) to construct specialized historiographies that can in turn serve to 'authenticate' the ideologies or pre-theoretical persuasions that drive them.

One sees this prominently among almost all varieties of post-structuralism, where it has become virtually standard procedure, but perhaps nowhere more unabashedly than in Rorty's ultra-pragmatism. In an essay entitled 'Overcoming the Tradition' which pits post-subject thinking (whose forerunners and masters for Rorty are Heidegger and Dewey) against thinking that leaves consciousness, intention and reference at the centre, Rorty candidly admits that 'insofar as there is any sensible question of the form "Who is right, Heidegger or the others?" it is going to be a question about historiography'.[14] The problem of a more or less *legitimate* historiography based on the intentions of the original writers, or any sort of semantic content or substance of the texts themselves, never arises here. Rather, a historiography is deemed to be legitimate or authoritative – or, in Rorty's terms, the genuine 'experts' or 'critics' are 'distinguished from the amateur, the philistine, the mystic, or the belletrist' – based solely on 'the depth and extent of their commentary on the details of the tradition'.[15] Rorty's own ultra-pragmatist historiography centres around a selective reading of Dewey and James (and Heidegger) which dispenses, in his words, with 'the bad parts' of their writings.[16]

It is here too, in the ideological reinterpretation of historical texts, that the free-floating holism or coherence (as opposed to normatively stable epistemological coherence), which I mentioned briefly in chapter 1, begins to come clearly into play. We can now address that distinction somewhat more fully. As already intimated, what all of these anti-rational post-subject methods share in common is a commitment to associations rather than to substance in building their cases: a commitment to the syntactical over the semantic, a commitment to questions of tactic and polity over questions of 'aboutness', meaning, intention and reference. And because of this, that is, because texts or writings themselves (i.e., as raw material) have no inherent jurisdiction over how they come to be interpreted, or because they have no unique character or 'presence', they can be used entirely in the service of the ideology in relation to which they are brought to discussion. But now the further, and present, point is that post-subject outlooks will always, in one way or another, come to build their ideologically tactical application of historical texts around appeals to 'coherence' as in, for example, John Milbank's description of Radical Orthodoxy as coming to expression within a 'complex but *coherently* executed *collage*'.[17] However, 'coherence' in these contexts denotes something fundamentally different from any of the philosophical 'coherence theories' of truth, including the

---

14. Rorty, *Consequences of Pragmatism*, p. 41.
15. Rorty, *Consequences of Pragmatism*, p. 41.
16. Rorty, *Consequences of Pragmatism*, p. 214.
17. 'The Theological Critique of Philosophy in Hamann and Jacobi', in John Milbank, Catherine Pickstock and Graham Ward (eds.) *Radical Orthodoxy* (London: Routledge 1999), pp. 21–37; p. 2.

more contemporary coherence theories in analytical philosophy, as advocated, for example, by Dummett, Putnam, Davidson or Quine. In all of these philosophical cases, both the 'coherence' and the 'conceptual relativity' around which it often comes to expression are defined within certain normative or authoritative horizons or constraints. That is, they remain at bottom philosophies-of-the-subject,[18] operating around concerns of consciousness, intention and reference. By contrast, any post-subject (roughly post-structuralist or ultra-pragmatist) construal of 'coherence' and conceptual relativity is utterly devoid of any such trans-internal normativity. In other words, it is a *radically free-floating coherence*.

The same sorts of distinctions must also be made with respect to the term 'holism'. There is a normative, genuinely philosophical, intentional-referential holism (different strains of traditional idealism, or what is currently called 'anti-realism' are usually holistic in this normative sense, as we shall see in chapter 3); and there is a radically free-floating holism which answers *only* to the 'collage' within which it comes to expression. Post-subject methods are constantly seeking to blur these distinctions, thereby gaining by association a level of normativity or stability that they do not possess by themselves. Rorty, for example, on several occasions tries to make Davidson a cohort of his free-floating coherence[19] but Davidson refuses the association. He admits that his own 'giving up [of] the dualism of scheme and content amounts to abandoning a theme central to empiricism in its main historical manifestations'. 'But', he goes on to say, 'I do not think, as friends and critics have variously suggested, that my argument against empiricism makes me, or ought to make me, a pragmatist . . . or an "internal" realist. All these positions are forms of relativism that I find as hard to understand as the empiricisms I attack.'[20] The point is that the kind of coherence and conceptual relativity from which Davidson here distances himself is precisely the radically free-floating, moorless and horizonless 'coherence' of the post-subject (anti-intentional-referential) outlooks.

With all of this in mind, we can now return to the point I was beginning to make earlier. I was suggesting that what Rorty, in comparative

---

18. Albeit in a continually redefining and self-reflective sense, as in Hilary Putnam, *Realism with a Human Face* (London: Harvard University Press 1990); or in Donald Davidson's recent *Subjective, Intersubjective, Objective* (Oxford: Oxford University Press, 2002).

19. cf., e.g., Rorty, *Consequences of Pragmatism*, pp. xviii, 5–9.

20. Donald Davidson, *Inquiries into Truth and Interpretation* (Oxford: Oxford University Press 1984), p. xviii. See also 'On the Very Idea of a Conceptual Scheme', pp. 183–98 in the same volume.

literature, or Milbank, in theology (along with many other post-subject compatriots), seem essentially to be appealing to, in constructing what I have been describing as their free-floating ideological historiographies, is a somewhat less consistent form of an art of intellectual traversal which is most purely and ingeniously displayed in Derrida's goal of 'strategic rhythm' (or 'undecidability'). Let us now turn to Derrida himself and try to make this clearer.

1.2   Intentional reference, 'dualism' and the 'feel' of meaning

One of the reasons that post-structuralism rejects not only philosophies that emphasize consciousness (philosophies-of-the-subject), but also philosophies that emphasize structures (structuralism) is that both of them operate, each in its own way, on the basis of fundamental oppositions or dualisms in thinking. Structuralism operates, as we have seen, on the basis of qualitative phenomenological oppositions and dichotomies such as small/large, male/female, odd/even, appearance/reality, false/true, and philosophies-of-the-subject on the basis of differentiations between subject/object, scheme/content, intention/reference and so on. Now there are two basic reasons, often broadly implied but seldom clearly articulated, for post-structuralism's rejection of dualism in either of these contexts. The first has to do with the intrinsic *stability* that both philosophies-of-the-subject and structuralism claim for reason or for assessment of meaning on the basis of these oppositions. Post-structuralism objects to this, countering that the alleged stability or normativity claimed by these two strains of 'dualistic' thinking is not reflective of anything intrinsic to reason at all, but is entirely arbitrary and self-serving. Or conversely, while it may be granted that these oppositions do indeed give rise to an *apparent* stability, this stability itself derives entirely *from* these (imposed) oppositions and so, again, the whole enterprise is manufactured and self-legitimizing. The second reason involves the post-structuralist contention that the dualistic tendencies within both consciousness-based and structure-based philosophies unavoidably result in the arbitrary division of reality into dichotomous sectors. The charge here again is that because this is nothing natural but is rather something imposed, either kind of 'dualistic' thinking actually violates the integrity of reality, or does violence to reality by partitioning it for self-perpetuating (i.e., rationally or semantically stabilizing) purposes.

But there is one particular 'dualistic' problem that even these post-subject outlooks must sooner or later come to confront. And this is the ineluctable fact that the very act of thinking seems to involve the most basic and obvious kind of bivalence or dualism: both because thinking is always 'thinking about' and, relatedly, because of the seemingly unavoidable distinction within conscious awareness between the thinker per se and the thinker's thought. Nevertheless, the more obviously and the more inexorably these bivalences seem to manifest themselves, the more energetically they are denounced as hegemonic and self-perpetuating.

One way to understand more clearly the reasoning behind this is to return to what I said in chapter 1 about the basic equivalency of the terms 'meaningfulness', 'intentional reference' and 'aboutness'. As I explained there, we do not require anything like a theory of meaning to authorize the equation of these terms, or to establish the truth of that equation, since the claim is merely trivially true, or true by the definition of the terms involved as these pertain to human discourse. In other words, what I *mean* by a statement *just is* what I *intend* that statement to *refer* to, or to express or to be about. Now the point in the present light is that post-subject outlooks will pick up on this very claim and declare that what philosophies-of-the-subject find to be 'tautological' or self-evident here is not tautological at all but 'hegemonic'. In other words, post-structuralism will readily grant that our experience of meaningfulness in discourse *as* intentional reference is indeed *ineluctable*, but it will immediately add that this is *not* because the identification of meaningfulness with intentional reference expresses something necessarily true with respect to human reasoning, but rather merely because this way of thinking has come to have a kind of stranglehold on our minds. It is not 'tautological' but 'hegemonic' and these can be easily confused because their psychological effects can be roughly the same. (It will be clear that this also points us back precisely to the distinction between reason as need and reason as power.) Contemporary anti-rational thought will thus try to derail all of this talk of meaning and intentional reference by declaring the whole philosophical enterprise to be a 'ruse', or to be fabricated and self-perpetuating in the first place.

But in thus declaring tautology to be hegemony, what post-subject outlooks commit themselves to is a rejection of 'dualism' that is so total and indiscriminate, often even obsessive, that they effectively lose touch with reality, or at least with anything that a conscious enquirer could in any way construe as *mattering* to the human experience of life. In other words, by rejecting the legitimacy of all semantic talk of 'aboutness' or intentional reference or, as Derrida puts it, by rejecting 'all the ruses of end-oriented thinking', post-subject and post-structure thinking enters a terrain of pure tactic, a terrain – at least for the real purists – without advocacy, without critical horizon or defining context. And it is here that we come to the distinction between Derrida and the rest of the post-subject field. For the fact is that only very few post-structuralist or post-subject thinkers are willing to remain 'real purists' here. Most, as we shall see, are more apt to perceive the barren terrain of non-reference and non-advocacy at the post-subject terminus as merely bleak rather than pure, and thus ultimately to abandon it for some foreign prospect of fruitfulness or purpose. In other words, for the majority of post-subject thinkers, the question now becomes how to re-integrate such utterly barren (to say nothing of counter-intuitive) commitments successfully with actual discourse; or even more deeply, how to re-introduce at least the *feel* of meaning[21] into anti-subject discourse so that this accords with the thinker's actual experience of life. And it is ironic here that the re-introduction of any sort of 'feel' of meaning will invariably seek to replicate precisely the 'feel' of *aboutness*, that is, the 'feel' of the kind of end-orientedness that was dispensed with in the first place in the rejection of 'dichotomizing' intentional-referential discourse.[22] In short, the 'tautology' that has been rejected as 'hegemony' is in fact always returned to by post-subject thinking when it tries to re-infuse the 'feel' of meaning into discourse, for the feel of meaning is always at bottom the feel of aboutness or the feel of intentional reference.

All of this can be made clearer still by citing some of the different methods employed by post-subject thinkers for undertaking this re-infusion of aboutness or end-orientedness in discourse. The names under which these techniques have come to be identified will be familiar enough, but their particular function as meaning-inducing strategies, as just described, is less well recognized. Rorty, for example, finds his end-orientedness in 'neo-pragmatism' (ultra-pragmatism), in 'solidarity' or in 'social hope'. Foucault's end-orientedness or aboutness comes to be focused around his 'archeo-genealogy', which, in any of its manifestations, is built around the unabashedly subject-centred category of power. Derrida, in a related

21. On the feel of meaning, see Rorty's 'Pragmatism, Relativism, Irrationalism', in *Consequences of Pragmatism*, especially pp. 174–5. See also Descombes, *Modern French Philosophy*, p. 79.
22. It will of course be claimed, however, (though not demonstrated) that this 'feel' of aboutness is now re-introduced somehow in non-dichotomizing and non-stable ways.

yet importantly different way, employs the tactics of 'deconstruction', 'strategic rhythm' and 'undecidability' to achieve a similar sense of focus or purpose (although Derrida himself would avoid these terms). The point remains that all three of these – roughly, ultra-pragmatism, archeogenealogy, deconstruction – constitute techniques for attempting to re-infuse some sense of meaning at the 'constituent' level, or at least a 'feel' of meaning or purpose, into post-subject ways of thinking. But the inclusion of Derrida in this group cannot be made without a crucial caveat. Whereas virtually all other post-subject thinkers reach into the positive terrain of advocacy to re-infuse the feel of meaningfulness (aboutness), and this with devastating effects to the consistency or conceptual soundness of their programmes,[23] only Derrida seeks to remain entirely within the negative openness of the purely tactical terrain. Derrida's post-structuralism, in other words, is unique among post-subject outlooks; and because of its prominence as such it will require some further scrutiny in order for us to come to a fully adequate assessment of this negative end of our spectrum of rational obligation (anti-rationality).

Derrida himself makes clear how, from his earliest essays (1950s) onwards until his cluster of seminal post-structuralist works of 1967, he had refused, even against the still-prevailing structuralist consensus of the 1950s, to accept any kind of *rapprochement* with structuralism.[24] From the very beginning, Derrida had consistently rejected any suggestion that

---

23. The point is that both Rorty and Foucault, in their endeavours to re-introduce the feel of meaning (aboutness), openly abandon the purely tactical post-subject and post-structure terrain. Rorty reaches for the decidedly anthropologically driven principle of communal usefulness and solidarity to yield his ultra-pragmatism; Foucault reaches even more intrepidly back into the subject-centred category of power to yield his archeo-genealogy. They do this moreover without any sign of concern for the disastrous effects it has on the conceptual soundness of their programmes. In fact, Rorty does not see the loss of conceptual soundness as a disaster at all but rather as something liberating, since to him conceptual soundness is just another legitimizing technique for philosophy construed as a competition between arguments. Truth here is not to be measured in any sense theoretically, whether in terms of coherence or as any sort of correspondence with fact, still less by anything like a trueness-to-self in a Hegelian sense (things do not have or reflect essences), but rather at bottom only by what works. Even our references to external objects are merely 'coping mechanisms' that help us speak about certain kinds of stimuli in our experience (cf., e.g., Rorty, 'Realism, Anti-realism, and Pragmatism', p. 166; Richard Rorty, 'Is Truth a Goal of Inquiry?: Davidson vs. Wright', *Philosophical Quarterly* 45. 180 (July 1995), pp. 281–300). With regard to Foucault, the blatant contradictoriness of his programme is as undisputed as his brilliance is acknowledged (cf. Dews, *Logics of Disintegration* pp. 169–70; Allan Megill, *Prophets of Extremity* (Berkeley: University of California Press, 1985), pp. 254–6; and Descombes, *Modern French Philosophy*, pp. 110–17, especially the last two pages).Vincent Descombes speaks euphemistically of how 'the conjunction of positivism and nihilism [i.e., power-legitimation conjoined with post-structuralism] in the same intelligence produces a "surprising mixture"' (Descombes, *Modern French Philosophy*, p. 117).
24. See Dews, *Logics of Disintegration*, p. 4.

there might be stability in what structuralism saw as thought's fundamental oppositions, and he viewed structuralism's claims to the contrary as simply leftovers of enlightenment impositions. In other words, Derrida's post-structuralism never came via structuralist dualism but rather was always in opposition to it. Now Derrida's extraction of himself in this way from the influence of structuralism may well be sufficient grounds for his claim to be able also to dispense with the standard *phenomenological* dualisms that occur in structuralism. However, the final or inexorable 'dualism' between thought and thinker, between writing and writer that we are now addressing – a 'dualism' that is implied in the very terms 'meaningfulness' or 'aboutness' – cannot be simply and summarily dispensed with in the same way. As the simplest act of writing or thinking alone makes unavoidably obvious, the distinction between thought and thinker, writing and writer is too inexorable simply to deem invalid by declaring it 'hegemonic' or by including it in structuralism's phenomenological dualisms. The question that must be answered is: *How* is this final ineluctable dualism too just another ploy or machination of end-oriented thinking? How is this 'final dualism' just another *phenomenological* dualism which reflects nothing *intrinsic* (orientating, obligating) about thinking or reason but which rather has its origins entirely in a particular historical development of western philosophical thought?

1.3   Reason as 'ruse'

In my view, a 1983 Cornell inaugural lecture given by Derrida, 'The Principle of Reason: The University in the Eyes of its Pupils', may be read as a serious attempt to demonstrate just this.[25] In a display of remarkable creative ingenuity, Derrida may be read as attempting to recast even this final distinction between thought and thinker in terms of what he sees as Kant's division of reason into pure and practical realms: that is, as something rooted in a particular episode within the historical development of European philosophical thought and not in anything about reason itself. It is highly significant to begin with that the university itself (to Derrida the very bastion of the self-perpetuating end-orientedness of thinking, and as such the engine of modernity) is his chosen arena for

25. Jacques Derrida, 'The Principle of Reason: The University in the Eyes of its Pupils', *Diacritics* 19 (spring 1983), pp. 3–20. I am indebted to Christopher Norris's, *Derrida* (London: Fontana, 1987) in directing my attention to this essay. On pp. 156–63 Norris comments at some length on it, and a portion of my own comment in this and the following paragraph, builds from glosses of his insight. The rest of the discussion is entirely my own responsibility.

this study, for it signals what will turn out to be an implicit recognition on his part (in stark contrast, for example, to Foucault or Lyotard or Rorty) of the need for post-structuralist (post-subject) discourse, despite its anti-rational commitments, to work *within* the structures of rationality, within intentional-referential epistemology, that is, within 'modernity'.

In this address, Derrida focuses on Kant's attempt to define the place of philosophy vis-à-vis the other scholastic disciplines. He cites Kant's contention that philosophy's prestige within the university setting derived precisely from its implicit recognition that its proper place, alone among the disciplines, remained solely within the university. More broadly this meant that, in return for minding its own speculative business and not meddling in matters of law or state, the state reciprocated and granted to philosophy an unparalleled and unfettered freedom of enquiry and expression within the university context itself. Philosophy came to be recognized as 'a place of pure rational knowledge, a place where truth has to be spoken without controls and without concern for "utility", a place where the very meaning and autonomy of the university meet'.[26] But now, Derrida reasons, this mutually agreed-upon division of intellectual labour comes itself to be directly reflected in Kant's philosophy, in the separation he places between pure and practical reason. In other words, the Kantian blueprint for the modern liberal university – that is, the reciprocal agreement that philosophy may operate freely and without fear of state repression as long as it confines itself to matters of pure theory and does not meddle in practical affairs – this blueprint, in Derrida's view, also implicitly signals the inauguration of the division of reason or knowledge itself into pure and practical domains. Derrida's point as such is that this division of reason is entirely fictitious and does not reflect anything inherent in the structure of rationality. He attempts to illustrate this by showing that the intermingling of the pure and the practical can be seen to take place 'naturally' even in the most abstract reaches of theoretical reasoning. For example, '[a]t the service of war, of national and international security, research programs have to encompass the entire field of information, the stockpiling of knowledge, the workings of all semiotic systems, translation, coding and decoding, the play of presence and absence, hermeneutics, semantics, structural and generative linguistics, pragmatics, rhetoric'.[27]

26. Derrida, 'The Principle of Reason', p. 18.
27. Derrida, 'The Principle of Reason', p. 13.

But it is the next step that is the really crucial one. It is not explicitly stated by Derrida but it is clearly implied in everything that follows. The point is, of course, that the intentional reference or aboutness of reason can itself always be seen as something 'practical' inasmuch as to be 'about', or to be 'intentionally referential', *just is* to be 'end-oriented'. Therefore the division between pure and practical reason that Derrida takes himself to have shown to be fabricated (i.e., rooted in a specific historical-philosophical development and not reflective of anything intrinsic to reason itself) also shows the aboutness or intentional reference of reason per se to be not tautological but artificial. And this in turn implies that the distinction between thought and thinker or between writing and writer (a distinction that 'aboutness' entails or, for Derrida, even comprises) is also merely a fabrication or ruse. We thus come to the first of two primary ways in which Derrida's post-subject approach differs from that of others. Whereas others invariably appeal to a kind of specialized ideological historiography, not only to justify their initial anti-rational stance but also putatively to authenticate their own insertion of purpose-inducing alternatives to re-infuse the feel of meaning (aboutness), Derrida himself turns the tables on this. He remains *within* reason and claims to show that the *apparent* inherent obligation or orientation we find in it – aboutness or intentional reference – is *itself* something merely 'ideological' and historicist inasmuch as it has its roots in a very specific, cultural-historical definition of the modern university, and does not identify anything intrinsic within reason itself.

Derrida's approach is thus by far the most carefully consistent, sophisticated and intricate of all post-subject outlooks. Yet even he cannot in the end resist inserting a 'feel of meaning' – that is, the feel of aboutness or of intentional reference (and as such a feel of purpose, obligation, responsibility) – into his post-structuralist enterprise in order to keep its purity from degenerating into mere bleakness.

The point is that, in the end, Derrida himself cannot help but frame all of this in terms of what he calls a 'new kind of thinking' centred around a 'new responsibility'. Granted, this new responsibility advocates an activity that is entirely negative: the responsibility is to 'unmask – an infinite task – *all the ruses of end-oriented thinking*'.[28] And it can also be granted that it is only in the purely negative sense of exposing all purpose-inducing or meaning-inducing endeavours as false and misbegotten in the first place,

28. Derrida, 'The Principle of Reason', p. 16, emphasis added.

that we can speak of a re-infusion of the feel of meaningfulness (aboutness, advocacy, intentional reference) in Derrida as much as in his less careful post-subject compatriots. Yet the feeling of purpose and advocacy that it brings is as undeniable as if it were positive. Derrida himself may resist this construal by objecting to it in the following compound way: First, he might grant that insofar as this activity of exposing such enterprises as 'ruses' is seen as anything like an *endeavour*, that is, as somehow *advocating* the 'deconstruction' of these, then it does indeed seem to become something 'end-oriented'. But he would immediately add, secondly, that this very activity must itself be simultaneously deconstructed in precisely the same way, so that its 'advocacy' is entirely replaced by 'undecidability' within a non-intentional terrain of 'strategic rhythm'.[29] But again,

---

29. The extent to which Derrida is willing to remain consistent to his principles of undecidability and non-advocacy (non-aboutness) even with regard to historical occurrences such as his own physical birth is remarkably illustrated in an interview cited in 'A "Madness" Must Watch Over Thinking', reprinted in *Points . . . Interviews* (Palo Alto: Stanford University Press, 1995), pp. 339–43. An excerpt:

Q.: Let us imagine your future biographer. One may suppose he will write, in a lazy repetition of the public record: Jacques Derrida was born July 15, 1930, in El Biar, near Algiers. It is up to you perhaps to oppose this biological birth with your true birth, the one that would proceed from that private or public event in which you really became yourself.

J. D.: For starters, that's a bit too much. You go so far as to say: 'it is up to you [*il vous revient*]' to say when you are born. No, if there is anything that cannot be 'up to me', then this is it, whether we're talking about what you call 'biological birth' transferred to the objectivity of the public record, or 'true birth'. 'I was born': this is one of the most singular expressions I know, especially in its French grammatical form. If the interview form lent itself to it, I would prefer, instead of answering you directly, to begin an interminable analysis of the phrase '*je, je suis, je suis né*' in which the tense is not given. Anxiety will never be dispelled on this subject, for the event that is thereby designated can herald itself in me only in the future: 'I am (not yet) born', but the future has the form of a past which I will never have witnessed and which for this reason remains always promised – and moreover also multiple. Who ever said that one was born just once? But how can one deny that through all the different promised births, it is a single and same time, the unique time, that insists and that is repeated forever? This is a little what is being recounted in *Circumfession*. 'I am not yet born' because the moment that decided my nameable identity was taken away from me. Everything is arranged so that it be this way, this is what is called culture. Thus, through so many different relays, one can only try to recapture this theft or this institution which was able to, which had to take place more than once. But however iterable and divisible it remains, the 'only once' resists.

Q.: Do you mean to say that you do not want to have any identity?

J. D.: On the contrary, I do, like everyone else. But by turning around this impossible thing, and which no doubt I also resist, the 'I' constitutes the very form of resistance. Each time this identity announces itself, each time a belonging circumscribes me, if I may put it this way, someone or something cries: Look out for the trap, you're caught. Take off, get free, disengage yourself. Your engagement is elsewhere. Not very original, is it?

Q.: Is the work you do aimed at refinding this identity?

J. D.: No doubt, but the gesture that tries to refind of *itself* distances, it distances itself again. One ought to be able to formalize the law of this insurmountable gap. This is a little

it is undeniable – and Derrida's own language here of a 'new responsibility' reinforces this – that deconstruction, undecidability and strategic
rhythm are all activities that are introduced to restore at least a 'feel' of
end-orientedness, a 'feel' of meaningfulness as aboutness. And, putting
this into Kantian terms, it would be difficult to know how to account for
this unexplained urge to restore the feel of meaningfulness as anything
other than a fundamental *need* of reason.

But now to complete the Derridean derivation of some of the terms I
have been employing here: Derrida continues on to say that, in order to
unmask and expose any of these endeavours as ruses and fabrications, the
responsibility underlying this new kind of thinking 'cannot be simple. It
implies multiple sites, a stratified terrain, postulations that are undergo-
ing continual displacement, a sort of *strategic rhythm*.'[30] Again, it should
be emphasized that this new thinking does not, in Derrida's own words,
'set [itself] up in opposition to reason, [or] give way to "irrationalism"'[31]
as other post-subject thinkers have done. Rather, it 'continue[s] to assume
within the university, along with its memory and tradition, the imperative of professional rigor and competence'.[32] But precisely because it is engaged around 'the principle of uncertainty' and 'a certain interpretation of
undecidability', *within* the established forms of rationality, Derrida maintains that this new kind of thinking will find its strategic rhythm in the
'possibilities that arise at the *outer limits* of the authority and the power of
the principle of reason'.[33] Hence it will be (what Derrida himself identifies
as) the most 'marginal' and most highly abstract disciplines such as critical theory that will operate most fruitfully in these conceptually distant
and difficult regions.

In light of all of this, it is not hard to see why Derrida holds such strong
appeal in some theological circles. His desire to break free from the epistemological constraints of the enlightenment conception of rationality,
coupled with a commitment to philosophical rigour and a deep respect
for the 'memory and tradition' of modernity – a great rarity, as we have
seen, among post-subject thinkers – sits well with theology's intrinsic and

what I am always doing. Identification is a difference to itself, a difference with/of itself.
Thus *with*, *without*, and *except* itself. The circle of the return to birth can only remain
open, but this is at once a chance, a sign of life, and a wound. If it closed in on birth, on a
plenitude of the utterance or the knowledge that says 'I am born', that would be death.
30. Derrida, 'The Principle of Reason', p. 17, emphasis added.
31. Derrida, 'The Principle of Reason', p. 17.
32. Derrida, 'The Principle of Reason', p. 17.
33. Derrida, 'The Principle of Reason', p. 14, emphasis added.

indispensable connection with its own 'modern' tradition and past, while prima facie seeming to provide a suitable vehicle for the task of theological reasoning by dispensing with the strictures of objectification, representation and normative intentionality. Nevertheless, what remains at bottom as clear in Derrida as in the other less resolute post-subject thinkers, is his inability (or unwillingness) to uphold the *integrity* of reason, which, to anticipate what is to come, orthodox theology with its inherent claim to authority by definition demands. In other words, Derrida's rejection of end-orientedness in thinking is precisely the most carefully considered negative answer to our question of whether there is any intrinsic orientation or obligation in reason. That is, it is the most articulate contemporary expression of what Kant called 'rational unbelief'. Thus, to state this in the terms outlined in chapter 1, while there may on the surface seem to be certain theological benefits of following these kinds of outlooks as just expressed, this will inevitably lead at best to some form or other of positivism (because of the rejection of the integrity of reason), or more worryingly, to a kind of gnosticism.[34]

2 Consequences of anti-rationalism

2.1 Post-structuralism and the haemorrhaging of subjectivity

Under the broad and growing influence of this post-subject (post-structuralist, ultra-pragmatist) mentality, what has resultingly arisen in the past three decades or so, especially in North America and Britain, is a confident and often rather strident espousal of 'the end of epistemology', or of 'pure procedural knowledge',[35] or a of a kind of 'irrationalism' that encourages us to 'think with our blood'.[36] However, in the face of this – beginning about the time when such slogans began to become popularized in North America and Britain[37] – in France itself, the nurturing ground

34. I have discussed this tendency within Radical Orthodoxy in another essay. (See 'Radical Orthodoxy and the New Culture of Obscurantism'.)
35. See, e.g., Rorty, *Philosophy and the Mirror of Nature*, 'Realism, Anti-realism, and Pragmatism'; Ian Hacking, 'Is the End in Sight for Epistemology?', *The Journal of Philosophy* 77. 10 (October 1980), pp. 579–88; Christopher Kulp, *The End of Epistemology: Dewey and his Current Allies on the Spectator Theory of Knowledge* (London: Greenwood Press 1992); Catherine Zelgin, 'Epistemology's End', in *Considered Judgment* (Princeton: Princeton University Press, 1996), pp. 3–20.
36. Rorty, *Consequences of Pragmatism*, p. 171. This is not how Rorty describes his own anti-rationalism but the less 'considered' irrationalism of others.
37. That is, in the late 1970s to mid 1980s, especially, at that time, among sociologists, ethnographers and critical theorists. See, e.g., James Clifford and George E. Marcus (eds.),

of post-structuralist thought, there has been a significant shift of tide underway. Writing back in 1980, French philosopher and historian Vincent
Descombes recounts the judgement of Jean Beaufret who in 1947, as an
anticipatory supporter of post-structuralism then just at its threshold,
warned against remaining 'within the Cartesian perspective of philosophies of consciousness'. Beaufret claimed that so long as the subject remains the root of philosophy's certainties, philosophy 'is condemned to
organise only the invasion of the world by a haemorrhage of subjectivity'.[38] But Descombes himself then asks, some three decades later: In the
wake of what Beaufret saw as so promising in post-structuralism, 'has
this haemorrhage of subjectivity announced by Jean Beaufret in 1947 been
staunched – more especially over the course of the recent years during
which "anti-humanism", the "liquidation of identity" or the "disappear-
ance of the subject" have played leading roles?'[39] In other words, have
these post-subject, anti-rational kinds of thinking actually achieved the
sort of radical liberation from the strictures of consciousness-based reasoning – and by implication, the fulfilment of human freedom on some
level – for which they initially strove? Descombes not only answers this
question negatively but observes that the condition had grown worse.
For in France itself the post-subject or anti-subject character of post-
structuralism actually gave way historically to a kind of intellectual *anti-
humanism*. And anti-humanism by definition undercuts the very liberation from the strictures of consciousness-based reasoning (in the sense
that this is a *human* liberation) that post-structuralism had promised. In
other words, this is not only self-defeating, but it actually, to continue with
Beaufret's metaphor, prolongs and exacerbates the haemorrhaging. For it
bleeds away, in the denial of freedom (anti-humanism), everything it purports to supply in intellectual liberation (anti-subject post-structuralism).

But now looking beyond the metaphor to real historical developments in French thought, Luc Ferry has noted that, because this post-
structuralist anti-humanism undercut and crippled the human individual, it actually led straight back into a new kind of authoritarianism. It
did so 'either by giving rise to [or reverting to] a panoply of master thinkers

Writing Culture: The Poetics and Politics of Ethnography (Berkeley: University of California Press,
1986) and George E. Marcus and Michael M. J. Fischer, *Anthropology as Cultural Critique: An
Experimental Moment in the Human Sciences* (Chicago: University of Chicago Press, 1986).
38. Jean Beaufret, *Introduction aux philosophies de l'existence*, quoted in Descombes, *Modern French
Philosophy*, p. 76.
39. Descombes, *Modern French Philosophy*, pp. 186–7.

(such as Hegel, Marx, Nietzsche, Heidegger, Foucault, Derrida) who produce hermetic systems of oracular discourse that admit of no falsification, or by elevating non-human things, such as the natural environment, to a point where humanity is rendered insignificant if not odious'.[40] The point is that post-structuralist thinking at its most consistent (i.e., without reintroducing 'aboutness' arbitrarily and ideologically as discussed above) has the undeniable 'feel' of fruitlessness and of utter immateriality to the enquiring observer.

The result has been that since the late 1970s post-structuralism has no longer been a 'living force' within France itself, however much it continues to hold sway in significant sectors of North American and British thought.[41] It is now seen broadly in France, because of the anti-humanistic ramifications just discussed, as an inherently foredoomed and misconceived intellectual endeavour. Predictably this backlash has come to be referred to as 'anti-post-modernism'. Descombes sums up the semantic vacancy at the root of the anti-post-structuralist ('anti-post-modern') sentiment in this way:

> In postmodernism [post-structuralism] there is *no original*, the model for the copy is itself a copy, and the copy is the copy of a copy; there is no *hypocritical mask*, for the face covered by the mask is itself a mask, and any mask is thus the mask of a mask; no facts, only interpretations, and any interpretation is itself the interpretation of an older

40. Ferry refers here of course to the 'deep ecology' movement which he shows to be tied to post-structuralist thought. See Luc Ferry, *The New Ecological Order* (Chicago: University of Chicago Press, 1992), pp. xxvii, 70–6. This is actually a quote from Reginald Lilly's essay on 'Post-Modernism', in Edward Craig (ed.), *Routledge Encyclopedia of Philosophy*, 10 vols. (London: Routledge, 1998), vol. VII, p. 595, who gives this apt gloss on Ferry.

41. See, e.g., Dews, *Logics of Disintegration*, pp. xi–xvii; Thomas Pavel, 'The Present Debate: News from France', *Diacritics* 19. 1 (spring 1989), pp. 17–32; Descombes *Modern French Philosophy*, especially pp. 180–90; Luc Ferry and Alain Renaut, Cattani (tr.), *French Philosophy of the Sixties* (Amherst: University of Massachusetts Press, 1985), pp. xxiv–xxix, 208–27; Ferry, *The New Ecological Order*, pp. xix–xxix; Lilly, 'Postmodernism', pp. 593–6. It must be added that it is not as if this signals the emergence of some new cohesive philosophical outlook in France. For example, the particular group of thinkers among which Luc Ferry, Alain Renaut and Pierre Manent are prominent exemplars in no way signifies a new 'norm' in French thought. Vincent Descombes' recent work, for example, although not entirely unsympathetic, is much different. (The excellent Princeton book series entitled 'New French Thought' is informative here.) Instead, in Peter Dew's words, the undermining of the 'dogmatic avant-garde consciousness of post-structuralism has made possible a fragmentation and pluralization of philosophical activity in France' (p. xii). The further point is that the backlash against anti-subject (post-subject) thinking has led to the re-evaluation of an array of thinkers who had been 'unjustly marginalized by the predominance of structuralism and post-structuralism' in the 1960s and early 1970s, including Levinas and especially the subject-affirming hermeneutics of Paul Ricoeur (Dews, *Logics of Disintegration*, p. xii).

> interpretation; there is no *meaning proper* to words, only figurative
> meanings . . . there is no *authentic version* of a text, there are only
> translations; *no truth*, only pastiche and parody . . .[42]

Indeed, as a result of the sheer vacancy of human constituency in post-structural or post-subject thinking, along with the loss of meaningfulness as intentional reference which by definition accompanies it (as discussed in chapter 1), French thought has recently been witnessing what many agree is a renewed sympathy for the enlightenment and modernity.[43] This has been marked specifically by a 'rediscovery of the urgency of epistemological questioning' and a return 'toward a conception of human activity' which accentuates 'the roles of consciousness, intentionality and human agency'.[44] Of course this does not signal any wholesale reversion to the tenets of modern epistemology, but rather indicates something along the more moderate and self-critical lines of the contemporary anti-realism versus realism issues that we will be discussing in the next chapter.

2.2 Post-subject thinking and the forsaking of intellectual virtue

We thus see a decidedly anti-humanistic outcome in the development of French post-structuralism which has produced an 'anti-post-modern' or anti-post-structuralist backlash in France itself.[45] This backlash, however, has not materialized to the same degree in Britain and North America. And this seems understandable enough given that a post-subject reaction against *analytical* philosophy will be less likely to spawn the same degree of anti-humanistic sentiment as continental post-subject reactions against the more visceral and historical systems of, say, Sartrean existentialism or the romanticism-tinged Hegelianism. Or in other words, perhaps the kind of analytical philosophy that serves largely as the antagonist for Rorty's ultra-pragmatism, for instance, is too technical and clinically conceptual to allow for the same kind of anti-humanistic haemorrhaging of which Descombes speaks. Whatever the reasons for the backlash not

---

42. Descombes, *Modern French Philosophy*, p. 182, original emphasis.
43. Dews, *Logics of Disintegration*, p. xiv. See also Pavel, 'The Present Debate: News from France', pp. 25–6. Vincent Descombes' new book, *The Mind's Provisions* (Princeton: Princeton University Press, 2001) is a prime example of the originality and contemporary relevance with which enlightenment themes are again being revisited and explored in new French thought. See also footnote 41 above.
44. Pavel, 'The Present Debate: News From France', pp. 25–6.
45. The new humanism that is re-emerging, however, is decidedly atheistic. See, e.g., Luc Ferry, *Man Made God* (Chicago: University of Chicago Press, 2002).

having materialized in the same way, it is clear that the human sciences and theology in Britain and North America are today heavily influenced by this post-subject mindset (most prominently again by way of Rorty and Derrida). In light of their continuing popularity and increasing influence within Anglo-American religious thinking then, I conclude this chapter by looking at one further worrying consequence of anti-rational outlooks for theology, beyond those associated with their failure in France.

The point to be made is that the contemporary move away from the *subject* (i.e., away from questions involving consciousness, intention and reference) will also inevitably turn out to be a move away from many of the *intellectual virtues* traditionally associated with philosophy at its best: virtues of clarity, logical consistency, argumentative integrity (e.g. avoidance of gratuitous circularity), modesty, circumspect self-critique, and a commitment to certain basic principles of intellectual charity and attentiveness. I do not mean that anti-rational or post-subject devotees never manifest these virtues or never implicitly strive for them. I mean only that insofar as they do aspire to them they are not being true to their own post-subject commitments inasmuch as all of these virtues by definition constitute *intentional-referential* behaviours or dispositions. Each of them presupposes the central involvement of a conscious, intentional subject striving to uphold what are taken to be certain basic standards of right thinking. This is why the most ingenious and tactically adept[46] among post-subject thinkers are careful to avoid giving any legitimacy whatsoever to what normal philosophical virtue terms purport to identify. Instead, the post-subject response here will be to treat these virtues not as constituting anything like high-water marks for thinking,[47] but rather, as we have seen, to expose as a 'ruse' what they appear to demand: for instance, either by deconstructing their intentional-referential 'end-orientedness' (Derrida) or by deflating them as reflective merely of a false construal of discourse in the first place as a 'competition between arguments' (Rorty). The point is that these virtues *always* show up as a *manifestation* of end-orientedness, such that when end-orientedness is declared by post-subject outlooks to be a 'ruse', all possibility of engaging these virtues also collapses. Stated in more formal terms, these virtues logically entail end-orientedness or intentional reference (i.e., they cannot be defined apart

---

46. I do not say logically consistent for that would imply the presence of normative horizons which adherents would resist.
47. This would be implicitly to legitimize epistemology, or the idea that thinking has certain basic normative features.

from end-orientedness). And it is thus the *formal* (i.e., logical) loss – and this means the utter loss – of their ability to speak in these terms that makes post-subject outlooks most truly obscurantist and anti-rational or anti-philosophical: they eschew the kind of virtue or intellectual wisdom – humility, modesty, circumspection, deference – that philosophy at its best always strives for.

Yet having said this, it is in a sense not difficult to understand the kinds of benefit that many today continue to perceive for theological thinking in following these non-end-oriented (or non-intentional-referential) post-subject outlooks. For a transcendent God can never be anything like a focus of end-orientedness; and the unavoidable need to make theological reasoning end-orientingly 'about' God *anyway*, that is, in spite of this impossibility, is a restatement of precisely the impasse encountered in the 'formal' question of Christian thinking with which I started this whole study. Or conversely, it is easy to see the prima facie theological appeal of non-end-oriented approaches inasmuch as it is exactly the *demand* for end-orientedness in theological discourse – and the impasse resulting from that demand – that gives rise to the opposing misleading 'solutions' of reductionism and positivism. Reductionism, as we saw in chapter 1, sacrifices the integrity of transcendence in order to preserve genuine end-orientedness (meaningful reference) in religious discourse. Positivism to the contrary dispenses with the demands of reason in order to enable end-orientedness to be genuinely 'about' the transcendent, by resorting to a kind of reference that is entirely inscrutable (positivistic) and arbitrary. Why then should theology not follow these post-subject methods and dispense with the problem of end-orientedness altogether if it is precisely *this* demand that is the source of the impasse?

The reason why theology cannot do so is of course that any claim to Christian *orthodoxy* cannot tolerate such a move. To illustrate this, and also thereby to show how the claim to orthodoxy cannot be merely positivistic (or radically fideistic) but must involve a claim to rational integrity, let us look at just one intellectual virtue – one particular expression of end-orientedness – and ask how orthodox theology could conceivably do without it. Let us look at the virtue addressed in a different context near the beginning of this chapter: that of allowing speakers and writers with whom one is engaging to *speak for themselves*, or the virtue of attentiveness. Now it will be immediately clear that there are two fundamental reasons why post-subject outlooks could never tolerate such an intellectual virtue or allow for its genuineness. The first reason is that genuine attentiveness involves or entails a kind of 'presence' or the possibility of an ontological integrity (independent authority) within that which one is seeking to be attentive *to*; and as our discussion above of structuralism and post-structuralism showed, this is precisely what post-subject outlooks most fundamentally deny. The meaning of a text or of a statement (or of a dogma) is determined entirely from its relation to other texts and statements and never from any intrinsic, persisting 'presence' or integrity per se. The second reason, as we have just been discussing, is that attentiveness is an intrinsically 'end-oriented' disposition of a conscious, thinking, listening subject; and all such dispositions have been declared to be fabrications by post-subject anti-rational approaches. And this now leads to the real point of concern for Christian thinking for when we come to the question of *orthodoxy*, we find not only that orthodoxy by definition demands this very virtue of attentiveness which post-subject outlooks cannot tolerate or contemplate, but also that it demands the intellectual virtue of attentiveness *for precisely the same reasons* that post-subject outlooks reject it. Let us look at these reasons again more closely with that in mind.

The first point was that post-subject outlooks cannot accommodate the intellectual virtue of attentiveness because it involves a claim to 'presence'. Yet the claim to orthodoxy *just is* such a claim to intrinsic 'presence', and this in the full and unmistakable sense of a claim to an authority that is genuinely general. Three qualifications must be made here. To begin with, we are not yet in this assertion about orthodoxy and intrinsic presence simply declaring that *transcendence* can be 'present'. For that would be to address a much different question.[48] Secondly, by speaking in these rather bold terms of intrinsic and universal authority we do not commit ourselves to an inappropriate kind of dogmatism either, for this language does not signify that we now expect Christian orthodoxy to be systematically expressible in some rigidly incorrigible or foundational way which can be ascertained utterly independently of human context. Nor, thirdly, and relatedly, is it to deny that orthodoxy will always come to expression *within* some context, and will reflect and be responsive to that context.[49] It is only to say that the claim to orthodoxy *just is* a claim to an intrinsic authority whose jurisdiction holds *on its own terms* across all contexts, and

48. Indeed, *how* the claim to *orthodoxy* can be a claim *about transcendence* would be precisely another way of stating the formal problem of Christian thinking as outlined at the beginning of the first chapter.

49. In fact, these are questions that begin to pertain to the problems of realism and anti-realism to be addressed in the next two chapters.

whose 'presence' as such no context can *fundamentally* alter, diminish or negate.

The second point was that post-subject, anti-rational outlooks declare all intentional-referential end-orientedness to be a ruse or a fabrication. Yet orthodoxy, because it is centred in faith, demands precisely the kind of human attentiveness that can only arise as some sort of end-oriented disposition. Again, as in the previous point, this is not of course to expect that faith could be exhaustively defined or accounted for *merely* or purely as an end-oriented disposition, as if that were essentially what faith *is*. It is only to say that faith cannot be expressed apart from the intellectual virtue of attentiveness *as* an *end-oriented* disposition; indeed faith is unintelligible apart from a sense of end-orientedness. This now leads in turn to a very interesting and important result. If there is one way in which faith can indeed be said to *need* reason or rational integrity, or if there is one way in which reason or rational integrity can be said to be *indispensable* to faith (and hence also to Christian orthodoxy), it is in this sense of faith demanding the presence of the kinds of intellectual virtues that cannot be had apart from rational integrity. For faith cannot come to expression without the presence of these intellectual virtues as conscious, end-oriented dispositions.

In sum, there is a fundamental incompatibility between any of these 'radical' anti-rational post-subject approaches and orthodox theology. For the attack on reason or on rational integrity can be shown (as I have just done) to entail an attack also on any claim to orthodoxy, since orthodoxy cannot come to expression apart from the end-oriented (intentional-referential) intellectual virtues that comprise the elements of rational integrity. We thus set the anti-rational outlooks aside in our enquiry into Christian thinking or theological cognition and begin an exploration, for theological purposes, into different approaches historically for upholding the integrity of reason in intellectual endeavour.

3

Philosophy's perpetual polarities: anti-realism and realism

I have spoken of the anti-rational outlooks in mainly negative terms in the last chapter. But there is also an extremely valuable service they have provided with respect to our own main goal of preserving rational integrity in theological thinking. In demonstrating the attack on reason to be most essentially an attack on end-orientedness or intentional reference in thinking, they have refocused and given a new and sharpened relevance to what must be the main task for any endeavour that wants to speak on behalf of the integrity of reason. Put simply, a defence of rational integrity will have to show how end-oriented thinking, that is, intentional-referential reasoning, is *not* a ruse, *not* merely a fabrication or an imposition, but rather the reflection, in Kantian terms, of something like a fundamental *need* of reason. In other words – and here we come back to one of the pivotal assertions of chapter 1 – the primary task in making the case for the integrity of reason will be to provide compelling and if possible indefeasible ways of accounting for *obligation* in reason or, what amounts to the same thing, of accounting for the intrinsic, self-orienting nature of reason.

To provide such an account of rational integrity for theological purposes is the first of the two major concerns of this book; and it is to that task that we now turn in the present and the following three chapters. We begin this enterprise with a discussion of some of the central aspects of what has become well known in contemporary discussion as the anti-realism/realism debate. There are two key benefits to initiating the question of rational integrity from within this debate, beyond the current prominence of the dispute itself across a wide array of academic disciplines. The first is that for all its disparateness and many-sidedness, the debate is at bottom most essentially concerned, as we shall see, with precisely these issues of rational obligation and authority, especially in response to the peculiar character of these concerns in today's rather turbulent epistemological climate. More specifically, the relationship between anti-realism and realism is most properly and fundamentally understood when these terms themselves are seen as essentially designating the two most basic diverging intellectual dispositions in explaining rational integrity, or in accounting for rational obligation or authority. But there is a second reason for broaching our subject matter initially from within the anti-realism/realism debate. And this is that the current dispute is not simply an isolated contemporary debate, but is actually connected to a perennial philosophical conflict, a conflict that has a long and multi-faceted history within epistemological disagreement, so that the enquiry into the current debate actually also addresses something much deeper within philosophy itself.

What I propose to do in this chapter then is to begin by contextualizing the anti-realism/realism debate both within contemporary discussion and with respect to its philosophical heritage, before focusing on individual exemplifications of each side of the debate in Hilary Putnam and Thomas Nagel. The surveys of Putnam and Nagel here will serve a double purpose. First, they will provide prominent examples of the ways in which rational integrity (or rational obligation or authority) is being defended today from opposing standpoints and thus help to focus our own agenda within contemporary concerns. (Putnam's *Reason, Truth and History* and Nagel's *The View from Nowhere* have become near classics in the current discussion.) But just as importantly, they will serve as a backdrop to the continued discussion of anti-realism and realism in the next chapter in the work of Donald MacKinnon, whose illuminating and highly relevant contributions to these matters have been all but lost in contemporary treatments and whose insight opens the debate to theological problems in enormously productive ways. These three together, with the subsequent chapter on act and being, will in turn serve as an even broader backdrop to the discussion of Kant in chapter 6, where all of these polarities will be turned fundamentally on their heads.

1   Anti-realism and realism present and past

1.1   Two ironies of empiricism
It must surely count as one of the strangest anomalies in the history of intellectual endeavour that today, at precisely a time when to the lay observer the 'hard' sciences seem to be yielding increasingly indisputable 'hard'

facts, or when the science journals announce that externally 'testable' knowledge about the physical world expands exponentially several times over in the space of the average single lifetime, or when what have hitherto been perceived as the radically private subjective mysteries of mind, mood, disposition and behaviour can be pinpointed, with ever-deepening accuracy, as corresponding to 'publicly observable' microscopic biochemical goings-on in the brain – it is strange that all of this should be accompanied by a sharp and ever-widening academic debate about whether there is such a thing as an 'objective reality' existing independently of the observer. In one sense this can be seen as just the latest reflection of the seemingly inescapable ironies of the Anglo-American empiricist heritage. Empiricism did away with the intangible, with innateness, with the a priori and the 'metaphysics' of the continental rationalists in order to rid philosophy of what it considered to be superstitions and obscurantisms; or more specifically to rid philosophy of any system of epistemic justification that is not traceable to sensory observation or experience. Yet ironically it is precisely this insistence on the sensorily experiential and verifiable that has historically engendered the most thoroughly *un*realistic viewpoints. Radically empiricist philosophies, it seems, will almost invariably comport themselves towards what they most want to avoid: namely towards a new kind of immaterialist and thoroughly subjective idealism, and as such also inescapably towards scepticism of one sort or another. Hence Mill's account of physical objects as simply 'permanent possibilities of sensation' and Berkeley's even more radical view (especially when the theistic presuppositions are removed) of objects as nothing more than collections of ideas.

But surely the sophistication and supremacy of contemporary science has changed this subjectivist face of empirical enquiry. To the commonsense day-to-day reality that most of us inhabit, it is prima facie difficult to see how anyone could not be willing to admit that the *reason* that science gives us consistent and 'publicly verifiable' results on its findings is simply that the world *real*-ly *does* exist 'in certain ways', independently of whether it is scientifically or pre-scientifically observed as such or not. But the subjectivist roots of empiricism cause it to judge even modern science harshly: for now, beginning from the second half of the twentieth century, out of the very precision and consistent regularity in the gleanings of scientific practice, arises a new kind of 'post-empiricist' dogma.[1]

---

1. It is commonly agreed that W. V. O. Quine's pivotal essay 'Two Dogmas of Empiricism' (in *From a Logical Point of View* (Cambridge, MA: Harvard University Press, 1961), pp. 20–46)

Post-empiricism begins from the observation that the more precise scientific enquiry becomes, the more it is essentially engaged with comparisons of sets of theoretical interpretations and no longer with the actual, observed, 'uninterpreted' world of simple empirical experience. In the light of this it claims that any cognitive encounter with the world is already interpreted, that any scientific observation is accordingly already 'theory-laden' and furthermore that any such scientific theory is itself at least partially (the post-subject anti-rational outlooks would say *entirely*) a cultural/historical construct, and not the 'discovery' of some pure algorithmic constant whose proper application will be capable of yielding objective truths of fact. From here of course it is not a very long distance to the denial of any privileged epistemological status whatsoever for scientific 'knowledge'. Science comes to be viewed as a discipline on a par semantically with other essentially interpretive (i.e., 'hermeneutical') activities, whether cultural or literary. Commenting on this radical and swift reversal from the glory days of scientific positivism, Christopher Norris remarks that 'where it was once a matter of "rescuing" poetry from science . . . now it appears that the tables have been turned with all the benefits accruing to the other side'.[2] He then cites this sardonic summation from Charles Taylor: 'old-guard Diltheyans, their shoulders hunched from years-long resistance against the encroaching pressure of positivist natural science, suddenly pitch forward on their faces as all opposition ceases to the reign of universal hermeneutics'.[3]

Back in 1981, in the introduction to his landmark book, *Reason, Truth and History*, Hilary Putnam spoke of a 'bold minority' of philosophers who, on the strength of this post-empiricist trend, but still against a prevailing tide of realism with respect to universals (I will explain what this means below), were at that time putting forward a 'subjectivist view with vigor'.[4] In the past two decades the ranks of this 'bold minority' have grown to such an extent that 'anti-realism', in varying grades of 'holism' or 'coherence', has now become easily the predominant, even the conventionalist or

provided a 'decisive impetus' for a rejection within many prominent Anglo-American intellectual circles of both traditional empiricism and logical positivism; cf., e.g., Hilary Putnam, *Reason, Truth, and History* (Cambridge: Cambridge University Press, 1981), pp. 82–5; and Christopher Norris, *New Idols of the Cave: On the Limits of Anti-realism* (Manchester: Manchester University Press 1997), p. 7.

2. Norris, *New Idols of the Cave*, p. 8.
3. Charles Taylor, 'Understanding in Human Science', *Review of Metaphysics* 34 (1980), pp. 25–38, quoted in Norris, *New Idols of the Cave*, p. 8.
4. Putnam, *Reason, Truth, and History*, p. ix.

default view within the human sciences.[5] Even in philosophy the trend is pervasive enough so that any genuinely 'external realist' position, which continues to affirm the ontological independence of a world extending beyond the reach of our minds (Nagel), must unquestionably be characterized as the current dissenting view. When one adds to this certain apparently parallel developments in the philosophy of science and in the physical sciences, especially in quantum theory, both of which seem to reinforce the 'mind-dependent' view of the world,[6] the stage is set for what has emerged with increasing momentum over the past two decades as an anti-realist/realist debate within philosophy itself, whose ramifications and divisive lines run through virtually every branch of academic study.

1.2   Anti-realism and realism: an old controversy renewed

However, considerable confusion continues to reign over what the anti-realism/realism dispute essentially is.[7] There are several reasons for this.

5. See, e.g., Joseph Margolis, *Pragmatism without Foundations: Reconciling Realism with Relativism* (Oxford: Blackwell 1986), pp. xvi–xvii; Norris, *New Idols of the Cave*, pp. 1, 6, as well as the valuable and extensive bibliography, pp. 36–37; David Papineau, 'Does the Sociology of Science Discredit Science?', in Robert Nola (ed.), *Relativism and Realism in Science* (Dordrecht: Kluwer Academic Publishers, 1988), pp. 37–57, pp. 37–9.

6. For example, within the philosophy of science, Thomas Kuhn's *The Structure of Scientific Revolutions* is of course pivotal (Chicago: University of Chicago Press, 1962). Kuhn questioned the hitherto universally accepted 'cumulative nature' of scientific discovery and proposed instead that science was essentially a reflection of the particular historical, cultural and sociological milieu from which it came to be practised. In other words, the perspectival paradigm of any given milieu or the discrete cultural hermeneutic onto which it seeks to make the world fit, is as much a contributor to scientific 'discoveries' as is whatever raw material the external world might contain. Kuhn's further claim, that these paradigms are 'incommensurable' (this is why they are 'non-cumulative'), although by no means uncontroversial, nevertheless coincided with a general increase in Anglo-American interest from the 1950s onward in the relationship of scientific development to the historical/social perspective from which scientific enquiry is practised. Hence also the continually increasing presence of 'history and the philosophy of science' departments in universities around the world (cf., e.g., Robert Nola (ed.), *Relativism and Realism in Science* (Dordrecht: Kluwer Academic Publishers, 1988), p. vii and especially Papineau's excellent and concise overview of science and the 'new sociology of science' in the same volume pp. 37–57).

The most frequently cited support for anti-realism from physical theory is the postulate, roughly, that quantum theory (hailed as the best explanatory material theory available 'to date') cannot itself be interpreted in a way that permits the description of phenomena without reference to some observer (Thomas Nagel, *The View from Nowhere* (Oxford: Oxford University Press 1986), p. 16; see also John Polkinghorne, *Science and Theology, an Introduction* (London: SPCK/Fortress, 1998) for an accessible review of the state of this issue within current scientific debate). In other words, quantum theory appears to make the world somehow 'observer-dependent', which is the anti-realist position. There are, however, many 'realist' responses to this paradox – including that of Niels Bohr himself (cf. e.g., Norris, *New Idols of the Cave*, pp. 173–92, which includes an extensive bibliography (p. 192) on the current discussion; see also Nagel, *The View from Nowhere*, pp. 16–17).

7. See Norris, *New Idols of the Cave* for one of the most helpful and comprehensive accounts of the current debate; see also Kulp, *Realism/Antirealism and Epistemology*.

One is the multi-faceted and cross-disciplinary nature of the debate it-self, especially in the wake of recent developments on the anti-realist side as discussed above. Another is the prevalent practice of conflating anti-realism with the kinds of anti-rationalism we discussed in chapter 2, or treating these as parts of the same 'relativistic' lump. Along these lines, perhaps the most common mistake is to view the anti-realism/realism debate as a conflict essentially between traditional 'modern' epistemology and something roughly construed as 'post-modern' (i.e., along the post-subject or post-structural lines discussed in the previous chapter). This is false. In fact, despite all the genuinely new developments that anti-realists claim as fresh support for their side of the debate, what the anti-realism/realism dispute most essentially *is* (as the next two chapters will show) is only the latest manifestation of what is better known historically as the idealism/realism dispute, a conflict that has been at the centre of philosophical debate in different forms since the time of the Greeks, and that continues to re-emerge in new ways. The conflict is often described in the broadest of terms within contemporary discussion as reflective of the two most basic and mutually exclusive dispositions or temperaments of philosophical enquiry: one 'internalist', espousing a perceiver-dependent view of reality (idealism or anti-realism), the other 'externalist', espousing a perceiver-independent view of reality (realism). While this description can give rise to oversimplifications, nevertheless it is a helpful distinction because it is capable of capturing virtually all traditional versions of both realism and idealism within it.

Before explaining this further, we can give ourselves a starting point by defining realism – that is, the 'perceiver-independent view' – in the simplest of terms, as the view that what exists and the way in which it exists is independent of any perception of it.[8] Anti-realism, or idealism – that is, the 'perceiver-dependent view' – in the simplest of terms, denies this. But the 'perceiver-dependent' label does not of course signify that anti-realists contend that the world of human experience is *purely* a con-struction of the mind. Anti-realism is not solipsism. Anti-realism claims only that since anything that can be said meaningfully about reality or the world *must* be said from some perspective, therefore it is not possible to engage in intelligible dialogue about reality *independent* of any perspective.

---

8. See, e.g., John Searle, *The Construction of Social Reality* (London: Penguin, 1996), p. 155; Edward Craig (ed.), *Routledge Encyclopedia of Philosophy*, 10 vols. (London: Routledge, 1998), vol. I, p. 115.

Or in other words, we do not know what we mean or refer to when we speak of reality apart from any perspective. Now there will of course be those who will want to press this point to an extreme and dispense with the realist claim about perceiver-independence altogether. They will maintain that such a realist statement is nonsense to begin with since the claim to the perceiver-*in*dependence of reality is itself a 'perceiver-*dependent*' claim. But all that such a blanket appeal to the necessarily anthropocentric nature of all of our enquiries amounts to in the end, as we shall see, is a facile deflationary move which serves at bottom only to avoid facing difficult questions. Such a view, as MacKinnon nicely puts it, makes the fundamental mistake of 'convert[ing] awareness of anthropocentrism [perceiver-dependence] from a problem into a solution' and, as such, merely 'into a recipe for dissolving a multitude of problems'.⁹ This is a deflationary danger which all anti-realist positions must face and which the most conscientious among them seek to avoid.

But with these clarifications in mind, let me now return to what I was describing as the heuristically helpful character of the 'perceiver-dependence versus perceiver-independence' distinction, especially for accommodating all the various historical versions of idealism and realism.¹⁰ So, for example, what came to be known in the first half of the twentieth century as 'atomic realism', associated famously with the 'logical atomism' of Russell, Moore and early Wittgenstein, promotes at bottom such a mind-independent or perceiver-independent view of the world. The world on this view is composed ultimately of a totality of 'atomic facts' that exist or obtain whether they are perceived or not. In other words, atomic realism is a kind of scientific or even *physical* realism. As such it is in certain ways significantly different from the *metaphysical* realisms of, say, Spinoza or Wolff where the focus of perceiver-independence is not sensible, spatio-temporal facts, but rather 'more ultimate' *supra*-sensible and time*less* realities or principles, which exist (or subsist) whether they are (rationally) perceived or not. Yet despite these differences, both are a type of realism since they affirm a perceiver-independent or mind-independent view

9. Donald MacKinnon, *Explorations in Theology* (London: SCM Press, 1979), p. 150. One way in which the claim to perceiver-independence can be made plausibly will be demonstrated by our discussion of Nagel below.

10. I do not speak of the plethora of 'realisms' that abound today which redefine the term at will. In an age where pragmatism holds such sway across so many disciplines, it often seems as if everyone wants to be a 'realist', even the most relativistic of outlooks. So we see talk of 'pragmatic realism', 'cultural realism', 'holistic realism' and so on. Even Putnam enters the fray here, as we shall see, with his 'internal realism'.

of reality, whether this is physical (scientific) or metaphysical. The same point can be made with regard to what we might call Plato's eternal realism, in which the Forms (even though they are also sometimes called the Ideas) are said to be eternal or ultimate realities that exist whether they are perceived or not, or, perhaps better in this case, whether they are materially instantiated or not. Similarly, from the other side, the 'mind-dependent' distinction is capable of capturing the whole disparate array of traditional idealisms as well, whether we are looking at Berkeleyan empirical idealism or the vastly different metaphysical idealism of Hegel, or indeed the more recent Bradleyan idealism that served as the antagonist for logical atomism.[11] All of these are types of idealism since they make reality in some way – even if in vastly different ways – mind-dependent or perceiver-dependent.

But there is also another, perhaps less divisive way of configuring this whole perennial philosophical disagreement: and this is in the even more estimable and long-standing formulation as a fundamental disagreement about whether *sensation* or *intellect* should be given priority in philosophical questioning. This disagreement came to be expressed prominently in Greek philosophy as the distinction between *aisthesis* and *noiesis*. The philosophies of Democritus (who privileges sensation) and Plato (who privileges thinking) are perhaps most traditionally contrasted here,[12] but it can be seen in pre-Socratic philosophy as well, for example in certain ways that Heraclitus is opposed to Parmenides. Now the basic point towards which this is building is as follows. If we draw all of these elements together, we can come to a kind of hybrid formulation that can serve to provide a basic definition of what has in the meantime come to be known as the 'classical' idealism/realism dispute. The basic definition of the classical dispute, then, is this: It is a conflict fundamentally between *empirical idealism*, that is, the perceiver-dependent view favouring sensation in philosophical reasoning, and *metaphysical realism*, that is, the perceiver-independent view favouring intellect in philosophical reasoning.[13] Within modern philosophy of course this has come most

---

11. Bradleyan idealism owes much to Hegel and spawned what came to be known as 'logical holism' in contrast to logical atomism. The Moore/Bradley debates are most well known here.
12. Aristotle arguably sought a harmonization of the two, even though he is often somewhat misleadingly contrasted with Plato here, as privileging sensation over Plato's privileging of intellect.
13. So simple a delineation can of course by no means be either exhaustive or exclusive. Hegel, for example, is more difficult than other idealists to place on this configuration, but it remains informative even in that context.

prominently and massively to expression in the conflict between British empiricism – especially where this is manifest as empirical idealism, most classically in Berkeley but also in Mill (Hume does not work here, as we shall see) – and continental rationalism, for example as seen in Spinoza, Wolff and Mendelssohn.[14] So the summary point is this: It is in connection with this long and venerable history, but *especially* as an expression of the dispute between empirical idealism and metaphysical realism that the contemporary anti-realism/realism debate is most properly placed.

But having thus set the present debate into that broad historical context, we can now return to the initial reason given for commencing our enquiry into rational integrity from within the anti-realism/realism debate. That reason, again, was that in any of their historical guises, and especially in their contemporary forms, anti-realism and realism (internalism and externalism) are most fundamentally and authentically understood as the two most broad and diverging philosophical ways of accounting for *rational obligation* or for *orientation* in reason, and thus tying precisely into our own overarching concern. This will become manifestly clear as we move into our surveys of Putnam and Nagel. But the first obvious indication we get of this is the way each side appeals to theories of truth. It will be helpful to outline this briefly before turning to Putnam and Nagel themselves, where the claim will be demonstrated more fully.

Stating it in the simplest of terms: the realist undertakes a defence of rationality based on some version of realism's most essential corollary, the correspondence theory of truth. The anti-realist or idealist undertakes a defence of rationality based on some version of anti-realism's most essential corollary, the coherence theory of truth or what is now often called a holist theory of truth.[15] For current purposes we may define these very basically as follows. Correspondence theory says roughly: A statement is true if it 'matches' or accurately 'corresponds' to some picked-out feature of reality or the world, where the world is understood as existing independently of and externally to any perception of it or belief about it. Coherence (or holist) theory says roughly: A statement is true if it 'fits' or 'coheres' within a given system of established beliefs or within a given cognitive picture. Finally, as we now turn to Putnam and Nagel themselves, I will follow what has become common practice in these kinds of debates and refer to

14. And to a lesser degree also Descartes and Leibniz, although Leibniz is especially difficult to place here.
15. Although 'holism' here again must be understood with the crucial caveat cited in chapter 2 held clearly in mind.

anti-realist outlooks as 'internalist' outlooks (because they make the interpretation of reality perceiver-dependent and thus in some way 'internal' to perception), and I will refer to realism as 'externalist' in disposition because it allows for existence independent of perception ('external' to perception).

2   Hilary Putnam's anti-realist ('internalist') account of rational obligation

Hilary Putnam is a reluctant anti-realist. He prefers to call his version of internalism by the names of 'internal realism' or 'pragmatic realism'. But this does not diminish its character fundamentally as a perceiver-dependent interpretation of reality, and so he remains anti-realist or idealist in the strict sense of these terms as I have defined them above. Putnam begins his book *Reason, Truth and History* by depicting the traditional debates between what he calls 'metaphysical realism' and 'cultural relativism' (by this he means roughly the kind of anti-rationalism we discussed in chapter 2) as 'outdated ... predictable and boring', describing these as 'alienated views', which 'cause one to lose one or another part of oneself and the world'. In a clear indication of his alignment with coherence or holist theories of truth, Putnam then declares his intentions to sketch the leading ideas of what will amount to the composite picture of a *'non-alienated* view of truth and a *non-alienated* view of human flourishing'.[16] He explains this non-alienated position more fully as follows:

> I shall advance a view in which the mind does not simply 'copy' a world which admits of description by One True Theory. But my view is not a view in which the mind *makes up* the world either ... If one must use metaphorical language, then let the metaphor be this: the mind and the world jointly make up the mind and the world ... Vision [for example] does not give us direct access to a ready made world but gives us a description of objects which are partly structured and constituted by vision itself ... Vision is 'good' when it enables us to see the world 'as it is' – that is, the human, functional world which is partly created by vision itself.[17]

In this light, let us look more closely at the extremes that Putnam himself is rejecting: metaphysical realism and cultural relativism. With regard to the former, Putnam was himself at one time a strong advocate

16. Putnam, *Reason, Truth, and History*, pp. x–xii; Hilary Putnam, *Representation and Reality* (Cambridge, MA: MIT Press, 1988), p. 1, original emphasis throughout.
17. Putnam, *Reason, Truth, and History*, pp. xi, 146, original emphasis.

of it.[18] What he formerly found most 'seductive' about metaphysical realism, he says, had not so much to do with how it seemed to resonate with our basic intuitions concerning the nature of reality. Its appeal was rather in 'the idea that *the way to solve philosophical problems is to construct a better scientific picture of the world*'.[19] Underlying this whole scientific realism approach – the central postulate that made it so convincing for Putnam – was the idea that 'the world consists of some fixed reality of mind-independent objects [and that] there is exactly one true and complete description of "the way the world is"'.[20] Putnam's favourite caption for this description of reality is the 'God's Eye Point of View' or the 'One True Theory'.

In the end, however, it was Putnam's equal conversancy not only in philosophy, but also in physics and mathematics that drew him over to the other side. For his expertise in these other areas convinced him that the more deeply one is able to delve into science the more implausible and incoherent any idea of the One True Theory becomes. A very simple example of this runs as follows:

> We may partly describe the contents of a room by saying that there is a chair in front of a desk, and partly describe the contents of the same room by saying that there are particles and fields of a certain kind present. But to ask which of these descriptions describes the room as it is 'independent of perspective', or 'in itself', is senseless.[21]

Putnam's point of course is that both accounts describe the room as it 'really is'

Now so far there is very little to argue with here, even, as we shall see in Nagel, with respect to current realist accounts; for the kind of 'metaphysical realism' that Putnam repudiates here will turn out to be little more than a strawman version of realism, a view that is extremely easy to defeat, and which no realist participants in the debate today would hold.

---

18. Putnam, *Reason, Truth, and History*, pp. 107–20. The decisive shifts within the course of the development of Putnam's thought are well publicized. (See, e.g., Conant in Hilary Putnam, *Realism with a Human Face* (London: Harvard University Press, 1990), pp. xv–lxxiv, and especially pp. xvi–xvii and xxxi; or Putnam himself in Samuel Guttenplan (ed.) *A Companion to the Philosophy of Mind* (Oxford: Blackwell, 1995), pp. 507–13.) In a circa 1976 about-face, which heavily impacted most aspects of his thinking, Putnam, until then a 'robust realist', began attacking 'metaphysical realism' as an essentially incoherent position, putting forward in its place his doctrine of 'internal realism'. Putnam still holds the internalist view and continues to develop it, albeit in increasingly pragmatic terms.
19. Putnam, *Representation and Reality*, p. 107, original emphasis. Actually, with respect to the overview above, it is clear that what Putnam is really rejecting here is not metaphysical realism, but more like a version of atomic realism. But the effect is the same.
20. Putnam, *Reason, Truth, and History*, p. 49.
21. Putnam, 'Comments and Replies', in Peter Clark and Bob Hale (eds.), *Reading Putnam* (Oxford: Blackwell, 1994), pp. 242–95, p. 243.

The hard part for any internalist outlook is Putnam's second objective: namely, avoiding the relativism to which any purely perceiver-dependent or subjectivist view of reality seems to lead. On the one hand, the extent of Putnam's commitment to internalism could hardly be clearer, as evidenced, for example, in his assertion that 'there is no fixed ahistorical *organon* which defines what it is to be rational'.[22] The question in light of this strong commitment is: how does he propose to provide the kind of rational obligation or authority that will be required to fulfil his promise to avoid relativism? The following passage will give a preliminary indication of how he attempts to accomplish this purely from within internalism:

> Internalism is not facile relativism that says, 'Anything goes'. Denying that it makes sense to ask whether our concepts 'match' something totally uncontaminated by conceptualization [i.e., something mind-independently real] is one thing; but to hold that every conceptual system is therefore just as good as every other would be something else. If anyone really believed that and if they were foolish enough to pick a conceptual system that told them they could fly and to act upon it by jumping out of a window, they would, if they were lucky enough to survive, see the weakness of the latter view.
>
> What makes a statement, or a whole system of statements . . . rationally acceptable is, in large part, its coherence and fit . . . Our conceptions of coherence and acceptability [in turn] . . . define a kind of objectivity, *objectivity for us*, even if it is not the metaphysical objectivity of the God's Eye view. Objectivity and rationality humanly speaking are what we have; and they are better than nothing.[23]

What we continue to look for is a genuinely *internalist* account of rational obligation that is robust enough, or 'objective' enough, to avoid relativism. And this prospect has now in the light of the above quotation been rearticulated as a task of harmonizing two seemingly conflicting statements: (a) that 'there is no fixed ahistorical *organon* which defines what it is to be rational'; and (b) that *nevertheless* not 'every conceptual system is just as good as every other'. Let us look at this task more closely.

The basic problem for Putnam's internalism is that it wants to make rational obligation (or truth) at bottom something inexorably internal (in order to avoid either the restrictive dogmatism or the absurd relativism of his 'alienated' views); and yet it wants equally to be able to appeal to

22. Putnam, *Reason, Truth, and History*, p. x.
23. Putnam, *Reason, Truth, and History*, pp. 54–5, original emphasis throughout.

rationality as holding at least some minimal normative sway or authority across any plurality of perspectives. In other words, the fundamental problem with respect to rational obligation for internalism is that it
can never speak about obligation in reason *per se*, that is, as something
'objective' *about* reason or truly intrinsic to reason, something that humans reflect and perceive simply by virtue of being rational. Rather, internalism or anti-realism can only speak about rational obligation in terms
of this or that instance of it (or, at best, even all instances of it); in other
words, it can be at most a de facto feature (even if this is a *universal* de facto
feature) of rational human beings. But it can never allow as such that these
instances are manifestations of anything truly final, anything genuinely
intrinsic (or as such anything genuinely 'objective') *about* reason itself. It
is this absence of any possibility of genuine finality in internalism, moreover, that makes the demand for rational obligation so difficult to satisfy.
All we can ever have or hope for, on Putnam's own account, is 'objectivity
for us'; and so he must now work within 'objectivity for us' to try to locate
a kind of finality that is robust enough to sustain the claim to rational obligation. In undertaking this task Putnam will appeal to three key concepts,
two of which are cited in the foregoing quotations. The first is the notion
of 'conceptual relativity'; the other two, 'rational acceptability' and a certain version of 'fallibilism', are a pair of ideas that belong together and that
are designed to show how mere 'objectivity for us' can provide the kind of
obligation needed for rational integrity, yet which can work in harmony
with the principle of conceptual relativity.

2.1   Conceptual relativity

Conceptual relativity is best approached via an example I have already
cited above: the one that asked why the table-and-chairs version of the con-
tents of a room should be any more 'correct' than the particles-fields version, and which concluded that there is no single 'way' that the room – or
the world – can be said to exist. Now for Putnam there is a principle that
underlies our legitimate recognition or judgement that both of these versions are 'correct', and he calls this principle 'conceptual relativity'. The
central and most obvious problem that conceptual relativity faces is how,
in the absence of any possible appeal to finality (within internalism), it can
avoid becoming the mere free-floating cultural relativism that we encountered in the post-subject anti-rationalisms of chapter 2. Or more straightforwardly, how can Putnam's 'objectivity for us' deliver a kind of objectivity or a kind of obligation that is more than mere cultural convention or

intersubjective agreement? Putnam responds to this question in the following way:

> Once we are clear about how we are *using* 'object' (or 'exist'), the question 'How many objects exist?' has an answer that is not at all a matter of convention . . . [for] what is in one sense the 'same' world (the two versions are deeply related) can be described as consisting of tables and chairs . . . in one version, *and* consisting of space-time regions, particles and fields, etc., in other versions.[24]

In other words, as he argues elsewhere, it makes no sense to think of the world as dividing *itself* up into 'objects' independently of conceptual schemes. Instead,

> it is *we* who divide up 'the world' – that is, the events, states of affairs, and physical, social, etc., systems that we talk about – into 'objects', 'properties', and 'relations', and we do this in a variety of ways. 'Object', 'entity', 'property' (and 'relation') have not one fixed use but an ever-expanding open family of uses. Because 'exist' and 'entity' are conceptually linked, the same is true of 'exist'.[25]

It is this last move into 'existence' that brings us most obviously to the genuinely idealist heart of Putnam's internalism or anti-realism. For Putnam's point is that, just as 'object', 'entity' and 'property' have no place or meaning whatsoever outside of a conceptual scheme (i.e., since even all of these very basic terms are still at bottom *elements* of a conceptual scheme and not somehow elements of 'the world' independently of any such scheme), in the same way, even our understanding of 'existence' can have no meaningful place outside a conceptual scheme but belongs purely within it. And this gives rise to the wholly idealist result that 'what exists' in the mental picture, once the frame of reference has been established, are not simply representations or signs, but *the actual, the 'factual', objects themselves*. But again, we must not, in Putnam's conclusion as such, impute to him the view that the world is a mere construction of the mind. He is not saying that there is no genuine discipline of physics. Rather, what he is claiming here can be understood in the following way.

The claims of internalism are always entirely epistemological and never ontological. Internalism avoids ontology and ontological pronouncements altogether. Indeed, if Putnam is forced to speak ontologically he will merely convert 'ontological' talk into 'metaphorical' talk, as we have

24. Putnam, *Representation and Reality*, p. 20, original emphasis.
25. Putnam, 'Comments and Replies', p. 243.

seen in his own words above: 'If one must use metaphorical language, then let the metaphor be this: the mind and the world jointly make up the mind and the world.'[26] In other words, it is precisely here, in the avoidance of ontology, or in the explanation of ontological claims in terms of episte-mology (and, when pushed, in terms of 'metaphor'), that we see the full extent of the 'reductionist' character of idealism or internalism. It is what Nagel has in mind when he says that anti-realism (internalism, idealism) operates at heart according to a 'broadly epistemological test of reality'. In a way, as such, we can begin to see a kind of metamorphosis of ideal-ism at work within *Reason, Truth and History* itself. Putnam begins by cit-ing a kind of Berkeleyan empirical idealism and moves towards what in-creasingly resembles a kind of Hegelian metaphysical idealism.[27] Putnam actually hints at the Hegelian connection on two occasions in the book but he does not follow up on the suggestion. Instead he will return to his more analytic (but ultimately also pragmatic) roots and appeal to a kind of Rawlsian principle of 'reflective equilibrium' to make his case. We will come to that presently in the next section. But the preliminary point in the light of the above is that Putnam now takes himself to be authorized to speak genuinely about 'facts' within the internalist picture. But we must now ask further about these 'facts'. What are they exactly; and how, given their 'internal' status, can they provide the genuine kind of finality that Putnam requires for rational obligation?

2.2   Rational acceptability and fallibilism

It is here that Putnam turns to the two remaining pivotal concepts in ac-counting for rational obligation or orientation in reason: the notions of 'rational acceptability' and 'fallibilism'. To begin with then, with respect to accounting for the authority of these 'internal facts', Putnam asserts that 'the only criterion for what is a fact is what it is *rational* to accept'.[28]

---

26. It should also be noted however that Putnam is concerned to emphasize the way in which this particular kind of idealistic result separates his own internalism or anti-realism from the 'sheer linguistic idealism' (i.e., the free-floating holism) that underlies cultural relativism. The difference is that in Putnam's internalism 'a sign that is employed in a particular way by a particular community of users can correspond to particular objects *within the conceptual scheme of those users*. '"Objects" do not exist independently of conceptual schemes . . . [Instead,] objects *and* signs are alike *internal* to the scheme of description, [and because of this] it is possible to say what matches what' (Putnam, *Reason, Truth, and History*, p. 52, original emphasis).

27. The distinction between empirical and metaphysical idealism will be explained more fully in chapter 6.

28. Putnam, *Reason, Truth, and History*, p. x, original emphasis.

But how do we determine what it is rational to accept? We begin by structuring our enquiries loosely around a kind of fallibilism (together with an initial idea of rational acceptability in embryonic form) in which errors are determined by, and corrected according to, a roughly defined set of 'probabilistic operational constraints'.[29] From this starting point, we then initiate a pursuit towards what Putnam calls an *'idealization* of rational acceptability' or an *'idealization* of justification'[30] in which, with decreasing error, we engage in a venture of projecting what rational acceptability *would* be like under 'epistemically ideal conditions'. Even though it can be freely admitted that such conditions will never actually be attained, they can nevertheless eventually be approximated to a high degree of accuracy in much the same way as, say, frictionless planes in physics are approximated. In Putnam's terms, just as 'frictionless planes' can have 'cash value' for the way we actually do physics, so our theoretical approximation of 'idealized justification conditions' can have real 'cash value' for internalism in matters of epistemology. The way this actually works is that these operational constraints are themselves 'revisable upward' as the interpretive theory evolves and develops. They are thus neither arbitrary nor rigid but are rather always an estimation of what 'rational inquirers *would* impose, if they observed and experimented and reasoned as well as possible' – an approximation, that is, of the constraints that rational enquirers would adopt in a state of 'reflective equilibrium'. In other words, we engage in a kind of fallibilism whose ideal state is reflective equilibrium, yet which never actually reaches this idealized state but only continually approaches it: 'We use our criteria of rational acceptability to build up a theoretical picture of the "empirical world" and then as that picture develops we revise our very criteria of rational acceptability in the light of that picture and so on and so on for ever.'[31]

However, in order to be able to speak legitimately about genuine *obligation*, Putnam is eventually forced to admit that 'such revision cannot be unlimited: otherwise we would no longer have a concept of anything we could call *rationality*'. But this brings us back precisely to the 'internalist' problem from which we started. How are we supposed to determine,

29. For these Putnam suggests the form 'An admissible interpretation is such that *most of the time* the sentence S is true when the experiential condition E is fulfilled' (Putnam, *Reason, Truth, and History*, p. 30, original emphasis, cf. also p. 134).
30. *Realism and Reason, Philosophical Papers* (Cambridge: Cambridge University Press 1983), vol. III, p. 84; Putnam, *Reason, Truth, and History*, p. 55, original emphasis.
31. Putnam, *Reason, Truth, and History*, p. 30, original emphasis; p. 134.

purely from within internalism or subjectivism, what these limits are or what this finality is? Putnam's response here is to say that these limits 'are not in general possible for us to state'.[32] The most that Putnam is willing to admit is as follows: 'The fact is that we have an *underived*, a *primitive* obligation of some kind to be reasonable, not a "moral obligation" or an "ethical obligation", to be sure, but nevertheless a very real obligation to be reasonable.'[33] Now the distinction at this point between Putnam's terms 'primitive' or 'underived' and the very different term 'intrinsic' is vital. For it is this distinction that in the end will permit Putnam to claim to be able to locate his own 'underived' finality, not within reason itself but within pragmatism. More fully, in the face of this ineluctable and primitive 'obligation to be reasonable', Putnam invokes a pragmatic application of Wittgenstein and says simply, 'here I have reached bedrock and this is where my spade is turned . . . this is what I do, this is what I say'.[34] He then immediately reinforces the internalist denial that even this bedrock might be something intrinsic or genuinely general or necessary:

> Recognizing that there are places where one's spade is turned . . . where our explanations run out, isn't saying that any particular place is *permanently* fated to be 'bedrock', or that any particular belief is forever immune to criticism. This is where my spade is turned *now*. This is where my justifications and explanations stop *now*.[35]

The crucial point in all of this of course – the point that keeps Putnam's anti-realism or internalism from becoming realist or externalist – is that this underived primitive obligation is itself *not* something *about* reason, something intrinsic to it, but rather something pragmatic about 'human flourishing'. But unfortunately this also means that whatever finality or 'obligation to be reasonable' Putnam does manage to achieve, this will not be accomplished without jeopardizing the epistemological integrity of his entire project. For the move into pragmatism is itself one that is not – indeed, by pragmatism's own stipulations, *may not* be – *rationally* justified (if it were, it would not be a pragmatic move but a rational, epistemic one), but must rather be undertaken as a kind of non-rational, non-justified 'leap', that is, as a kind of positivism.

We can thus in conclusion venture two different kinds of assessment with regard to Putnam's programme. Firstly, insofar as it remains

32. Putnam, *Reason, Truth, and History*, p. 84, original emphasis.
33. Putnam, *Representation and Reality*, p. 84 original emphasis.
34. Putnam, *Representation and Reality*, p. 85.
35. Putnam, *Representation and Reality*, p. 85, original emphasis.

genuinely internalist, anti-realist and 'holist' – seeking to avoid the dichotomies (but also the putative 'alienations') around which realism attains its stability – it also remains a thoroughgoing form of idealism: one that seems to begin along quasi-Berkleyan lines but that, as it approaches its ideal state of reflective equilibrium, takes on more of a quasi-Hegelian character. At bottom, however, it remains (in either idealistic form) 'a broadly epistemological test of reality', which reinterprets the realist's claim to ontology (independent authority) in epistemological terms, or where such claims persist, reinterprets ontological claims metaphorically. As a form of idealism it may indeed accomplish a kind of non-alienation on one level (i.e., 'holistically') but then it reintroduces alienation in a new way on another. For inasmuch as it cannot supply the kind of finality or rational obligation it requires in order to avoid relativism, it contributes to yet another – and in many ways deeper – instance of the perennial conflict between realism and idealism.

Secondly, insofar as it imports pragmatism as something essentially non-rational (primordial, underived) in order to ground Putnam's idealism in the kind of finality it needs for rational obligation and to avoid relativism, to this extent, it actually resorts to a new kind of *positivism* because the move into pragmatism is itself (by definition) not rationally justifiable. As such, on the pragmatist interpretation it escapes the polarization between idealism and realism only by unilaterally removing itself from the demands of rational scrutiny. It thereby compromises the integrity of reason (reason is seen as insufficient to provide a defence for the move into pragmatism) and thus fails to provide the kind of robust account of rational obligation needed to answer the attack on reason mounted by the radical post-subject anti-rational critiques.

3   Thomas Nagel's realist ('externalist') account of rational obligation

The summary point of the above discussion is that, depending on whether it is construed as at bottom a form of idealism or pragmatism, Putnam's programme is in the end either reductionist or deflationary. In its reductionist or idealist form, it commits what for Nagel is the error of 'treating our capacity to engage in reason as the primary clue to what it is',[36] or in

36. Thomas Nagel, *The Last Word* (Oxford: Oxford University Press, 1997), pp. 74–5.

other words, treating reason as having no intrinsic character or essence but as fully accounted for by instances of rationality in human beings. As Putnam's idealism becomes 'grounded' in pragmatism, however, it becomes openly deflationary by committing the error cited above by MacKinnon: that is, the error of converting the necessary anthropocentricity of all of our endeavours 'from a problem into a solution', thereby unilaterally declaring itself authorized to avoid a host of philosophical difficulties. Like MacKinnon, Nagel too decries all such attempts to turn philosophy 'into something less difficult and more shallow than it is' maintaining that 'to redefine the aim [of philosophical enquiry] so that its achievement is largely guaranteed, through various forms of reductionism, relativism, or historicism, is a form of cognitive wish-fulfillment'. 'In the name of liberation', he goes on to say, 'these movements have offered us intellectual repression'.[37]

In a way, Nagel's 'view from nowhere' also attempts to put forward a 'non-alienated view', although, as a robust kind of realism, it is fundamentally different from Putnam's venture under the same description. Whereas Putnam builds his view around a kind of coherence that seeks to undermine or dissolve the disparities and polarities of thought, Nagel's approach, building around a correspondence theory, will be based on 'a deliberate effort to juxtapose the internal and external or subjective and objective views at full strength, in order to achieve unification when it is possible and to recognize clearly when it is not'.[38] In other words, as we see clearly from the second phrase in this quotation, Nagel's attempted harmonization of internal and external views will not have what he calls the 'pretensions to completeness' that internalism (idealism) based on holism or coherence usually does. Indeed, he maintains that any aspirations toward highly unified worldviews inevitably lead to the most fundamental philosophical mistakes: usually, again, to one form or another of reductionism, which always at bottom involves a reinterpretation 'of the content of our beliefs . . . so that they claim less'.[39] Nagel maintains to the contrary – and here, his own goal of harmonization notwithstanding – that

---

37. Nagel, *The View from Nowhere*, p. 10; Nagel's unhelpful propensity to lump all non-objectivist viewpoints together is evident here.
38. Nagel, *The View from Nowhere*, p. 4. This sounds quasi-dualistic. However, it should be noted that, although his basic allegiances reside clearly with Descartes (cf., e.g., Nagel, *The View from Nowhere*, pp. 70–1; Nagel, *The Last Word*, pp. 18 ff.), Nagel resists Cartesian dualism and paints a picture instead of humans not as dichotomous but rather as *complex beings without a naturally unified standpoint*' (cf. e.g., Nagel, *The View from Nowhere*, p. 29).
39. Nagel, *The View from Nowhere*, p. 68.

any endeavour that seeks uncompromisingly to demonstrate the integrity of reason must in the end be willing to accept the ways in which 'life and thought are split, if that is how things are'.[40] Underlying this view is the conviction that 'certain forms of perplexity . . . embody more insight than any of the proposed solutions to those problems'.[41]

Now, the prospect of integrating internal and external views wherever possible and where not to ascertain the limits of the disparity, Nagel continues, can itself be broached (in genuinely realist fashion) from either side: subjective or objective. Both attempts face implicit hurdles. In fact, most traditional defences of realism, or of 'perceiver-independent reality', begin from the subjective side. On such an approach, I will immediately encounter the familiar and standard correspondence theory problems of how, based simply on my own experiential perspective, I can come to any 'true' conception of reality *independent* of this perspective. Or, stating this in even more typical terms, I face the problem of how I can show indefeasibly that my internal mental 'representations' are *really* similar to the external objects to which I take them to 'correspond'. As such, this approach to realism must be able to answer to, or to guard against, the inevitable counter-tendencies towards scepticism, idealism, relativism or solipsism. The objectivity approach, on the other hand, in which 'the given is objective reality . . . and what is problematic by contrast is subjective reality', runs into the opposite difficulty. Here the problem is how to accommodate myself and my point of view (and relatedly other like selves with their own points of view) in a world that 'simply exists' without any perspectival centre. It is this second, less travelled objectivity approach that becomes the focus of Nagel's attention in his project of subjective/objective or internal/external integration.[42]

3.1   Reality, objective reality and non-completeness
Nagel maintains that in most current discussions objectivity is both underrated and overrated, often by the same thinkers: 'It is underrated by those who don't regard it as a method of understanding the world as it is in itself [and] overrated by those who believe it can provide a complete view of the world on its own, replacing the subjective views from which it has developed.' These opposite tendencies to overrate or underrate, moreover,

---

40. Nagel, *The View from Nowhere*, p. 6.
41. Nagel, *The View from Nowhere*, p. 4.
42. Nagel, *The View from Nowhere*, p. 27.

have a common source: 'they both stem from an *insufficiently robust sense of reality* and of its independence of any particular form of human under-standing'.[43] In other words – and here we come to a claim that is pivotal to Nagel's entire project – 'reality' and 'objective reality' are not equivalent terms and indeed are to be strongly differentiated from one another. Nagel's implicit complaint is that the opponents of realism commonly and falsely construe it as claiming that reality exists in some ultimately *objective* or 'thematizable' way – a construal that Putnam's formulation of 'metaphysical realism' based on the notion of a 'God's Eye View' exemplifies exactly. Nagel rejects this portrayal, claiming to the contrary that 'to insist in every case that the most objective and detached account of a phenomenon is the correct one' will probably lead to similar sorts of reductive errors as did the subjectivist coherentism or holism of the anti-realists. (One could think here again, for example, of some of the radically reductive physicalist philosophies of mind.) While the 'seductive appeal' of simply equating 'reality' with 'objective reality' is undeniable, this equation for Nagel depends on a mistake. Contrary to the stereotypical interpretation, for the realist, 'the truth is not always to be found by travelling as far away from one's personal perspective as possible'.[44]

In other words, objectivity is not to be thought of as the test or criterion of reality in the same way that the anti-realists (erroneously for Nagel) are searching for 'a broadly *epistemological* test of reality'. 'Objectivity' is instead simply *one way of understanding* reality. This means that an objective conception of reality does not purport somehow to circumscribe all of reality 'per se'. Reality is by definition complete (and unknowable as such) whereas 'any objective conception of reality must include an acknowledgement of its own incompleteness'. Importantly, however, this admission of incompleteness does not mean that we have 'given up the [realist or correspondence theory] idea of the way the world really is, independently of how it appears to us or to any particular occupant of it. We have only given up the idea that this coincides with what can be objectively understood. The way the world is includes appearances and there is no single point of view from which they can be fully grasped.'[45] The task, accordingly, is to articulate a version of objectivity that is somehow capable of accommodating both the external and the perspectival (internal) aspects of reality. This

43. Nagel, *The View from Nowhere*, p. 5, emphasis added.
44. Nagel, *The View from Nowhere*, p. 27.
45. Nagel, *The View from Nowhere*, pp. 4, 25–6, 91.

task will lead ultimately to what Nagel calls the 'view from nowhere', and the path to this runs crucially through scepticism.

3.2   Scepticism, self-transcendence and objective advance

Now if one looks at objectivity carefully it will soon become clear, as we shall see, that scepticism is not the antagonist of objectivity but is actually its corollary. For Nagel, the dynamic interplay between objectivity and scepticism will critically and centrally determine the way in which his objectivity-approach to external/internal integration will proceed.[46] To effectively situate the relation, I quote at length from Nagel.

> Objectivity and skepticism are closely related: both develop from the idea that there is a real world in which we are contained, and that appearances result from interactions with the rest of it. We cannot accept those appearances uncritically, but must try to understand what our own constitution contributes to them. To do this we try to develop an idea of the world with ourselves in it, an account of both ourselves and the world that includes an explanation of why it initially appears to us as it does. But this idea, since it is we who develop it, is likewise the product of interaction between us and the world, though the interaction is more complicated and more self-conscious than the original one. If the initial appearances cannot be relied upon because they depend on our constitution in ways that we do not fully understand, this more complex idea should be open to the same doubts, for whatever we use to understand certain interactions between ourselves and the world is not itself the object of that understanding. However often we may try to step outside ourselves, something will have to stay behind the lens, something in us will determine the resulting picture, and this will give grounds for doubt that we are really getting any closer to reality.
>
> The idea of objectivity thus seems to undermine itself. The aim is to form a conception of reality which includes ourselves and our view of things among its objects, but it seems that whatever forms the conception will not be included by it. It seems to follow that the most objective view we can achieve will have to rest on an unexamined subjective base, and that since we can never abandon our own point of

---

46. We should, however, be aware of the distinction here between scepticism as a method and scepticism as an inevitable destination. Nagel's largely Cartesian rationalist outlook here embraces scepticism in the former sense, as a philosophical method, and seeks to avoid scepticism as the destination towards which subjectivist empirical idealist approaches ultimately tend, as explained above.

view, but can only alter it, the idea that we are coming closer to the
reality outside it with each successive step has no foundation.[47]

According to this passage, we may say that the root problem of objectivity has to do with its 'non-examinable subjective base' and the uncertainty that this can bring to all of our beliefs. And since we cannot literally get out of our skins or escape ourselves as subjects,[48] Nagel will now
suggest further, as a response to scepticism, that any improvement in our
beliefs will have to be the result of forming some sort of 'detached idea
of the world that includes us, *and includes our possession of that conception as
part of what it enables us to understand about ourselves*'.[49] He describes the basic principle that we see here in germinal form as 'self-transcendence'. In
other words, it is this *second* 'inclusion' that critically allows me somehow
to get epistemically 'outside myself' in the sense that, while I myself do of
course continue to appear inside my own conception of the whole world,
nevertheless *this* conception (i.e., the actual conception with me in it; not
the event of my having this conception) is not itself tied to my particular point of view (since anyone could have that view of the world with me
in it). Or, stated in somewhat simpler terms, while my conception of the
world in the above case does indeed in one sense involve my point of view,
it does so only instrumentally and not essentially. Now we already know,
as asserted negatively at the opening of this section, that the aim of this
process is not 'completeness'. The real positive aim of this whole project
of self-transcendence, instead, is 'a gradual *liberation of the dormant objective
self, trapped initially behind an individual perspective of human experience*'.[50] Or
in other words, the goal is a conception of the world that does not leave the
perceiver ineluctably at the centre, it is the goal of a detached 'view from
nowhere' which reflects no single perspective but which rather aspires to
what might be described as a kind of 'universalized subjectivity'.

Now each successive step in this 'gradual liberation of the dormant objective self', or each successive step in this project of 'self-transcendence',
involves what Nagel calls an 'advance in objectivity', an advance that is
not the product of scientific but of epistemological insight. Explaining
this more fully, advances in scientific knowledge are merely 'additive'
(Kuhn notwithstanding), but the epistemological advances in objectivity

47. Nagel, *The View from Nowhere*, pp. 67–8.
48. This is precisely what the unworkable post-subject outlooks cited in chapter 2 attempt
to do.
49. Nagel, *The View from Nowhere*, pp. 69–70, emphasis added.
50. Nagel, *The View from Nowhere*, pp. 70, 74, 85–6, emphasis added.

of which Nagel speaks are conceptually or noetically 'progressive'.[51] The point is that most new discoveries, even some exceedingly difficult ones, simply add knowledge to an already existing framework of awareness and do not fundamentally alter our epistemic relation to the world. Examples of such merely 'cumulative' advances in the non-epistemic category would include things like discoveries of previously unknown astronomical bodies or of hitherto unrecognized formative influences on an historical figure, or even things as complex and ingenious as the discovery of the structure of DNA – since this was essentially an extension into genetics of previously understood methods of chemistry. By contrast, 'an advance in objectivity requires that already existing forms of understanding should themselves become the object of a new form of understanding, which also takes in the objects of the original forms . . . All advances in objectivity subsume our former understanding under a new account of our mental relation to the world.'[52] As an example, Nagel cites the distinction we now ascribe between primary and secondary qualities, a distinction that has been the precondition for the development of modern physics and chemistry.[53] A second, less generally accessible example involves Einstein's special theory of relativity.[54] In short, what was required in either of these cases was an advance in objectivity itself, involving the epistemological transcendence of the earlier view: a requirement in turn that arose precisely from the incapacity of the earlier view of the world to include and explain itself.[55]

51. It must be added, however, that this progressive and open-ended nature of objective advance is simply a feature of given reason and should by no means be construed as anything evolutionary about rationality. Nagel offers powerful arguments against any sort of evolutionary component to rationality (cf., e.g., Nagel, *The Last Word*, pp. 75, 131–42; Nagel, *The View from Nowhere*, pp. 78–82).

52. Nagel, *The View from Nowhere*, p. 75.

53. Briefly glossing Nagel's more detailed account: It is our recognition that certain of our perceptions of objects depend both on their physical properties and on our own sensory-psychological ones while other perceptions have a physical stability that seem to obtain pan-perspectivally which enables us to ascribe qualities like colour as secondary and size or shape as primary. Moreover from this point it seems but a short and very natural step to the further postulate that secondary qualities may in turn be caused by other primary qualities of objects which we can then attempt to discover (cf. Nagel, *The View from Nowhere*, pp. 75–6).

54. Again, without elaborating the details, the main point is that the previous 'received theory' of absolute space-time was incapable of yielding or explaining the 'new' appearance (granted, an appearance yielded via electrodynamics rather than more basic perception) that we 'actually' occupy 'relativistic' space-time (i.e., the 'objective' location of events in 'viewpoint-dependent' space-time). It is, of course, the conjunction here of 'actual' and 'relativistic', of 'objective' and 'viewpoint-dependent' that is decisive.

55. Nagel, *The View from Nowhere*, p. 76.

3.3   The objective self

But having thus roughly glossed the leading ideas of Nagel's objectivity enterprise, we are still left with the central problem addressed at the beginning, about how such a universalized view can accommodate *my* particular subjectivity. The whole purpose behind objective advance and self-transcendence, after all, has been precisely to attain to more general and less perspective-specific accounts of the world, eventually leading to a fully universalized view from no particular perspective at all. The real heart of the problem here as such is this: How can a genuinely centreless view-from-nowhere-world accommodate *me*, who inherently, and even in the very act of contemplating such a view from nowhere, continues to view myself as its centre? Nagel addresses this final question by developing the idea of what he calls the 'objective self':

> How do I abstract the objective self from the person TN?[56] By treating the individual experiences of that person as data for the construction of the objective picture. I throw TN into the world as a thing that interacts with the rest of it, and ask what the world must be like from no point of view in order to appear to him as it does from his point of view. For this purpose my special link with TN is irrelevant. Though I receive the information from his point of view directly, I try to deal with it for the purpose of constructing an objective picture just as I would if the information were coming to me indirectly . . . The basic step which brings [the objective self] to life . . . is simply the step of conceiving the world as a place that includes the person I am within it, as just another of its contents – conceiving myself from the outside, in other words. So I can step away from the unconsidered perspective of the particular person I thought I was.[57]

Now, although this may go some way to reconciling the idea of a 'theoretical me' with the centreless view from nowhere, the real problem remains undiminished, as Nagel himself admits. The problem is that my ensuing awareness of my 'objective self' with its somehow 'universal' character still does not seem to answer to the fact that I also perceive myself as an individual being with a private empirical perspective. Indeed, this leads Nagel himself to acknowledge that, unavoidably, 'objective advance produces a split in the self and as it gradually widens the problem of

---

56. 'TN' designates the 'self' which is 'Thomas Nagel' among the set of human individuals and is not meant to include his recognition of himself as such.
57. Nagel, *The View from Nowhere*, pp. 62, 63.

integration between the two standpoints becomes severe, particularly in regard to ethics and personal life'.[58] What this means in practical (i.e., empirical) terms is that I may not take too literally the image of my 'true self' imprisoned within the individual perspective but must rather try to view the world 'both from nowhere and from here' – in other words to develop what Nagel calls a form of 'double vision' and then seek to live accordingly.

Let us now, as we did with the Putnam survey, try to draw this together and focus it on our own basic concerns, especially in anticipation of MacKinnon in the next chapter and then of Kant in chapter 6. Nagel's realism, together with his whole objectivist endeavour, is concerned with the problem of how to establish the genuine and universal authority of the objective while at the same time acknowledging that this authority is always only subjectively encountered or experienced. It is this problem that Nagel is fundamentally seeking to address in his method of 'objective advance'. Although he grants that it is never completely possible to divest ourselves of the subjective, anthropocentric nature of our enquiries, nevertheless he claims that we can approximate such a view in which my own private empirical *subjectivity is absent* (thus, 'the view from nowhere') by pursuing an enterprise of progressive detachment from the self towards an objective idea of the world that *includes* me, the enquiring subject.[59] However, this is the point at which Nagel's project becomes least convincing, for the radically detached view that it seeks is ultimately *so* detached from any human experience of reality that it becomes hard to associate intelligibly with anything recognizable as *realism*.[60] There are several reasons for this. To begin with, the 'view' to which it aspires is purely, even *necessarily* theoretical, and as such it is a thoroughly *idealized* view. It is a view that, accordingly, begins to bear a strange resemblance to what I cited above as a quasi-Hegelian metaphysical *idealism* in Putnam's destination of 'reflective equilibrium' (a result that Nagel would surely not want). Secondly, as something essentially theoretical (ideal) – and notwithstanding Nagel's provision of a 'double vision', which I shall

---

58. Nagel, *The View from Nowhere*, p. 86.
59. Clearly, this detachment from self or a self-transcendence is meant in a fundamentally different sense than anything advocated, for example, by Gabriel Marcel or Søren Kierkegaard.
60. It might be added that Nagel's ethical and political theory stands in sharp contrast to his epistemology and metaphysics in this regard. I comment on this further in the following paragraphs.

address further momentarily – it is a 'view' from which the contingencies of particular subjectivity are absent and thus one that no human could ever actually hold (Nagel freely admits this).

But it is the third point, to which both the previous ones lead, that is the really troubling one. For the very notions of a purely *objective* 'view', and of an 'objective self' are incoherent or more exactly contradictory, *if one takes subjectivity seriously*. Perhaps the most essential element of a proper treatment of subjectivity is the full recognition – beyond the mere lip-service that Nagel in the end seems to pay to the stipulation – that we can never 'get to' subjectivity, or we can never 'treat' it itself. For as soon as we claim to do so, we find that we are no longer treating subjectivity but only an idea of it. And any idea of it, even if it is an attempted 'universalization' of it, is an objectification of it and as such is *at bottom* as much an abandonment of subjectivity as the most blatant traditional forms of dogmatism or, in more recent philosophy, as the most strident forms of radically reductivist physicalism in the philosophy of mind. In other words, as it eventually turns out, when Nagel speaks of his intentions to 'juxtapose subjective and objective views at full strength' in order to come to his 'view from nowhere', he clearly does not have *genuine* subjectivity in mind (i.e., the essentially unobjectifiable *having* of the 'view'), but rather a conceptualization, a 'universalization', that is, an *objectification* 'at full strength' of subjectivity.

Again, it is this third point that leads from what otherwise might have remained a rather more technical concern to the real central problem of Nagel's endeavour. For what we witness here is an initially tacit, yet nonetheless inexorably progressive disintegration or even excision of the subjective or anthropocentric element from epistemology. As such, in what must be seen as a very odd result indeed, Nagel manages inadvertently to achieve the same absence of subjectivity that we saw in the post-subject outlooks addressed in chapter 2, on the radically opposite end of the spectrum. For the 'view from nowhere' does not even allow subjectivity its minimal status philosophically as something like a pretheoretical ground or unanalysable causal origin of all human experience and endeavour, but treats it instead as something like a mere interloping nuisance, an unwelcome intruder in the pursuit of a 'truer' objectivity project. Now granted, Nagel does see the need for developing what he calls a 'double vision' here, but it is unmistakably clear which of the two 'selves' he prefers, at least for epistemology. (In fairness to Nagel, his ethics and political theory are nothing like this, in that they seem to take genuine subjectivity, as just described, much more seriously. But this merely raises questions about whether one can really remove epistemology so utterly from 'ethical' concerns and responsibilities in the way that Nagel's 'view from nowhere' aspires to do.)

Kant, as we shall see, is harshly critical of any such strategies of pure objectivity, referring to them as instances of 'dogmatism'. For Kant, the term 'dogmatism' designates strategies that aspire somehow to divest human discourse of the subjective constraints to which it is deemed to be 'shackled'. These ventures then seek, accordingly, by a kind of intellectual coercion or 'despotism', to transport discourse impossibly onto a domain of pure objectivity, a domain that is somehow supposed to provide direct knowledge of 'external' things apart from their mediation or 'contamination' through human sensory faculties, that is, in Nagel's case, through human subjectivity. Now Nagel's otherwise careful and measured approach may not really qualify as 'despotic', since in certain important ways (notably, for example, in his distinction between 'reality' and 'objective reality') he does seem to be concerned to present an objectivist position which does not succumb to such inclinations. Nevertheless, when he states his aim as involving the 'gradual liberation of the dormant objective self, trapped initially behind an individual perspective of human experience',[61] he clearly betrays persisting dogmatist tendencies. Ironically, such a 'realist' manifesto, which ultimately equates the real with pure objectivity (or at least an approximation of it by aspiring to render the subjective objectively), shows itself in fact to be highly *un*realistic inasmuch as it utterly undermines or minimizes the ineluctable *empirical* heart of every human experience of reality, an empirical reality from within which even the most abstract declarations about the essentially non-empirical 'nature' of reality must be made.

In conclusion then, even though Nagel's realism remains an exemplary model in drawing our attention back to the importance of the rigours of reason, especially in the present time in which we seem especially prone to lapse in those areas, nevertheless, for our purposes especially, it fails on the two main counts. First, by viewing human experience as an entrapment and as a hindrance to truth in discourse rather than as a kind of ground and origin of discourse, even if only in the 'minimalistic(!)' sense of

61. Nagel, *The View from Nowhere*, pp. 85–6.

providing the *actual* condition for its possibility, Nagel's programme in the end effectively reinforces and exacerbates the old divisions between idealism and realism at even deeper and more accentuated levels. Secondly, and on these same grounds, it does little to answer the radical critiques of reason addressed in chapter 2 (actually it ignores them).

4

Philosophy's perpetual polarities: making and finding

Despite the unsustainable results, no less of Nagel's realism than of Putnam's idealism (that is, since both in the end merely re-emphasized the polarizations between realism and idealism, and were unable to respond properly to the anti-rational attack on reason), there is still an obvious and unavoidable sense in which orthodox theological reasoning cannot be at bottom idealist or anti-realist but must remain in some way at least oriented toward realism. Theology, after all, wants to claim to be able to speak 'about' God both *genuinely* and *meaningfully*, and in making this claim, it is understood that when we engage in Christian discourse we do not merely take ourselves to be participating in a specialized kind of play with our imaginations or to be engaging merely in some particularly sublime form of human ingenuity. And this in turn leads to an interesting and important preliminary result. If indeed we want our speech about God to be both *genuine* (that is truly about *God*) and *meaningful* (that is truly *about* God, in the way that meaningfulness was shown in chapter 1 to be definitionally equated with 'aboutness'), then we cannot avoid treating the problem of Christian thinking as, in some way, a question of intentional reference, and hence also as a question of correspondence.

Now at a time when the correspondence theory of truth (or at least a standard stereotype of it) has become highly polemicized as designating the basic justificatory mechanism for a certain bankrupt foundationalist kind of thinking that 'longs to build for itself its own foundations in a consciousness deceptively pure and an identity deceptively secure',[1] in such an environment the above result (about the need for 'correspondence')

---

1. David Tracy, 'The Post-Modern Re-Naming of God as Incomprehensible and Hidden', *Cross Currents* (spring–summer 2000), p. 1.

will for some be an unwelcome and even unacceptable outcome. And so there will immediately be the temptation to return in some way to one of the three responses we have already rejected: anti-realism, anti-rationalism or positivism. If we choose idealism (or anti-realism), we will be attempting to avoid the 'correspondence result' by resorting to ever-widening holisms, so that God in the end is no longer 'alienated' by the strictures of normal intentional-referential discourse but is somehow included in it.[2] But we soon realize that any of these attempts are just ever more sophisticated kinds of reductionism which make theological discourse essentially the product of human endeavour, whether epistemological or sociological. Or again, we might, in the face of the stereotypical view of correspondence, simply try to deflate these questions altogether. We might ask why we should be forced to make such a choice in the first place, arguing that such a demand in effect holds theology hostage and is merely part of the 'hegemonic' hold that intentional referential thinking (i.e., reason) has over all our deliberations. But I have shown decisively in chapter 2 that any claim to orthodoxy or general authority cannot simply dispense with rational (intentional-referential) authority because orthodoxy by definition involves the kinds of intellectual virtues that are precisely the sine qua non of rational integrity, and which as such are unavailable without rational integrity. Or thirdly, we may choose a form of fideistic positivism and as such simply pre-empt the question of rational integrity from the outset in a different way from the anti-rationalists. The summary point is that, if we want theological reasoning to be both genuine and meaningful as just described, we will inevitably be brought face to face with the realist question of intentional reference and hence to the question of correspondence. I will come to deal with the full ramifications of the question of theological reference in the final two chapters of this book, but I must first continue to lay the groundwork in the remaining portion of this chapter and in the next two to make that endeavour possible.

1 Donald MacKinnon's conciliatory realism

Donald MacKinnon is one of the few recent theologians (Bonhoeffer is another) who has been bold enough not to shrink from asking the theological question in precisely these realist and referential terms, while

2. Certain recent Trinitarian epistemological approaches tend in this direction. As important and refreshing as they are, especially in complementing and opening up the predominantly Christological focus of a generation of German theology, there is currently a worrying

remaining fully aware of the pitfalls and dangers involved in doing so. MacKinnon recognizes that 'the absolutely central problem raised by religious and theological language ... is the problem of *how reference to or characterization of the transcendent is possible*'.[3] Now it will be very obvious right from the outset that any example of realism or correspondence that we have encountered thus far – whether the strawman atomic version vilified by Putnam or the highly abstract metaphysical (universalized) version defended by Nagel – neither of these, nor any in between, will be suitable to the task of theological reference or correspondence as MacKinnon has just stated it. In order to create a proper context for what this chapter, building from MacKinnon's insights, will offer in its place, let us revisit the anti-realism/realism issue briefly by way of a particular example.

What realists or correspondence theorists are taken to be affirming when they speak about things 'being the case apart from any conceptual scheme' can be illustrated in the following way. Oceanologists and meteorologists tell us that the world's largest ocean current is the Antarctic Circumpolar Current of the Southern Ocean. The current is 21,000 km in length and is said to transport roughly 130 million cubic meters of water per second. Now it seems obvious, in some very basic sense, that even though the *actual* flow of water from point A to point B on any given day, say 12 June 1999, was not perceived or may not even be precisely measurable, that nevertheless there are certain 'facts' about the flow of water on that day – the amount of it, the strength of the ocean currents, the magnitude and movements of marine life within it, the effect on weather patterns and so on. Again, these 'facts' are said by realists to be 'mind-independent' inasmuch as they 'obtain' whether perceived or not. Furthermore, statements about these 'facts' are said to be true in the degree to which they 'correspond' with the facts and false in the degree to which they do not.

However, the anti-realist or the coherence theorist (holist) will now typically respond that precisely all of these terms of 'length' and 'volume' and 'facts about the flow of water', even 'Antarctic Circumpolar Current of the Southern Ocean', *just are* already elements of a particular conceptual scheme that come to be applied, in Putnam's words, against certain 'experiential inputs'. And indeed, it is hard to argue with the claim that any of these measurements *as* measurements are *not* something about the

tendency in some cases precisely to treat the Trinitarian 'relational' emphasis as a licence to re-engage in suspect kinds of idealism cloaked in 'holism'.
3. Donald MacKinnon, *Explorations in Theology* (London: SCM Press, 1979), p. 75, emphasis added.

reality of the world's largest ocean current 'in itself' but are rather measurements within the conceptual scheme *itself* as this is applied to these 'experiential inputs'. In Putnam's words, 'internalism does not deny that there are experiential *inputs* to knowledge; knowledge is not a story with no constraints except *internal* coherence; but it does deny that there are any inputs *which are not themselves to some extent shaped by our concepts*, by the vocabulary we use to report and describe them'.[4]

Now the first thing that we realize about MacKinnon's realism as we bring it to bear on this stand-off is that MacKinnon does not, committed realist though he is, simply dismiss such anti-realist or internalist concerns *tout court* as 'reductionist', but allows for their obvious legitimacy and importance as genuine challenges to realism. Indeed, for MacKinnon the central question on which realism and idealism most often *both* go wrong, and within which we might as such begin looking for the possibility of a conciliation, is in their *equally* unsatisfactory responses to the anthropocentric challenge faced by all philosophical endeavour (that is, the ineluctable fact that philosophy is always engaged from some human perspective and unavoidably reflects that perspective to some degree). Looking at this more closely with Nagel and Putnam as representatives: Nagel's objectivist realism, in its aspirations toward a subject-less 'view from nowhere' does not take the ineluctability of the anthropocentric challenge seriously enough, inasmuch as it seeks (impossibly) completely to do away with the human element. Nagel's programme as such yielded an untenable kind of dogmatism. Putnam's anti-realism makes the opposite mistake when it, in the end, allows anthropocentrism to transform from a problem into a solution in its arrival at Putnam's primordial and underived anthropocentric (i.e., pragmatic) 'bedrock'. The point is that in seeking to avoid both of these extremes, or in seeking to avoid this kind of mutual exclusivity, MacKinnon's realism does not define itself *essentially* in opposition to anti-realism but seeks a conciliatory approach wherever possible while remaining at bottom the kind of genuinely realist doctrine that Christian orthodoxy demands.

1.1 MacKinnon's realism: against atomism

In light of this whole preamble then, MacKinnon insists that those who, like himself, want to 'identify truth fundamentally with correspondence... [must] realize the need for the utmost sophistication in

---

4. Hilary Putnam, *Reason, Truth, and History* (Cambridge: Cambridge University Press, 1981), pp. 54–5, original emphasis.

analysis of that correspondence'. He is thus, as a *realist*, repeatedly at pains to distance himself from what he calls 'a *simpliste* model of correspondence' which buys into the 'logical mythology of "atomic propositions" corresponding with "atomic facts", and the implied ontology of ultimate simples'.[5] Of course, what MacKinnon is referring to here is precisely the strawman version of 'metaphysical realism' (or more correctly, atomic realism) repudiated by Putnam, a realism that in his words contends that 'the world consists of some fixed totality of mind-independent objects', that 'there is exactly one true and complete description of "the way the world is"' and that 'truth involves some sort of correspondence relation between words or thought-signs and external things and sets of things'.[6] MacKinnon refers to such a *simpliste* construal of realism or correspondence as the 'picture theory' of truth. All of the characterizations of realism we have been considering so far (i.e., 'atomic realism', 'metaphysical realism', the 'One True Theory' view, the 'God's Eye' point of view and so on) are for MacKinnon versions of the 'picture theory', and as such they all represent a fundamental misconstrual of the true import of correspondence. MacKinnon clarifies what he has in mind here by means of the following example.

One gets the notion of correspondence wrong, he maintains, if one takes as one's exhaustive paradigm 'the correspondence of the details of a photograph with its original'.

> Certainly in a criminal investigation one needs a very accurate photographic likeness of, for example, the sexual maniac the police are seeking. When one passes from photography to portraiture, however, the matter changes dramatically. In Bishopthorpe, the residence of the Archbishops of York near that city there is a portrait by the English portraitist Orpen of Cosmo Gordon Lang, Archbishop of York in the early part of this century [the twentieth century] and later Archbishop of Canterbury. It is an unforgettable study of prelatical arrogance, in which the artist has used the scarlet of the Archbishop's chimere and doctoral hood to emphasize the relentless pride of his subject. A Swedish ecclesiastic, seeing the portrait, said that the artist had painted him 'as the devil intended him to be; but by the grace of God he was not like that'. Yet Lang was a very ambitious man; this was part of his story, and the artist in a portrait, not a photograph throws that fact into relief.[7]

5. MacKinnon, *Explorations in Theology*, pp. 145, 73, 142.
6. Putnam, *Reason, Truth, and History*, p. 49.
7. MacKinnon, *Explorations in Theology*, p. 73.

The point is that the portrait, although technically not as exact a 'match' as the photograph, expresses something of the true character of the 'original' – a *fact* about the *man*, Archbishop Gordon Lang – that the photograph does not, and as such is in some real respect a truer representation of its subject. Or to state this another way, the deeper 'truth' expressed by the portrait is indeed found in the way it 'corresponds' to the man himself, but this 'correspondence' does not consist in some sort of exact similitude or perfect matching, but in something else. In fact the idea that there *could* be anything like 'exact similitude' between mental image and external object is manifestly absurd. Here one need only cite Putnam's restatement of Berkeley's argument against what Putnam calls the 'similitude theory of reference'.

> To ask whether a *table* is the same length as *my* image of it . . . is to ask an absurd question. If the table is three feet long, and I have a good clear view of it, do I have *a three foot long mental image?* To ask the question is to see its senselessness. Mental images do not have a *physical* length.[8]

It is easy to see that MacKinnon's rejection of the 'picture theory' of truth exactly parallels Putnam's rejection of the 'similitude theory' of reference. But the even deeper point as such is that MacKinnon *and* Putnam, externalist *and* internalist, are rejecting the *same* characterization of correspondence and external realism. The difference is that whereas Putnam takes the failure of the picture/similitude theory as providing conclusive grounds for rejecting truth as correspondence, MacKinnon sees the picture/similitude theory as a fundamental misconstrual of the real intent of correspondence.

1.2   MacKinnon's realism: openness to holism

One particularly important way in which MacKinnon's conciliatory stance is borne out is in his reconfiguration of the anti-realism/realism dispute in terms of a disagreement about learning. The key question here is: When we learn, do we 'invent' (anti-realism, idealism) or do we 'discover' (realism)? Do we 'make' or do we 'find'? Obviously there is a kind of ambivalence here (which actually opens the way for the possibility of conciliation) even in just framing the question in these terms; for the truth is, of course, that learning invariably involves both. But MacKinnon's point is well taken, both here and in the foregoing example, in which we were made aware that we could 'discover' something more *truly* about

---

8. Putnam, *Reason, Truth, and History*, p. 59, original emphasis.

Archbishop Lang, the *man*, through the creative ingenuity of the artist than through the exact similitude of the photograph. The tacit point here is that, although learning must at bottom involve a kind of finding (in order to count as genuine learning), nevertheless sometimes we 'find' more truly (i.e., in a more genuine sense of correspondence) via certain kinds of expertise and skills in 'making'. What all of this points to, in other words, is a kind of *openness to holism* and coherence that any properly integrated correspondence theory (or realism) will have to manifest. We will discuss this more fully later in the chapter but for now let me cite three brief examples of ways in which truth seems to be ascertained more on the basis of coherence than correspondence, and which as such a proper theory of correspondence must be able to accommodate.

One can look, for example, to a certain kind of scientific theory such as Newton's Inverse Square Law (which states that the intensity of an effect – e.g. gravitation, illumination – changes in inverse proportion to the square of the distance from the source). The point is that we affirm the truth of such a theory even though it is neither axiomatically invulnerable, nor theorematic, nor even scientifically demonstrable *in*ductively on the basis of some comprehensive set of empirical data gleaned from actual experience. Rather, the 'unrestricted generality' (i.e., a kind of seeming *universality* but not *necessity*), which we nonetheless attribute to the truth of such theories, resides in large part in their ability to 'organize and integrate vast amounts of theoretical material', that is, in their 'coherence' and explanatory capacity.[9]

A second example of the way in which realism based on correspondence must be able to accommodate kinds of learning which seem to be almost 'sheer coherence', can be found in the area of pure mathematics. Here we are reminded of Bertrand Russell's dictum that 'in pure mathematics we do not know what we are talking about, nor whether what we say is true'.[10] MacKinnon's point about Russell here (even though Russell remained one of the most influential proponents of logical atomism) is that learning in pure mathematics does not proceed on the basis of 'correspondence' to mathematical 'facts', but rather according to a 'hypothetico-deductive

---

9. MacKinnon, *Explorations in Theology*, p. 74. It is true that some of the most recent 'grand unification theories' place the 'unrestricted generality' of Newton's law into question. It is interesting, however, according to a recent report in *Physical Review Letters* (*Physical Review Letters* 86. 1418, 19 February 2001), that 'improved previous short-range constraints by up to a factor of 1000 find no deviations from Newtonian physics' and that Newton's Inverse Square Law is thus 'still correct'.
10. MacKinnon, *Explorations in Theology*, p. 74.

scheme where theorems are deduced from axioms and postulates'. This has led some to go so far as to suggest that in pure geometry internal coherence must be accepted not just as the *criterion* of truth but as the very *nature* of truth. Although MacKinnon will in the end dispute this claim (and we will discuss this later in the chapter), he acknowledges that the challenge it poses to realism based on correspondence must be taken seriously.[11]

In the same way, what we learn from great works of fiction, which can convey truth with great power and meaningfulness, is not a matter of straightforward correspondence of proposition with 'fact'. In MacKinnon's words, 'Where fundamental moral issues are concerned . . . one learns much more from e.g. William Faulkner's great novel *Absalom, Absalom!* (on the guilt of slavery), from Tolstoi's *Anna Karenina* (on adultery), from Conrad's *Lord Jim* (on the inward deception of the man who lives with a fantasy picture of himself), from Dostoevsky's *Brothers Karamazov* (the problem of the use of power) than from the writings of many moral philosophers and most (if indeed not all) moral theologians'.[12] In other words, even though we see sharp differences between, say, Dostoevsky and Tolstoi, nevertheless we recognize and assess the truth or falsity of what they write – i.e., we learn from them – in a profoundly different way than we measure the truth or falsity of careful newspaper reporting. Truth with respect to the latter is judged more as a matter of correspondence with the facts. In the former, our recognition of truth is rooted in large part in the immense feats of disciplined organization or, again, the 'coherence' that characterize such great works of fiction.

The pertinent point in all of this is to emphasize that any properly sophisticated account of external realism or truth as correspondence will have to be able to accommodate and account for the kind of truth or learning reflected in the foregoing examples: a truth or learning whose genuineness seems in some way beyond dispute, yet which at least prima facie appears to be more a matter of coherence than any sort of correspondence of proposition to 'what is the case' in the world. Yet even here, the following consideration can be added in defence of realism. It is undeniable that *The Brothers Karamazov* or Newton's Inverse Square Law project a kind of *unity*, and as such also a compelling sense of authority or finality. It is an authority that is not based merely on internal or private conviction, nor even based on a kind of intersubjective cultural agreement, still less on any

11. MacKinnon, *Explorations in Theology*, p. 74.
12. MacKinnon, *Explorations in Theology*, pp. 74–5.

sort of pragmatic outlook of 'what works' (especially in the case of the fiction). It is rather an authority or a unity that somehow has its own intrinsic integrity – a unity that both defines the subject of enquiry and sets limits and demands on how it may be properly interpreted. In other words, the openness to holism or coherence that a proper correspondence theory must exhibit 'is no soft plea for a kind of facile tolerance; rather it is a demand that we consider the system of projection to which [each of these examples] belong as a complex whole, vulnerable to falsification in different ways, but *still in itself what it is and not something else*'.[13]

This leads to the following twofold point. Not only does one reason falsely if one treats *The Brothers Karamazov* as if it were *Anna Karenina*, or Newton's Inverse Square Law as if it were the second law of thermodynamics, but the falsity of such reasoning stems ultimately from the limits and constraints that these entities themselves impose on their proper comprehension and interpretation. What we see emerging here then is a clear point at which the openness to holism or internalism, required of a properly sophisticated theory of intentional reference or correspondence, begins to reach a critical limit. The point at which strict internalism must be rejected is the point at which it fundamentally disallows that these systems can be 'invested with any sort of inviolability'[14] (i.e., despite the *relative* 'authority' it is willing to allow for conceptual systems). The most basic example of what MacKinnon is criticizing here can be seen in our foregoing study of Putnam, who was unwilling to admit that the epistemic 'bedrock' at the heart of any rational enquiry was itself anything inviolable about *reason*, but was rather at bottom essentially something about particular (or cumulative) instances of human flourishing.

But this increasing talk of 'finality', 'inviolability' and 'authority' may arouse suspicions that we are here after all reverting back to what some see as a particular kind of bankrupt 'modern' foundationalist programme (which I addressed briefly at the beginning of this chapter). But this is precisely what we are *not* doing, and so let us be clear about what the integrated external realist or correspondence theorist is truly asking for in this demand for finality or authority. The finality or inviolability that the realist requires has little to do with the 'indubitability' at the base of what is commonly referred to as Cartesian foundationalism. Our goal is not epistemic 'certainty' following a method of 'therapeutic doubt'

---

13. MacKinnon, *Explorations in Theology*, p. 75, emphasis added.
14. MacKinnon, *Explorations in Theology*, p. 145.

towards the articulation of clear and distinct ideas. The external realist is, in these 'holistic' examples, concerned rather with certain built-in 'horizons', 'frontiers', 'constants' or even 'backgrounds' that, as the examples themselves have already intimated, are integral to, and constitutive of, *any* intellectual enquiry aimed at learning. But in order to understand this point properly, we need to make it somewhat more structured, especially with a view to defining more exactly what MacKinnon means by a 'properly sophisticated theory of correspondence'. To begin with, such a properly integrated realist doctrine of correspondence or reference must be dynamic and indeed *realistic* enough to accommodate the full range of all the ways we encounter finality in the world; or, in different words, the full range of the ways we 'discover' or 'find' in the world. One way of formulating this task is to build on a distinction, vaguely implied by MacKinnon but not developed by him, and say that statements can correspond in a 'common sense' and in a 'focal sense' as well as in a range of ways in between. The further point is that it will be in relation to the range of ways that we encounter *finality* in the world that our sense of *correspondence* will also change. With this in mind, we may discern in MacKinnon a concern for the finality or authority of the objective on five different levels. I will deal with only four of these here, beginning from the more particular and non-theoretical, and proceeding onward in 'increasing generality' to the more universal and theoretical: (i) finality in common-sense empirical externality, (ii) finality in observational science, (iii) finality in theoretical science and (iv) finality in logic, mathematics and metaphysics. The fifth category, finality as encountered in tragedy, will be broached in a later chapter as we turn our attention to the impact of all of this on transcendence.

2   An integrated theory of correspondence: finality on four levels, from 'common sense' to 'focal sense'

2.1   Finality in empirical externality

To begin with then, we find ourselves most obviously and unavoidably confronted with the authority of the external on the straightforwardly common-sense level of everyday empirical experience. In the gradients of hills or the properties of natural gas, for example, we are confronted with a kind of authority that is not dependent on any conceptual scheme. Now at this juncture already there is an important contrast to be made with Putnam who, from an internalist perspective, addressed this same empirical authority in making his case against relativism. Putnam argued that internalism does not contend that every conceptual system is as good as every other, and made the point by saying that anyone who by jumping out of a window acts on a conceptual system that tells him he can fly will soon see the weakness of this view. But Putnam was unwilling to speak even of the authority of gravity in such a case as anything genuinely external or objectively final. He allowed that gravity has the status of a genuine 'experiential input' but at the same time denied 'there are any inputs *which are not themselves to some extent shaped by our concepts*'.[15] The most important aspect of what Putnam seems to be saying here is that there is no external authority for humans that is not, in his words, 'conceptually uncontaminated'.

It is at this juncture that some of the uniqueness and importance of MacKinnon's contribution to the current anti-realism/realism debate begins to emerge. For MacKinnon reads precisely the opposite tendency into our empirical interaction with the world. In other words, rather than, like Putnam, speaking about the inadvertent 'conceptual *contamination*' of all our interactions with the world, MacKinnon inverts this and points instead to the invariable human tendency actually to conceptualize empirical problems, or to account for them, in ways that give the appearance of bringing them under our conceptual *control*. MacKinnon's examples will explain further what I mean here. So, for instance, when a motorist encounters difficulties in controlling his vehicle on a steeply sloping road, he will attribute this difficulty to the poor condition of his brakes instead of the gradient of the hill, since the state of his brakes is at least partially within his control whereas the slope of the hill is not. Likewise, 'if a do-it-yourself enthusiast blows up his bungalow and nearly kills his wife, his two children, and himself, we find the cause in his belief that he could effectively service his gas-fired central heating installation himself, and not on the properties of natural gas'.[16] Now what I am suggesting here is that, when we invert the picture, from Putnam's point about *ineluctable conceptual contamination* to what I am calling MacKinnon's point about *invariable conceptual control*, we discover that this inversion enables us to see through the necessary anthropocentricity of all our endeavours and to speak about objective authority in ways that remain entirely hidden from Putnam's perspective. In other words, while we need to grant, on the one hand, that 'our knowledge of the world about us is directed, and enlarged and advanced by our concerns, and it assumes the kinds of form that it takes

15. Putnam, *Reason, Truth, and History*, p. 55, original emphasis.
16. MacKinnon, *Explorations in Theology*, p. 139.

partly by reason of its permeation by such interests', and although, in the same vein, we must acknowledge that 'when we hold [the world] at a distance from ourselves, as we do when we seek to enlarge our understanding of its order, the very act of doing so constrains the world to assume a different look from the one it has when we are living, breathing, eating, what you will'; nevertheless, on the other hand, 'when we recall the extent to which we are unquestionably part of the natural world, we find that we can do no other than to acknowledge the authority of the objective. The world is as it is, and not as we might want it. We can surmount the hill and keep ourselves and our families alive by having our brakes mended, or by admitting that gas-fired installations demand the skill of the professional. Yet it is because hills are as they are and natural gas is as it is, that we must adjust in ways in which we have to.'[17]

Two summary points can be made here then in contrast to Putnam. The first is that the experience of the gradient of the hill (as I approach a curve that is impossible to negotiate at my increasing speed) and the properties of natural gas (as I actually experience the house collapsing around me) are not (initially at least) even *part* of any 'conceptual scheme', and thus not necessarily 'conceptually contaminated'. They are empirical experiences of a certain kind, which are capable of giving rise to a kind of belief that the reformed epistemologists would call 'properly basic' – that is, warranted but non-inferred, or not believed on the basis of any other beliefs. But secondly, even if they are deemed to be ineluctably contaminated (and we see traces here of Putnam's tendency to convert anthropocentricity from a problem into a solution) it needs to be demonstrated how this contamination fully *nullifies* the genuineness of *every* empirically objective authority.

2.2   Finality in observational science

In other words, on the common-sense level of everyday experience, there is a certain straightforward ineluctability to the authority of the world outside my head, an authority that the charge of conceptual contamination cannot reach. (We will see a similar point made more strongly by Kant below.) But of course it would be short-sighted and naïve to suppose that our interaction with the world is just this simple, and to build a general case for external realism or correspondence theory around it. (This is exactly the caricature that anti-realists and relativists often paint

---

17. MacKinnon, *Explorations in Theology*, p. 139.

of realists even though no realist participant in the debate actually holds such a 'naïve' view. *Legitimate* 'common-sense realism' becomes *unjustifiable* 'naïve realism' only when it is taken to provide a *full* explanation of the 'external world'.) For clearly, not everything is this straightforward and frank, even on the empirical level. This becomes especially clear as soon as we step outside 'living, breathing, eating, what you will...' and begin to make the empirical world the subject of any sort of real *enquiry* – even the most uncomplicated observational enquiry. Remaining within our finding/making model of learning, it is evident that, when we engage in the task of scientific enquiry, for example, we are faced with a whole spectrum of ways in which we learn about the world, not all of which carry the same pre-theoretical common-sense pressure of everyday empirical experience. It seems clear, on the one hand, that what might be called the 'observational' sciences do involve an authoritative 'finding' (externality) in a manner not far from the common-sense examples just cited, involving the gradients of hills and the properties of natural gas. However, the straightforwardness of 'finding' and, along with it, the authority of the objective, seem to diminish in inverse proportion as we move in 'increasing generality' towards the theoretical.

In short, on this second level of finality, there is a move away from the straightforwardly common-sensical, but our focus is still primarily on empirical observation. The following example, in which MacKinnon accentuates in meticulous detail, and to full effect, the characteristic particularity of the observational sciences, or observational learning, illustrates this:

> There are important differences between the ornithologist patiently watching for hours birds coming and going in the vicinity of a sewage farm, and the experimental physicist working with others in the artificial environment of his laboratory, invoking the assistance of highly sophisticated laboratory technology... Where the bird watcher is concerned, we may say that he finds what flies into his sight. So on Sunday afternoon, 9 February 1978 at the estuary of the River Don on the north side of the city of Aberdeen, after almost twenty-four hours of weather almost unique in the area in its combination of snow, frost and gale force winds, the Professor of natural history at that time (Professor V. C. Wynne-Edwards, a most distinguished student of bird behaviour) insisted that he had seen birds he had never seen before outside the Arctic Circle.

After citing this example, MacKinnon continues with a characteristic recognition of the internalist (anti-realist) or of the 'making' side of learning (although now not without a certain dry humour): 'It was through perception (with its built-in ability to recognize birds of any and every species) that he was enabled to see (I use the word advisedly) the birds that were so surprisingly there.' Nevertheless, this being essentially an observational case, we find that we are once again led in the end to acknowledge the authority of the empirically objective: 'But they were brought there by the state of the weather, the sufficient, necessary conditions for their presence specifiable in terms of the state of the weather, their response to it ... and the nature of the estuary whither they had arrived.'[18] Against this 'common-sense' and observational backdrop, however, when we come to the more theoretical sciences, we find that what counts as learning, or advancement in knowledge, is much different – not nearly as straightforward.

2.3   Finality in theoretical science

When we come to theoretical physics, for example, we find that we have moved much further away from the common-sense idea of correspondence, so that our focus is now only tangentially on the observational. We are reminded here of Albert Einstein, who was deeply critical, not only of any attempt to do away with experiment and observation in theoretical physics (i.e., to do away with empirical realism and make physics into something like an extension of mathematics), but who likewise rejected the 'dogmatic empiricist' reduction of knowledge of the external world to mere patterns of sensation within the perceiver (idealism). Nevertheless, despite this, at heart, decidedly 'objectivist' view of things, Einstein was equally insistent that 'fundamental scientific progress must wait on the development, by spontaneous intellectual activity, of more powerful branches of mathematics'.[19] In other words, there is a two-sided character to Einstein's approach to physics. On the one hand, it must be granted (in support of the 'finding' component on the externalist or realist side) that physical theory can never be *purely* mental construction, since the subject matter, *physical* reality, can never, by its very material nature, be accessed directly through thinking, but is instead by definition 'found' and mediated through sense experience. Yet nevertheless, on the other hand (in support of the 'making' component on the internalist or anti-realist side), real progress in physics, the more theoretical it becomes, actually

18. MacKinnon, *Explorations in Theology*, p. 153.
19. MacKinnon, *Explorations in Theology*, p. 153.

and increasingly depends on inventive and creative cognitive strategies, especially mathematical ones. This dependence is accentuated even further in the increasing reliance of physics on technologies that are also products of human ingenuity aimed towards specific functional ends. In MacKinnon's words, 'No one can suppose that in the natural sciences, let alone the historical study of human economic, social and political institutions, one can easily draw up the frontier lines between observation (and its counterpart in historical study) and imagination [as found in] the flash of intuitive perception that is one of the marks of genius, [or in the] inventive virtuosity in the choice of questions to be attacked and of the means to seek their answer etc.'[20] The point then, for present purposes, is that, as we move away from empirical particularity and towards generality, *what* we 'find' in the world is increasingly informed by the constructive imaginativeness and creativity that we bring to our enquiries. And it is here that the frontier lines between internalism and externalism become noticeably more blurred. For it was in part the innovativeness of Einstein's thinking (internalism/construction) that brought him to 'find' the *real impasse* (externalism/discovery) in his attempt to unify field theory with the general theory of relativity. And it will likewise be through innovativeness and creativity that new kinds of theory may perhaps be suggested which (as some physicists hope today) might enable that impasse eventually to be overcome.

2.4   Finality in logic, pure mathematics, metaphysics

But what, then, about mathematics itself (and, along with it, other abstract disciplines like logic and metaphysics)? If it is true, as Einstein contends, that fundamental scientific progress must await the development of more powerful branches of mathematics, then it might seem that at least part of the implicit claim here is that mathematics is capable of providing a more fundamental or more universal finality – and hence, as some would want to contend, a more ultimate finality – than what is available through empirical enquiry by itself. But such 'a more ultimate finality' at these levels is not anything that a properly integrated theory of correspondence, or a properly integrated realism (i.e., one that does not lead towards dogmatism) would be able to claim. Let me explain why this is so. In the first place I am not of course saying that logic, mathematics and metaphysics, as intellectual disciplines, can just naturally and easily be lumped

20. MacKinnon, *Explorations in Theology*, p. 154.

together. Indeed some of the most heated philosophical disagreements can occur on the relation among these disciplines.[21] I am only suggesting, borrowing a category hinted at by MacKinnon, that, despite their differences, these disciplines can in a broad sense be seen as belonging together inasmuch as each of them wants to warrant its claims as having a kind of 'unrestricted generality'. Or in other words, all of these disciplines claim for themselves a kind of authority that is something like the antithesis of the authority claimed at the common-sense level of particular empirical correspondence. And so of course the question at this juncture becomes: What *is* this authority on the basis of which these realist claims to unrestricted generality are made? It is in response to this question that a

21. Among the most famous philosophical conflicts with respect to mathematics and logic, for instance, is the one between the ideas of Kant and Frege. Kant had maintained that mathematics is a 'synthetic' (roughly, partly intuitive) discipline and not purely 'analytic' (roughly, purely rational) in the way that logic is, because even the essentially abstract mathematical concepts like number and ratio depend on an awareness of *extension*. The deeper point here, of course, is that our very awareness of 'extension' cannot be anything purely rational since 'extension' by definition has its roots in space and time (spatial and temporal notions exhaustively define extension) and our comprehension of space and time is a matter of sensible intuition, not pure rational concept. Frege disagreed, claiming that mathematics could be explained purely in terms of logic. (Frege's 'logicism' in the philosophy of mathematics is, in current discussion, no longer regarded as viable.)

When we come to metaphysics, the distinction between it and logic can be made along the same lines in an even more obvious way. For 'metaphysics' is not concerned with the purely abstract rational functions of logic, nor even with the timeless and spaceless abstract entities of mathematics (even though number, distance, ratio etc., as *theoretically* 'extensive' entities, may require the presence of spatio-temporal 'intuitions', as just described). It is rather concerned, as the term itself implies, with the basic processes and structures underlying *physical* (extended, temporally and spatially) reality. Our notions, accordingly, of time, space, causality, existence, substance, quality, relation are all 'metaphysical' in this sense, and as such are seen to be different even from the mathematical entities (although there is hardly universal agreement on this point).

There are of course pejorative usages of the term 'metaphysics', stemming from one of two radically polar intellectual camps. On the one extreme, logical positivism, based on its verificationist principle, viewed metaphysics as little more than superstition. Significant traces of this anti-metaphysical view are still clearly visible among analytical and empirical philosophers in Britain and North America. At the other extreme, in post-structuralist and ultra-pragmatist relativism, metaphysics, like its close relative epistemology, is associated with terms such as 'hegemony' and 'violence' (as discussed in chapter 2). There is another kind of configuration of metaphysics which goes in the other direction and makes the metaphysical claim something purely conceptual so that it is almost impossible to reject. Vincent Descombes, for example, speaks of the word 'metaphysical' as 'that which directs our thinking, not toward speculative entities but toward the status, within our conceptual system, of classes of utterly familiar things' (*The Mind's Provisions* (Princeton: Princeton University Press, 2001), p. 78). My own use of the term is in the somewhat stronger yet still the moderate and broad philosophical sense, as simply denoting *claims about* the nature of reality or the way things are. The term as such is fully neutral, and need not even carry any external realist commitments. The point is that even a post-structuralist claim, or in different ways a nihilistic claim, that there is *no* way things are – not even an infinite plurality of ways as Putnam wanted to claim – is a metaphysical claim, albeit an entirely negative one.

properly integrated theory of correspondence will begin at last to speak of correspondence purely in its 'focal sense'.

Three basic points should be made briefly in this regard as I conclude this chapter. In the first place, any authority that may be generated by correspondence in its 'focal sense' on this general level should not be expected to occur by way of a conclusive demonstration. The integrated realist's aim at these levels of unrestricted generality is rather plausibility, believability, intelligibility, integrity. In other words, the really compelling demonstrations of correspondence theory (and hence realism) will always occur on the more straightforward empirical levels. Indeed, it can even be granted that when the authority that is sought for on these abstract levels is isolated, taken by itself, anti-realism or idealism based on coherence can often score at least equally as well, especially given that the very claim to 'unrestricted generality' is itself more a 'holist' claim about coherence than a referential claim about correspondence. But the realist's (correspondence theorist's) strongest argument, as will become especially clear in our study of Kant below, is always in the authority of the empirical, and as such, a *properly integrated* (i.e., non-dogmatic) realism will always seek to direct these abstract activities in some way back to empirical applications. But that is to jump ahead of ourselves. For in any case, the initial point to be made here is not that realism is able to deal with claims to unrestricted generality in more satisfactory ways than anti-realism, but merely to show that such claims can be adequately and plausibly accommodated within a correspondence theory of truth in its focal sense.

On this basis then, secondly, it can be freely granted that in the areas of abstract mathematics or theoretical physics, for example, it is indeed measurements like greater conceptual economy, comprehensiveness, simplicity, internal beauty (aesthetics), coherence and explanatory power – rather than any unequivocally demonstrable authority of the objective – that are taken as the main criteria for the realist claim that we are gaining a more secure grasp of 'what is the case' or 'the way things are' in the world. But the crucial difference is that for the realist these *remain criteria*. They are not merely self-enclosed, self-referential and ever more coherent constructions, as they must at bottom remain for the idealist (anti-realist). But they are rather, for the realist, indications that we are indeed getting closer to describing correctly (at least from one vantage point) something about the reality of the world we inhabit. For example, the fact that we retain central aspects of Newtonian physics despite frictions with quantum theory, which is taken to have superseded Newtonian physics in basic ways, certainly has much to do with the simplicity and conceptual economy in the explanatory capability of the former over the latter. But for the realist, what is most essentially of value here is not *only* the beauty and simplicity of the Newtonian structure per se – that is, it is not merely internal aesthetics or economy or pragmatics. Rather, the fundamental value for the realist is the belief that Newtonian physics (or equally, quantum physics) continues in important ways to express something true about the nature of the world we inhabit.

Now this last sentence brings to a head something that has been emerging with increasing clarity over the last few paragraphs. And this also brings me to my third point: As I move into these abstract conceptual regions of unrestricted generality, the question of whether or not we remain realists (correspondence theorists) will be less a matter of conclusive demonstration and more a matter of choice and conviction; and chances are that those choices will have already been made, those convictions already formed, at the more particular levels of empirical finality. Drawing this all together one might say then that the *overall* choice[22] for realism over anti-realism or idealism is most essentially the choice to be at home in the world rather than to be a stranger in it. I do not mean this yet in an any more complex theological or eschatological way, but rather, to begin with, simply empirically.[23] It is freely granted, because of the absence of conclusive demonstration or empirical finality in this focal sense of correspondence, that the scepticism that continues unavoidably to lurk within the realist claim, virtually as its corollary (as Nagel made clear), will continue to make its presence felt here in these abstract conceptual regions of unrestricted generality. But this seems decidedly more palatable, both intelligibly and empirically, and intuitively easier to tolerate than the relativism that lurks within the anti-realist claim. At any rate, based on a decision made more fundamentally on empirical levels, the integrated realist, or the integrated correspondence theorist, finds himself or herself dispositionally and temperamentally inclined to follow the intuitively more obvious approach and on investigation finds this also to be strongly sustainable intellectually.[24]

---

22. That is, the choice attending to the full range of correspondence (or realism) from common sense to focal sense, and not just restricting the choice to the latter.

23. Although this has immediate ethical connotations, as we saw in Nagel's unsustainable result. And indeed, as we shall see below, ethical finality turns out to be very closely related to empirical finality.

24. Some mention should be made of a group of cases involving a special instance of the focal sense of truth. I refer to the question of the ontological status (i.e., the finality or objective

3 Assessment

The kind of integrated realism that I have been pointing towards in this chapter, on the basis of certain latent ideas or recurring but unstructured and undeveloped categories in MacKinnon, anticipates Kant's empirical realism to a high degree, as we shall see. But it is not surprising to find that MacKinnon can be projected so easily in this direction, given his own deep respect for Kant and the formidable influence that Kantian philosophy exerts on all his thinking. The point here has not been to suggest any sort of philosophical victory for realism over anti-realism, as it has been developed along these gradients of finality, still less to say that some kind of compromise or truce has been reached (or *can* be reached) between the two sides of the perennial stand-off. Indeed, as we shall see more clearly in chapter 7 when we come to discuss finality in tragedy, MacKinnon's own commitments on these issues remain in the end largely negative, even troubled or anguished, perhaps precisely for fear of re-engaging in the kind of dogmatism to which realism can so easily succumb,[25] and the

authority) of such products of human ingenuity and creative construction as works of fiction, drama, music and art. In what way, for example, can human creations such as Shakespeare's *Hamlet* or Beethoven's Ninth Symphony be said to exist 'mind-independently'? It is surely not just the ideas in the playwright's or composer's head that constitute the drama and symphony, still less merely the ink and the paper on which they were originally documented. Nor would it be correct to say that *Hamlet* or Beethoven's Ninth exist as particular performances of them, or as a set of performances, even as the set of all the performances of them. In other words, such entities seem to reflect a finality or a unity or even in some sense a metaphysical 'essence' which extends beyond all the transcriptions and performances of them. Of course we are not, by describing them as metaphysical, claiming that they obtain in the world in the same way that Newton's inverse square law, if it is true, obtains in the world, or in the same way that the principle of sufficient reason obtains in all our reasonings about the world. (Philosophers sometimes describe such entities as 'subsisting' rather than 'existing'.) Its finality or 'ontology' is for the realist not rooted in 'the nature of things' or in the 'structure of reality' but rather in its own conceptual or compositional unity which makes it 'in itself what it is and not something else'. This unity is not rigid but it *is* authoritative in an 'objective' sense. That is, it does not spring merely from intersubjective agreement, but has its own kind of inherent finality which makes it possible to speak truly and falsely of Beethoven's Ninth Symphony quite apart from all transcriptions and performances of it. For example, it would be false to say that Beethoven's Ninth Symphony makes no requirement for human voices and true to say that the third movement is designated an *Adagio molto e cantabile*. Again, it is this intrinsic unity that sets certain pliable but inviolable limits as to what counts and what does not count as Beethoven's Ninth Symphony. For instance, the third movement could be performed as an *Andante moderato* and still be identified as belonging to Beethoven's Ninth; but it could not be performed as the third movement of Mahler's 'Tragic' Symphony without ceasing to be what it is, even if it were performed in the required *Adagio molto e cantabile*. The point of mentioning this here is not to claim, again, that realism accounts for the status of such entities more satisfactorily than anti-realism, but merely to show that they can be quite adequately accommodated within a properly integrated correspondence theory of truth.
25. What this means exactly will be discussed more fully in chapter 6.

consequences of which can be especially unwelcome as all of this works its way into ethics. But he remains a fully committed realist nonetheless, and in so doing models an intellectual integrity that is marked by a kind of reticence and attentiveness that must surely be indispensable as an initial disposition for any enquiry into Christian thinking.

The point to which this is leading, once again, is that we cannot help but be *realists* if we want to preserve the integrity of Christian thinking or theological reasoning on both our counts: that is, the integrity of reason and the integrity of transcendence. More than this, realism as an initial disposition for Christian thinking must remain *genuine*: that is, it must remain inherently connected to intentional reference as a kind of correspondence, despite all the obvious shortcomings and pitfalls associated with this. It may not simply be redefined as 'internal realism' or 'pragmatic realism' so that beneath its name lurks yet another instance of anti-realism (idealism) or anti-rationalism (i.e., in Rorty's sense of 'pragmatism', not Putnam's). For however much, or however importantly, anti-realist or anti-rationalist concerns may indeed need to inform a properly integrated account of realism, nevertheless, genuine theological thinking will never be able simply to revert back to these others as possible alternatives, as has by now been clearly demonstrated. *We cannot be anti-rationalists* in Christian thinking because the kinds of intellectual virtues that orthodoxy inherently demands are by definition intentional-referential virtues, that is, virtues *of* reason, or virtues that *define* rational integrity. Likewise, *we cannot be anti-realists* or idealists in theological reasoning either, because this always, in one way or another, reduces theology in the end to at best something like a sublime human endeavour.

But it is also important to emphasize at this juncture that there are *no other possible alternatives* than these three. Under whatever label 'new' theories of truth or new outlooks may emerge, they will always (a) have to engage in intellectual enquiry at bottom either realistically or idealistically, that is, as externalism or internalism, as a finding or a making (or some combination of the two), or else (b) by whatever means, declare all such intentional-referential endeavours invalid to begin with. (The point is that any outlooks that are not either externalist or internalist, realist or idealist, will inevitably, in one way or another, be variants of an anti-rational or deflationary outlook, even though these may come to expression in new terms and in a wide variety of ways.) Even the usual anti-rational ploy of rejecting my whole tripartite division here, on the grounds that it treats the anti-rational outlook as just another 'alternative' or 'option', whereas anti-rationalism (it will be claimed) wants precisely to *withdraw* itself from this whole 'fabricated' intentional-referential enterprise of 'alternatives' or of 'competitions between arguments', even this normal deflationary ploy will not work for theology. It may succeed in a certain way for atheistic outlooks,[26] but it cannot succeed for theistic outlooks, especially those aspiring to be orthodox. The reason for this is that orthodoxy, with its implicit claim to intrinsic authority, actually *implies* 'alternatives', 'options' and 'competition'. Orthodoxy by definition entails the possibility of heterodoxy[27] and heresy. In short, to aspire to orthodoxy as something 'non-competitive' would be a contradiction in terms, since orthodoxy by definition sets itself up as a challenge to that which seeks to undermine it.

So we are left with only these three alternatives, and in the face of them we have no choice but to return to realism, and this moreover in its *genuine* sense – and despite the well-documented perils of such an approach – as necessarily involving a kind of correspondence. For only realism as a kind of 'intentional reference as correspondence' does not close the door on either of the two counts of integrity that Christian thinking demands (even if realism cannot achieve this integrity itself), whereas the other alternatives by definition preclude the possibility of at least one and sometimes both. First, only realism, or intentional reference as a kind of correspondence, *can*[28] accommodate the independent integrity of its 'referent', or perhaps better, for theological purposes, can accommodate and respect the independent integrity of the source of its interrogative concern, in the way that anti-realist or idealist outlooks cannot. Secondly, only realism among our three alternatives does not shrink from seeking to engage *meaningfully* (i.e., intentional-referentially) *with* that independent source of concern in the way that anti-rational outlooks cannot. Specifically then, only realism does not shrink from asking, along with MacKinnon, the bold theological question (a boldness made possible precisely by his reticence and attentiveness): 'How is reference to or characterization of the transcendent possible?'

But again, it is clear that in all of this the most that realism can do, at this point, is to supply something like an appropriate initial disposition

---

26. Although even here, we have seen in chapter 2 the kind of anti-humanism and intellectual bankruptcy to which this ultimately leads.
27. Note that anti-rational responses would not even allow for the intelligibility of this term, since heterodoxy likewise implies the possibility of orthodoxy (the relation is a biconditional).
28. I stress 'can' here; I do not of course mean that realism always *does* this; the point is that anti-realism or idealism *cannot* do this.

for the task of theological thinking as a kind of referential thinking. Beyond this, realism remains effectively at the same impasse from which we started. For orthodox theology must still confess the reality of God in the following way: God is *real*, but not in any sense that our normal ontological categories could properly convey. And so it is on the basis of a certain ground gained, yet still in the face of the same fundamental dilemma of Christian thinking, that we now turn to yet another, and final, version of philosophy's perpetual polarities, in which these questions will come to be asked in a somewhat different way: the problem of act and being.

5

Philosophy's perpetual polarities: act and being

In the categories of 'act' and 'being' we come to what is arguably both the most basic and the most broad of all philosophical polarities. Act and being is a configuration that in modern times has come to expression more easily in continental philosophy than in analytical, and the categories themselves admit of broader application than any of the other dualities discussed thus far. One sees these categories strongly at work in Hegel, for example, and also in Heidegger, although in different ways and for different purposes. But in fact we have also already encountered this most broad and basic of philosophical polarities implicitly several times in this book, inasmuch as the problems with which this formulation is most fundamentally concerned are those arising out of the confrontation between thinking ('act') and being. The polar relation between thinking and being represents one of the most fundamental antitheses of Hegel's Logic; and perhaps Hegel served as something of an impetus for Bonhoeffer's development of these categories in his most neglected book, *Act and Being*, which will serve as a main focus of this chapter.[1]

So then, when stated in these terms, it becomes obvious that in the present study we have already encountered these categories, for example in Derrida's attempt to expose as a 'ruse' the 'final duality' between thinking and thinker (i.e., act and being), an attempt that ultimately failed. But we have also seen the polarity at work, perhaps less obviously but no less strongly, in what MacKinnon called the 'anthropocentric challenge' to philosophy, which refers to the problems posed by the ineluctable human-centredness of thinking or perceiving (act) for our enquiry into 'the world'

---

1. Bonhoeffer was deeply interested in Hegel's thought and lectured on him, even though the main philosophical influence in *Act and Being* is Kant.

(being). In the final analysis, not only Putnam's idealism or anti-realism, but Nagel's realism, too, faltered in the face of this challenge, both of them by minimizing or trivializing the demands of anthropocentricity and thus, in one way or another, the problem of act and being. Nagel minimized or trivialized the problem of *act* in the face of being in supposing that he could dispense with the anthropocentric challenge by projecting (even if never fully arriving at) a purely objective 'view from nowhere', a view that is precisely free from the constraints of any particular anthropocentric act of perception or thinking. Putnam conversely minimized or trivialized the problem of *being* in the face of act by, in the end, arbitrarily transmuting the anthropocentric challenge from a problem into a solution.

In a fundamental way, what this minimization or trivialization of anthropocentricity amounts to is a trivialization of subjectivity, and one should add here in this light that there seems to be a strong propensity in present-day epistemology generally to minimize such questions. As testimony to how deeply rooted this tendency to trivialize or marginalize subjectivity is, I cite Joseph Margolis, among the most respected, fair-minded and critically even-handed senior commentators on current epistemological issues. In the introduction to *The Persistence of Reality*,[2] in which he attempts a reconciliation of sorts between anti-realism and realism, Margolis makes the following remark: 'In an obvious, perhaps even trivial sense', he says, 'we are all realists no matter how hard we protest'. Now the realists that we all are, of course, pertains precisely to the reality that we all *already ineluctably inhabit*; and *that* point is indeed quite obvious. But is it really as 'trivial' – in any sense of this term, but especially in the philosophical sense in which it is meant here – as Margolis imagines? For if we look at this carefully we see that what we might call the 'of-course-ness' of my own existence, of my own subjectivity, or of my own 'objective capacity' as Nagel puts it, is not the same kind of 'of-course-ness' that Margolis implicitly wants to appeal to here: namely, an 'of-course-ness' in the philosophically or logically 'trivial' sense as something analytically true or true *by definition*. My point here is not to explore the relation of these two very different instances of 'of-course-ness', but only to say that existential ineluctability (or subjectivity) is often exempted from serious philosophical consideration on the tacit and false assumption that it can be

2. Joseph Margolis, *The Persistence of Reality: Pragmatism without Foundations, Reconciling Realism with Relativism* (Oxford: Blackwell, 1986).

relegated to the same status as the trivial or tautological truth or the definitional truth of logic.

We can summarize this brief introductory contextualization of the problem of act and being by highlighting two key points that will prove to be helpful in setting a basic framework against which Bonhoeffer's insightful but structurally confusing treatment of the problem can be explored. The first point is that the problem of act and being can arise in either one of two fundamental ways. (a) It can arise between the *act* of thinking and the thinking '*being*' from which this act of thinking proceeds, and which is the 'ground' or the condition for the possibility of thinking. (This is the distinction between act and being, or between thinking and thinker, that Derrida and some other post-subject thinkers want to declare a 'ruse'.) And (b) it can arise between the *act* of thinking (or perceiving) and the *being* of the world external to the conscious mind into which thinking enquires. (This is the problem of act and being that was unsatisfactorily 'settled' in opposing ways by Putnam and Nagel, as just discussed.) The second point is to re-emphasize that in all of the instances we have seen thus far, whether from the side of the anti-subject approaches, which seek fully to nullify it, or from the side of the anti-realism/realism debate, which trivializes it (from both idealist or realist perspectives): in *all* of these instances, the act/being distinction is either marginalized or somehow collapsed in contemporary discussion. So then, it is against this pervasive contemporary trend that Bonhoeffer's *Act and Being* is now best understood as targeting and problematizing, in a protracted way, this most basic, broad and obvious polarity or duality at the very centre of human self-awareness, for theological purposes.

Act and Being is hard to follow if one does not understand ahead of time what the book is seeking to accomplish. Unfortunately, the prospect of understanding the real aims of the book is made extremely difficult because the overall enterprise, as it is outlined and projected in the introductory chapter, is often very different from what the book actually goes on to develop (and even this frequently remains somewhat haphazard and opaque).[3] Perhaps this can be attributed in part to Bonhoeffer's youthful

---

3. It must be added that, for English readers, the task is made even more difficult, and at points virtually impossible, given that the new translation of *Act and Being* (1996), in the otherwise excellent English version of the *Dietrich Bonhoeffer Works* collection, makes several serious and at times almost fatal errors. The first half of *Act and Being* is highly philosophical in focus, and the terminology often intricate and subtle. At several crucial points translational errors are made that deeply shroud, or even fully invert, the German, yielding results that on some key points express virtually the opposite of what the German actually

age (twenty-three) when he wrote it as his *Habilitationsschrift*. Nevertheless, for all its youthful unevenness, the book contains frequent instances of the same brilliant original insight and sudden incisive lucidity to which his readers have become accustomed in his later, better known, more mature (and much less philosophical) writings. In this chapter I want to suggest a way of reading *Act and Being* (or at least the first two-thirds of it) that I believe will not only draw together and galvanize much of what otherwise remains uncentred and ambient in the book, but which in so doing will also be able to address our own concerns in important ways. This way of reading *Act and Being* can be outlined as follows.

To begin with, *Act and Being* should be understood – in its very *broadest* sense – as an enquiry into Christian thinking (i.e., is as an enquiry into the theological problem of thinking about God) via an enquiry into the two most basic configurations of the problem of act and being as I have just described them above: that is, (a) via an enquiry into the relationship between the *act* of thinking and the thinking '*being*' or subjective ground from which this act of thinking proceeds; and (b) via an enquiry into the relationship between the *act* of thinking (or perceiving) and the *being* of the external world. This overall focus and fundamental underlying structure of the book is obscured by Bonhoeffer himself, or made confusing in a number of ways, but in two really basic ones.

The first has to do with the terminology employed to designate the two kinds of configurations of the problem of act and being, as just described. Bonhoeffer divides up the epistemological portion of his study into what he calls a 'transcendental attempt' and an 'ontological attempt'. However, it is not at all clear, either on the basis of the book's introduction, or often even on what follows, what exactly is being 'attempted' here; and the reader comes easily to the erroneous conclusion that the 'transcendental attempt' has somehow mainly to do with the 'act' part of the book and the 'ontological attempt' with the 'being' part of the book. This is false. What Bonhoeffer is actually trying to do is to problematize precisely the two possible kinds of manifestations of the act and being polarity that we have already encountered in the present book, as just outlined. In other words (and now at the risk of being overly repetitive), the 'transcendental attempt' is the attempt of *thinking* (act) to understand the pre-theoretical

says. Granted, the task of translation is not aided by Bonhoeffer's own unevenness. But the original unevenness occurs more on a macro level; Bonhoeffer is quite consistent on the levels of terminology and syntax, which is where the translational errors occur. All translated quotations from *Act and Being* in this chapter are my own.

thinking being out of which thinking proceeds, or which is the condition for its possibility. The 'ontological attempt' is the attempt of thinking (act) to understand the being of that into which thinking enquires outside of itself (the world). Or more briefly (and again risking oversimplification leading to misunderstanding), the 'transcendental attempt' is the attempt of thinking (act) to understand the 'being' of subjectivity, or subjective 'being'; the 'ontological attempt' is the attempt of thinking (act) to understand the being of objectivity or objective being.

An important parenthetical note must be inserted here. It will be noted that I have placed the subjective 'being' of the 'transcendental attempt' in quotation marks, but not objective being. I follow Bonhoeffer's own practice here (unstated but consistently employed), and the reason for doing so should be obvious enough. For the term *being* is already an *objective* ontological (or ontic) category and as such cannot really be used properly to express the inherently subjective pre-theoretical ground or 'I' of thinking 'being'. (This is why the whole first 'attempt' is deemed to be 'transcendental', in the epistemological sense of this term, as we shall see.) So in short, the placing of 'being' into quotes is purely a provisional way of expressing the writer's implicit recognition (Bonhoeffer's or mine) of the unthematizable (i.e., unobjectifiable) 'being' of the subjective, and that this must remain different from any construal of objective being. This simple procedure will be found to pay certain dividends later on, when we address the unthematizable (unobjectifiable) 'being' of revelation.

The second way that Bonhoeffer confuses or hinders the clarity of the basic structure of *Act and Being*, as I am broadly outlining it here, is by framing the *whole* enterprise (i.e., transcendental *and* ontological attempts) as an enquiry into 'autonomous human self-understanding' (*autonomes Daseinsverständnis*). This is confusing because it can easily seem that only the former 'transcendental attempt' (i.e., the attempt of thinking to understand the 'I' or the pre-theoretical ground of thinking) is really an enquiry into human self-understanding. But in fact Bonhoeffer wants to ask whether *either* of these – the enquiry into pre-theoretical 'thinking being' *or* the enquiry into the world – is capable somehow of leading us *into the truth about ourselves*.

Finally, there is one more vital, clarifying point that must be made before proceeding to a discussion of Bonhoeffer's transcendental and ontological attempts themselves. This concerns Bonhoeffer's determination to engage in this enquiry in a purely *formal* way (or what Anglo-American readers might today be more familiar with as a purely *analytical* way). It is extremely important to recognize that what Bonhoeffer will be trying to do as such in this enterprise is to make sure that the basic *integrity* of thinking *as* 'act' is never compromised – that is, is never 'sullied' through any sort of premature, surreptitious or arbitrary introduction of being into the thinking process. This of course is not to say that there is anything 'impure' about being, but only that thinking, defined formally or analytically *as* 'act', may never inadmissibly or without full justification claim jurisdiction or ownership over being. Any such unjustified or premature move in which thinking claims jurisdiction or possession over being will always amount to some form of dogmatism.[4] The endeavour as such is to see whether thinking can, entirely of its own accord, come to any sort of truth about being or understanding of being; or at least, in the first place, to see where such a 'pure act' enquiry into being will lead. The more ultimate benefit for theology will be that only those noetic approaches that make no jurisdictional or possessive claims over being will be suitable for a further enquiry into the 'being' of revelation, which is entirely beyond human possession or jurisdiction, whether in the sense of a 'making' or of a 'finding', as discussed in chapter 4.

1   Bonhoeffer's 'transcendental attempt': thinking (i.e., act) enquires into subjective 'being'

Bonhoeffer opens the transcendental attempt – that is, the attempt of thinking (act) to understand the pre-theoretical thinking 'being' out of which thinking proceeds, as follows:

> Epistemology is the attempt of the I to understand itself. I reflect upon me, the I and me move apart and come back together again . . . The concept of genuine transcendentalism posits the referentiality of thinking toward transcendence, but not the jurisdiction of thinking over transcendence. All thinking stands doubly in reference to transcendence: referring *backwards*, in that *as* thinking it lays claim to a meaning which it cannot give to itself, and in this sense has reference to the knowing consciousness (*Logos*) of transcendence; referring *forwards* as the referentiality toward 'objects' (*Gegenstände*) in which thinking must truly stand over-against transcendence, if these 'objects' are genuinely to be considered as standing over-against.[5]

---

4. This term will be described further as we proceed, both in this chapter and the next.
5. Dietrich Bonhoeffer, *Akt und Sein*, Hans-Richard Reuther (ed.), Dietrich Bonhoeffer Werke, 16 vols. (Munich: Christian Kaiser Verlag, 1988), vol. II, pp. 27–8. It is unavoidable but to

This rather dense, cryptic and telegrammatic passage represents the conceptual heart of Bonhoeffer's 'transcendental attempt'. It presupposes a basic familiarity with aspects of Kant's *Critique of Pure Reason*. We will discuss Kant himself at length in the following chapter, but two points may be made here preliminarily in order to get a basic sense of bearing with respect to the above quotation. To begin with, we must clarify briefly the use of the term 'transcendence' as it occurs here, which has nothing to do with transcendence in a theological sense, but which rather denotes something purely epistemological or, perhaps even better, transcendence in a purely 'logical' sense. Kant's critical philosophy is commonly spoken of as having its transcendental centre in a single primary locus: that is, in the *Ding an sich*, or the 'thing-in-itself'. This is only half correct, as Bonhoeffer implicitly and quite correctly recognizes in the above quotation: Kantianism is constitutive not of one, but of two transcendental loci or 'poles'. The more famous is indeed the 'thing-in-itself': that is, what 'remains' of the empirical object once all empirical appearances have been (theoretically) abstracted. In other words, the *logically* transcendental character of the thing-in-itself is, in the first place, its transcendence by definition of human *sensory* capacities. More fully, this simply means that by definition (i.e., 'logically') the thing-in-itself 'transcends' sensory perception since all empirical (sensory) qualities have been (theoretically) abstracted from it. (We will discuss in detail this widely misunderstood aspect of Kantian philosophy in chapter 6.)

But now secondly, what is sometimes overlooked, and what Bonhoeffer correctly identifies and puts to unique use here, is that, when we turn our view back onto the perceiving human locus itself, we discover another transcendental 'pole': that is, the thinking 'being' or the 'I' that is the ground or the condition for the possibility of thinking. Kant himself refers to this subjective transcendental 'pole' as the 'unity of transcendental apperception' or sometimes more simply as the 'I think'. The *logical* transcendence of this 'pole' is even easier to demonstrate. In its most

render the term *Gegenstand* as 'object' even though this has the undesired effect in English of conflating *Gegenstand* in the sense in which it is meant here – i.e., as that which stands over-against the perceiving subject in an empirical way which transcends conceptual classification or thematization – with *Objekt* which denotes the determinate 'object' of cognition or intentionality. The German is more nuanced in this area. In Kant's *Critique of Pure Reason* itself, for example, *Gegenstand* and *Objekt* are normally kept separate (a regimen that Bonhoeffer follows carefully), the former term generally referring to 'objects' of empirical experience, and the latter to these being made objects of cognition (cf., e.g., Immanuel Kant, *Critique of Pure Reason*, Paul Guyer and Allen W. Wood (tr. and eds.) (Cambridge: Cambridge University Press, 1998), A104–A110).

straightforward sense it means quite simply that since human 'subjectivity', as the habitational ground of thought or as the pre-theoretical condition for its possibility, can never itself be an 'object' of thought (since subjectivity is that from which any activity of thought proceeds), therefore it logically 'transcends' the objective intentional-referential purview of thinking. In short, I can never 'get behind' myself to view my subjective experiencing as an object; and even if I could do so, I would find that what I was viewing would no longer be the subjective *having* of the experience, but only an idea of it, and as such an objectification of it. It is in reference to these two transcendental poles, then, that, according to the above passage, the genuinely transcendental attempt remains 'pure' act, pure thinking: always operational referentially and motionally between them – referring *backwards* towards the 'unity of transcendental apperception', referring *forwards* towards the 'thing-in-itself'. On this basis we can now go back to the opening sentences in the above quotation: 'Epistemology is the attempt of the I to understand itself. I reflect upon me, the I and me move apart and come back together again.' It is now clear that 'I' represents the logically transcendental 'unity of transcendental apperception' pole and 'me' represents the logically transcendental 'thing-in-itself' pole.[6]

But Bonhoeffer quite rightly perceives a persisting problem here for the 'pure act' integrity of thinking, inasmuch as there seems to remain some vestige of 'being' in each of these transcendental poles. For their very designations as '*thing*-in-itself' and '*unity* of transcendental apperception' seem to reflect the lurking presence of being, any traces of which must remain absent from a genuinely formal or analytical enquiry into the relation between thinking (act) and human being. As a response to this, Bonhoeffer, by returning to Kant, insists that 'only as long as the resistance of transcendence over against thinking is maintained, that is, only as long as the thing-in-itself and transcendental apperception are understood as *pure limiting concepts*, or as *pure boundaries*, may we speak of genuine transcendentalism'.[7] In other words, as soon as we speak of either transcendental 'pole' – either the thing-in-itself or the unity of transcendental apperception – as an entity per se or as somehow inhabited in a way that thinking could grasp, rather than simply as cognitive *limit*, two things will have occurred. First, we will have arrived at an understanding of being

---

6. It is questionable whether this second move (the transcendence of 'me') is entirely Kantian, but we can let it pass without doing serious damage to the Kantian programme, in order to follow the point that Bonhoeffer is wanting to make here.

7. Bonhoeffer, *Akt und Sein*, p. 28, emphasis added.

that is either *engendered* by thinking or somehow *discovered* by it ('made' or 'found'), and thus at a being over which thinking can claim jurisdiction or possession, at which point the 'poles' to which thinking refers are no longer genuinely transcendent, as they must remain by definition. Second, in so doing we will have already short-circuited the formal nature of the pure act enquiry. But by remaining true to this 'doubly purified' transcendental framework, we find that it now in turn yields the 'pure act' definition of human-being (*Dasein*): 'In knowing, or cognition (*im Erkennen*), human-being understands itself as suspended between two transcendental poles, and this "being-between" transcendence is "human-being" (*Dasein*).'[8] In other words, *Dasein* or human-being is never purely 'I' or purely 'me', but 'being between' these two poles, and thus any enquiry into myself must always likewise remain 'in reference to' these two poles.[9]

However, we now encounter an unexpected problem. For it soon becomes apparent that these very transcendental limits *as* limits to rationality, on which a 'pure act' approach to self-understanding depends, are *limits that are themselves set by reason*. It is reason itself that *posits* the boundaries of the confinement of human self-understanding to referentiality between transcendence. Reason as such becomes its own crisis, sets its own critical limit. This in turn yields the seemingly unwelcome result that human-being (*Dasein*), on this transcendental attempt, does not ultimately understand itself out of the transcendental limits at all, but rather out of the rationality or reason that posited the limits in the first place. And in the final analysis this means that the 'transcendental attempt' of thinking to understand human-being ends in a contradiction. For inasmuch as the I is the ground or the condition for the possibility of thinking 'the I *is logically prior to thinking*. Yet insofar as everything ascertainable *about* the I is thus ascertained *via* thinking, *thinking is prior to the I*.' The preliminary conclusion then is that the transcendental 'attempt to understand oneself out of oneself must fail since human-being (*Dasein*) is essentially not "in itself" but precisely "in reference to"'.[10] As Bonhoeffer puts it more fully:

> [I]n other words, thinking impinges or nudges against (*stösst an*) the boundary of the 'non-objective' [i.e., the subjective], without which there is nothing objective, precisely because it [i.e., the subjective, or

8. Bonhoeffer, *Akt und Sein*, p. 29.
9. Bonhoeffer's indebtedness, beyond Kant, also to Kierkegaard here is clear.
10. Bonhoeffer, *Akt und Sein*, pp. 29, 31, emphasis slightly altered.

the 'non-objective'] is the very condition (*die Bedingung*) of the conditioned (*des Bedingten*). It is the boundary of existence out of which the human being (*der Mensch*) lives, in that the unconditioned, that is, his existence is always before him but precisely always also behind him whenever human-being (*Dasein*) tries to understand itself out of itself.[11]

So then, out of this final conundrum, in which the thinking I comes up against the limits of its own non-objectivity, Bonhoeffer suggests that thinking can assume one of two dispositional stances. The first is to resort to a kind of metaphysical idealism in the vein of Fichte or Hegel, which, in Bonhoeffer's words, acquiesces to 'the great temptation of all philosophy and declares itself lord over the non-objective in that it arrogates to itself the still-thinking-I, seeking, in so doing, to establish the thinking I, now no longer as the limit or boundary of philosophy, but as its definitive point of departure'. He then observes that, as a result of this move, it seems initially as if idealism has indeed 'rescued' human-being (*Dasein*) from its 'embarrassing confinement' to referentiality between transcendence, and brought it into its own autonomous freedom within the pure-act domain of thinking. In metaphysical idealism, 'human-being is the returning-back, the homecoming (*Einkehr, Heimkehr*) of the eternal I, understood as eternal act, to itself... all concepts of being appear to have subsided and a purified act-concept governs epistemology and anthropology'.[12]

However, in this 'radicalization' of Kant[13] something surprising has occurred. 'Whereas in the original transcendentalism the human mind was suspended between transcendence, in indefeasible reference to it – here, by contrast, the cognitive movement has turned the mind in upon itself (*ratio in se ipsam incurva*, Luther) and as such has axiomatically come to rest [in being]', and accordingly is no longer genuine 'act'. Idealism as such is revealed as 'a merely apparent movement or a pseudo-movement within a self-contained state of rest'.[14] The further consequences of this kind of idealism, Bonhoeffer claims, turn out to be even more severe. For because 'philosophy, thinking, the I, succumbs to itself rather than to transcendence, the unboundedness of the claim of thinking is transmuted

---

11. Bonhoeffer, *Akt und Sein*, pp. 31–2.
12. Bonhoeffer, *Akt und Sein*, pp. 32, 34.
13. Actually it is less a radicalization and more of an inversion, as we shall see in the next chapter.
14. Bonhoeffer, *Akt und Sein*, pp. 34–5, 44.

into its exact opposite'. In this kind of idealism then 'thinking remains perpetually self-enclosed. Wherever thinking posits freedom from transcendence, from reality, precisely there it remains imprisoned within itself.'[15]

The second option is for thinking to return to its genuinely transcendental base, where now, in a kind of noetic modesty, reason willingly acquiesces to its self-imposed 'confinement' between transcendence and always remains 'in reference to' transcendence. Here, 'thinking submits to its own limitations';[16] it 'humbles itself' at the boundary which, *as* thinking-being, it has itself set as the 'condition' for its own activity. In other words, the thinking I tolerates the contradiction implicit in a pure act understanding of human-being, as such agreeing with Nagel that 'certain forms of perplexity can . . . embody more insight than any of the proposed solutions to those problems'.[17]

Nevertheless, at the very end of all of this, Bonhoeffer claims, even the most rigorous and genuine transcendental attempt is not able to remain in this purely referential state. For even transcendental 'pure act' thinking, 'despite intensive attempts to limit itself', leads finally to the evanescence of the very transcendental limits that define it; for because reason is essentially boundless, these limits are always 'thought away (*werden zerdacht*) until they are themselves no longer genuine limits'. Bonhoeffer's final judgement as such is that, even though in pure-act genuine transcendentalism the I is not subsumed under the 'lordship' of reason as it was in idealism, nevertheless there is a sense in which, in the genuine transcendental attempt too, 'reason ultimately gets entangled in itself'.[18]

As we shall see at the opening of the next chapter, this rather dismal outcome (including the conclusions Bonhoeffer will draw presently on the basis of it), while it is indeed the result of a faithful reading of Kant *as far as this reading goes*, is also the result of a crucially incomplete reading of Kant. What it leaves out is Kant's empirical realism which, as we shall see, is both the source and the goal of his entire transcendental or critical enterprise, such that when that is properly figured in, it is capable of yielding very different outcomes for both epistemology and theology. Nevertheless, Bonhoeffer's point on the purely transcendental level (even though, again, for Kant the logically transcendental can never be divorced from the

15. Bonhoeffer, *Akt und Sein*, p. 32.
16. Bonhoeffer, *Akt und Sein*, p. 32.
17. Thomas Nagel, *The View from Nowhere* (Oxford: Oxford University Press, 1986), p. 4.
18. Bonhoeffer, *Akt und Sein*, pp. 38, 48.

empirical, but actually springs from it) is well made and brings an important level of clarity, or at least depth, to some of these considerations; and so we can let it stand for now provisionally in order to follow Bonhoeffer to his own conclusions in section 3 below.

2   Bonhoeffer's 'ontological attempt': thinking (i.e., act) enquires into objective being (the world)

My treatment of this section of *Act and Being* will be brief, not because it is unimportant but because its key aspect for our purposes – the modest, non-possessive disposition of thinking vis-à-vis being – will be found largely to mirror what the transcendental attempt has already achieved. As we move into Bonhoeffer's 'ontological attempt' then, we find that this proceeds from roughly the same basic premises as the 'realism' (or externalism) of the anti-realism/realism debate that we have been discussing in previous chapters. In Bonhoeffer's words, 'it is the concern of *genuine* ontology to demonstrate the antecedence or ordinal *priority of being over consciousness* and to uncover and disclose this being. Ontology initially wants to claim no more than that there is real existence independent of consciousness, outside of the sphere of logic and the boundaries of rationality (*ratio*).' As such, Bonhoeffer continues, the central problem for ontology is that in it, 'two equally powerful claims encounter each other: *logos und ón*', that is rationality and being. But in contrast to the metaphysical idealism discussed earlier (where these two claims also met, and where *logos* declared 'lordship' over *ón*), here, being successfully resists the propensities of reason to encompass it, because the ontological method gives precedence to being over thinking. However, this seems merely to re-entrench the conflicting claims of *logos und ón* in a new way, since the precedence, given here to being, now in turn gives rise to the opposing question: 'How is *ontology* really possible as *Wissenschaft*', or as a discipline of *knowledge*, at all?[19] Or in other words: How is ontology, as a claim to *being*, possible as a form of *discourse*?

In view of this, Bonhoeffer then makes the summary assertion that 'the real problem of ontology lies in its *concept*'. And if we look carefully at this summary statement we will see that it is in effect a kind of inversion of any of the standard approaches to realism discussed thus far, which have generally wanted to speak instead of the 'correspondence' of thought to

---

19. Bonhoeffer, *Akt und Sein*, p. 53.

some independently referring 'ontological reality'. In other words, the basic problem *there* concerned the possibility of genuine reference to external being. The basic problem *here* concerns the very coherence of speaking of *ontology* in the first place as a *noetic* discipline. This inversion of the standard ontological case accomplishes two things. First, it ensures the vital recognition that in spite of its name, and despite the fact that it gives a kind of ordinal priority to being over consciousness, the ontological attempt does not thereby automatically gain some sort of favoured access to being, or access in a more privileged way than the transcendental attempt or any other philosophical approach. For at bottom ontology too remains a noetic or conceptual discipline, occurring entirely within the domain of concept and discourse, such that any claim to jurisdiction over actually existing external being is as much an instance of dogmatism, or what Kant will call 'proud ontology', as any of the most confident forms of idealism.

Secondly and relatedly, this makes the ontological problem not one most essentially concerned with establishing 'correspondence', but rather one of determining a mode of conceptualization that is 'appropriate' to ontology. And this in turn prepares the way importantly for the kind of 'critical' approach to ontology that in Bonhoeffer will come to expression around a principle of rational integrity which parallels the basic principle of the transcendental attempt. More precisely: just as in 'genuine transcendence' (transcendental reasoning at its most genuine or at 'full integrity') thinking always remained doubly *in reference to* transcendence (or subjective 'being') and never claimed jurisdiction over that 'being', so now likewise, in 'genuine ontology' (ontological reasoning at its most genuine or at 'full integrity'), thinking will again and again *suspend itself* in being, and will never claim jurisdiction over that being.[20] Or stating this the other way around, whenever the 'transcendental attempt' *does* declare lordship over 'being' – that is, does not remain purely *in reference to* subjective 'being' or transcendence – it will inevitably breed some form or other of metaphysical idealism (i.e., idealism in a German, post-Kantian vein). And likewise, whenever the 'ontological attempt' *does* declare lordship over being – that is, does not *suspend itself* in being – it will inevitably breed some form or other of metaphysical realism. *Both* of these are forms of 'dogmatism', as they will be identified and come to further discussion in the next chapter on Kant.

20. Bonhoeffer, *Akt und Sein*, p. 54.

3   Assessment

3.1   'Act and being' and rational integrity

Bonhoeffer's contribution to our twofold overall goal – preserving both the integrity of reason and the integrity of (theological) transcendence in Christian thinking – can be summarized on several levels. To begin with, by problematizing the 'final duality' between thinking and thinker (act and being), a distinction or polarity that post-subject outlooks want to declare a 'ruse' as discussed in chapter 2, or – what effectively amounts to the same thing – by problematizing the very anthropocentricity or the ineluctable human-centredness of discourse, which both Putnam (idealism, anti-realism) and Nagel (realism) minimize or trivialize in different ways, in this problematization Bonhoeffer has demonstrated two things. He has shown first that thinking (or 'act'), when it is *most true to itself,* that is, when it is operative at its *highest level of integrity,* cannot give itself being or cannot find being. In this result, without stating it openly, or perhaps without fully realizing it, Bonhoeffer has achieved something significant. At the very point at which the post-subject outlooks and some existentialist philosophers[21] have declared that thinking 'does violence to reality' (or to being), Bonhoeffer, while largely agreeing with that assessment itself, has inverted the emphasis of it. Rather than condemning thinking *tout court* for its frequent dogmatist excursions into being, he has instead brought out from the relation something positive for thinking, by demonstrating that thinking (act) *at its most genuine* makes *utterly no claims to being.* Or stating this somewhat differently, he has in effect agreed with Kant that when thinking *does* make jurisdictional claims over being it abandons its integrity and its genuineness and becomes dogmatism. But the really important point here is that he has been able to deny that thinking *must* come to this result (as is the post-subject charge). Indeed, he has shown that thinking *at full integrity* never *does* come to that result. In other words there is a strong convergence of sentiment here (between Bonhoeffer and the post-subject outlooks) on the question of the authority or jurisdiction of thinking over being. The difference is that, where the post-subject outlooks abolish the authority of reason altogether by focusing on the dogmatist excesses when thinking (act) oversteps its bounds into being,

---

21. Although I am by no means equating post-subject and existentialist outlooks by associating them loosely here; indeed in many ways they are radical opposites.

Bonhoeffer, following Kant, wants precisely to preserve the integrity, not only of reality or being (which *can* indeed be 'violated' by thinking), but also of thinking itself, by ensuring that reason always recognizes its proper limits and operates within them.

But we can now go beyond this initial outcome and use it to demonstrate two further results, results that will in fact turn out to be strongly at odds with each other, yet that precisely as such will be able to restate in a new way the original impasse of Christian thinking from which we began. On the one hand, by showing that thinking (act) can never of its own accord yield or reach being, and by Bonhoeffer's placing all of this within the context of human self-understanding, we have been given a penetrating and almost poignant demonstration of *how it is* that human beings cannot through thinking (act) *place themselves into the truth about themselves* as free rational *beings* (since, again, act or reason can never reach human-being). Nevertheless, on the other hand, and now more positively, it is precisely *this* kind of thinking that *recognizes* that it cannot place itself into truth: it is this kind of thinking that will be required for speaking 'about' the 'being' of God's self-revelation, that is, which will be required for genuine Christian thinking. For only a kind of thinking that has tested its limits to the furthest internal reaches (*bis ins Letzte hinein*), and recognizes, as such, that its only legitimate place remains within those limits, only a kind of thinking that makes no possessive or jurisdictional claims over being, but which always remains *in reference to* 'being' or *suspends itself* in being, only this kind of thinking will perhaps be predisposed to encounter the 'being' of revelation in similar appropriate ways.

But now, finally, it is important to note what has just occurred here as such. For we have been brought to an important result that Bonhoeffer himself does not seem fully to foresee, or at least does not bring to full effect. The point is that the only appropriate disposition of thinking or reason *in the face of revelation* is thinking or *reason at full integrity*. Or to state it the other way around, what *revelation demands* of thinking as it confronts and challenges it, is *the full integrity of reason*. But of course reason at full integrity, at its full level of 'goodness', at the heart of its genuineness, does not mean reason at its most overreaching, at its most dogmatic, at its most possessive and excessive, but rather reason at its most carefully self-orienting or self-critical and reflective. *This* result – that revelation demands the full integrity of reason – is the truly compelling aspect of what a deeper engagement with Bonhoeffer's *Act and Being* is capable of bringing to the problem of Christian thinking. Let us look at just one brief example of the further applicability of this 'full rational integrity' result for the question of theological thinking.

3.2   Act and being in the interpretation of revelation

Even at this early juncture in his writing, although still heavily influenced by Barth (this never really changed), Bonhoeffer takes issue strongly in *Act and Being* with Barth's development of the question of act and being on another, theological level, a development that can be seen to foreshadow Bonhoeffer's later critique of Barth's theology as somehow 'positivistic'. The question of act and being plays out in a very different, although not entirely unrelated way on the theological level. The focus here is less on the meaningfulness of discourse about God (that is, less on the *integrity of reason*) and more on the preservation of the *integrity of transcendence*, or the avoidance of reductionism of which I wrote in chapter 1.

The basic concern here is that there are certain perils involved in *any* being-interpretation of revelation (or theological transcendence), pitfalls that have led some theologians – Karl Barth and Jean-Luc Marion are among the leading recent examples – to avoid speaking of God in terms of being at all. For if God 'is' in revelation, in any perduring and intellectually 'visible' or graspable sense of 'being' or 'thereness', then this very visibility or graspability to human capacities, whether intellectual, sensory or affective, would by definition be a violation of the integrity (unconditionedness) of transcendence, as explained in chapter 1. This is why Barth insists that God's transcendence (inasmuch as *God's* transcendence is something 'about' *God* and not merely, as in logical transcendence, something about the limitation, or definition, of human cognition) involves God's ontological 'hiddenness',[22] and that God's self-revelation as such can never be the revelation of God's 'being', for the hiddenness of God's 'being' is part of the very nature of God's 'being'. Because of this, any sense we think we *might* have of God's 'being' must always be reinterpreted purely in terms of God's 'act'.[23] (Marion gives a different response to the same problem and we will discuss that in more detail in chapter 8.)

But Bonhoeffer objects to this for several reasons, two of which are most important. The first objection is that on such an act interpretation of revelation God once again retreats into the non-objective and as such

22. See, e.g., Karl Barth, 'The Hiddenness of God', in *Church Dogmatics II.i* (Edinburgh: T&T Clark, 1957), pp. 179–204.
23. See, e.g., 'The Being of God in Act', in *Church Dogmatics II.i*, pp. 257–72.

effectively into the non-accessible. Revelation becomes perpetually elusive, unable as such to provide the kind of tangible reference or aboutness that meaningful theological discourse 'about' God requires. Now it is true, of course, that a radically fideistic positivism (which Barth's theology is not)[24] could respond to this critique by appealing to a kind of occasionalism or voluntarism in which God pre-empts any concerns about natural human obligation (rational or even ethical), or overrides questions of human integrity, and simply answers this problem 'within Himself' as it were. But this is an untenable position and a difficult one to defend against the biblical view of human freedom, or even more strikingly against the Christian doctrines of creation, incarnation and reconciliation.

So setting these kinds of responses aside, the most obvious problem that we face, again on such a pure act interpretation of revelation, is that this seems to run counter to the very idea of what 'revelation' intrinsically signifies or means. In Bonhoeffer's words, 'If revelation is non-objective, this means theologically that God always remains subject and as such evades any knowable access by humans. On the other hand, however, if it is really *revelation* we are concerned with, then it must in some way become evident, recognizable to human beings; and of course the revelation of God in actual fact has somehow become recognizable and knowable in Christ.'[25] The same idea is expressed in a somewhat different way elsewhere:

> After all, what is at work in revelation is not so much the freedom of God on the other side of revelation – in the eternal self-remainingness and aseity of God – but much more God's moving out of himself in revelation, in his *given* Word; in his covenant (*Bund*) to which he has bound himself; and in his freedom – a freedom which is most powerfully demonstrated precisely in the fact that he has bound himself freely to historical human beings and made himself accessible to them. God is not free from human beings but free for human beings. Christ is the Word of God's freedom. God *is* present, that is, not in eternal non-objectivity but – stating it very provisionally for now – haveable, graspable (*habbar, fassbar*)...[26]

24. In fairness to Barth, the depiction of his theology here as purely act based does not entirely do him justice since he roots revelation as much in the love of God and the freedom of God as in the act of God (cf. *Church Dogmatics* II.i, pp. 272–321). Bonhoeffer did not have *Church Dogmatics*, but at the time of writing was proceeding on the basis of *Die christliche Dogmatik im Entwurf*, I (Munich, 1927).
25. Bonhoeffer, *Akt und Sein*, p. 86, original emphasis.
26. Bonhoeffer, *Akt und Sein*, p. 85, original emphasis.

An interpretation of revelation purely in terms of act, by contrast, seems to ignore this kind of presence or seems unable properly to accommodate it.

A second problem arising out of the interpretation of revelation purely as God's act has to do with two separate but related issues involving continuity: continuity with respect to revelation and with respect to human existence. Let me explain this briefly. Bonhoeffer has previously in *Act and Being* aligned himself with the (roughly) Barthian position that when God, through his self-revelation, 'touches' the human being, a 'new creation' or a 'new existence' is brought into being. (Bonhoeffer calls this new existence *getroffene Existenz*, or existence that has been 'touched' by God in revelation.) In light of this, on a pure act view of revelation, problems of continuity arise both on the level of human identity and on the level of revelation. The root of the problem is as follows: 'If it is only in the act of being touched by God (*nur im Akt des Betroffenwerdens*) that existence is in the truth, then with each passing of the act, existence already stands in untruth. Furthermore, since human existence is incapable of placing itself into truth, then existence "is" in the truth only always as the decision of God for it, which must of course in turn also somehow be conceived as its decision for God'[27] (i.e., because in the end it is God himself who somehow 'hears and believes in me'; one sees the traces of voluntarism or positivism arising here). The problem of continuity expressed here, then, is really twofold. The one difficulty concerns how even just *getroffene Existenz* by itself – the 'new existence' created by and for revelation – may be understood as any sort of unity or identity on a purely act-based understanding. But the further, less technical and more troubling problem, anthropologically (that is, for the meaningfulness of revelation to humans), concerns the question of how an act understanding of revelation can supply the needed continuity between human-being (*Dasein*) and the 'new being' (*getroffene Existenz*), a continuity, so to speak, of the old existence *and* the new existence.

But beyond these important theological questions, the real difficulty with respect to our own present epistemological concerns has to do with the basic loss of rational integrity that such a pure act interpretation of revelation ultimately involves. In later writings, Bonhoeffer implies that the only way Barth can regain the needed sense of reference or aboutness in theological discourse is to resort to a kind of 'positivism of revelation'.

27. Bonhoeffer, *Akt und Sein*, p. 91.

Although he himself does not explain this very satisfactorily, what he clearly means to identify and criticize in Barth is the compound view that in revelation God both 'posits' himself as a possible referent of rational discourse or thinking, and yet does so while contradictorily (and therefore 'miraculously') remaining entirely immune from the intrinsic obligations of the very rational discourse into which revelation posits itself. Or in other words, God 'gives' himself in the kind of 'aboutness' or intentional reference required for intelligible discourse without thereby becoming susceptible to the fundamental requirements of rational integrity, or of showing how that 'aboutness' or reference is possible. So it is not just the aloofness of positivism that is objectionable here but much more that such a view of revelation is actually incoherent or inconsistent, since it simultaneously takes away what it claims to provide for purposes of meaningful (intentional-referential) theological discourse.

In the light of all of this, I can now complete the point I was beginning to make at the end of the previous section. That completed point now runs as follows. If thinking (act) remains true to itself '*bis ins Letzte hinein*', or to the point of *full integrity*, then the danger of reductionism or the compromising of the integrity of transcendence that Barth had feared (and on the basis of which he had insisted on reinterpreting God's being in revelation always as God's act) can be avoided from 'the other side' as it were (i.e., from the side of thinking itself), while preserving the kind of 'being' in revelation that meaningful Christian thinking requires. In fact, far from demanding a voluntaristic or positivistic response, this result suggests something in precisely the opposite direction, again by demanding the full integrity of thinking in the face of revelation – that is, a kind of thinking (act) that will never make possessive or jurisdictional claims over the 'being' of revelation, and yet which *precisely in so doing* will leave the way open for an understanding of Christian revelation as the self-revelation of the non-thematizable 'being' of God.

But in a way, this is to jump well ahead of where we need to be at the moment, and is given merely as a preliminary indication of the productiveness of this notion of 'full rational integrity in the face of revelation'. Indeed, this is not really a result that *Act and Being* by itself would be able to yield. For remember where we were before we moved into this parenthetical treatment of act and being in the interpretation of revelation. Bonhoeffer's final point in the 'transcendental attempt' was that, even when thinking remains genuinely transcendental, with full integrity intact, even here the very nature of reason will ensure that these transcendental limits, which thinking remains always only 'in reference to', even these will be 'thought away until they are themselves no longer genuine limits'.[28] What Bonhoeffer does not say but what he might as well have done is that this 'self-entanglement' and confusion will unavoidably give way to a kind of scepticism and ultimately even to the 'rational unbelief' that I addressed in chapter 2. (Indeed it is not difficult to see aspects of the post-subject anti-philosophies in embryonic form in Bonhoeffer's 'self-entanglement' stage.) But again, we must also be reminded that when transcendental thinking in its genuine Kantian form is understood properly as a *corollary of empirical realism*, it leads to a very different kind of outcome, as we shall see in chapter 6.

This is where the really productive aspects of *Act and Being* come to an end. I assign a brief overview and assessment of the remaining, rather awkward, portion of the book to a footnote.[29] What we can say finally, however, is that at the conclusion of *Act and Being*, in light of its own rather esoteric and manufactured 'solutions' (as discussed in the foregoing footnote)

---

28. Bonhoeffer, *Akt und Sein*, p. 38.

29. Even though, as just stated, transcendental philosophy *need* not lead to the 'self-entanglement' result, nevertheless Bonhoeffer must himself now come to terms with that outcome in order to bring his theological enterprise of act and being to some sort of completion. To accomplish this he engages in what can only be seen as a pair of awkward, stilted moves leading to rather manufactured and ad hoc 'solutions'. (There is little doubt, from Bonhoeffer's later writings that he himself would readily agree with this assessment of the concluding portions of his youthful *Habilitationsschrift*.) The first of these is the strange and rather disconnected idea that because reason itself, even at full integrity, cannot place us into the truth, therefore we are 'expelled outward' (*hinausgewiesen*) towards revelation which *can* give us the truth about ourselves. This move is presented on the one hand as something quasi-reasoned (*because* reason fails, *therefore* we as *rational* beings, find ourselves directed outwards to revelation . . .). Yet, on the other hand, it is acknowledged that we may not understand this 'expulsion outward' to revelation as anything like 'the last possible step' of reason, as if it were something we were epistemologically led into, or any sort of rationally justifiable step. Instead, the step outward toward revelation must be seen paradoxically as 'one which must have already been undertaken, thus enabling us to take it' (*Akt und Sein*, p. 74). The awkwardness of this continues: Revelation then (once we arrive at it), upon encountering these previously purified transcendental and ontological dispositions, will be found somehow to 'return them back [to noetic discourse], albeit in an entirely new form' (*Akt und Sein*, p. 73). In this 'new form', the two key noetic principles – i.e., of thought remaining 'in reference to' transcendence and of the 'suspension' of thinking in being – will 'open themselves up to a distinctively theological interpretation and as such be able to assist also in the understanding of the concept of revelation' (*Akt und Sein*, p. 73). This is presented as a completion of sorts of the 'act' (thinking) requirement of theological reasoning.

Similarly, what Bonhoeffer offers as a 'solution' (especially now in light of the Barthian 'act' challenge) to the 'being' problem for theological thinking – i.e., a rather eclectic, insular and telegrammatically presented view of the Church – is equally unsatisfactory. But again, this should not be allowed to detract from the contribution *Act and Being* is able to make on the epistemological front for theological purposes. And anyway, these questions are dealt with, as we shall see, in much more promising ways in Bonhoeffer's more mature thought, even if only indirectly.

what Bonhoeffer seems to remain in search of, or what slips his grasp, is an appropriate theological approach to 'being' in all of this, that is, a way of speaking *ontologically* about transcendence or God. Yet there also is a tension in this very search, as Bonhoeffer implicitly recognizes, for any such 'ontology of transcendence', by very definition of these terms, would appear to violate the integrity or the unconditioned character of transcendence. Bonhoeffer's project of act and being thus remains decidedly incomplete at this point, yet the value of what *Act and Being* is capable of contributing to current discussions, in spite of its incompleteness and often cryptic character, should not be underestimated.

6

The Kantian inversion of 'all previous philosophy'

The guiding focus of our enquiry into Christian thinking continues to be the twofold preservation of integrity, both of reason and theological transcendence. If we now look back and take stock of the ground we have covered in this endeavour, especially over the last three chapters, we find that, although some important progress has been made, nevertheless at every turn we have in the end been thrown back onto some version of philosophy's perpetual polarities, or have been unable to get beyond these. Even the project of act and being, which seemed to offer a fresh promise by demonstrating that revelation (and by extension, theological discourse) demands to be approached in the full integrity of reason, even this could not deliver on that promise, but found itself succumbing ultimately either to a new kind of idealistic dogmatism, where thinking (act) declared itself 'lord' over being, or to a new kind of scepticism in the 'self-entanglement' of reason. Similarly, although MacKinnon brought us perhaps closest to a kind of conciliation between realism and idealism (or anti-realism), the progress there was mainly negative, pointing out the inadequacies of both sides and how each needed the other, yet not offering any positive way forward in the light of these polarities. In the end we were still left at the making/finding dilemma and could not advance beyond this. Furthermore, this invariable arrival at philosophy's perpetual polarities led in turn to unacceptable answers for our broader theological endeavour, inasmuch as these polarities will always seek to treat transcendence either merely as invention or discovery, or as some combination of the two, and thus by definition compromise its integrity. It seems then, if progress is to be possible beyond these, that we will have to find some different way of asking the question of rational integrity.

It is inevitable as such, having come to the same polarizing results over and over again – whether as *aisthesis/noiesis*, idealism/realism, empiricism/rationalism, internalism/externalism, anti-realism/realism, act/being and so on – that we must at some point be brought face to face with the Kantian project in philosophy, specifically as this is presented seminally in the *Critique of Pure Reason*. For it is precisely these perennial polarities, to which our own endeavours here have invariably led, that the *Critique* takes as its initial starting point and that it is intent fundamentally on overcoming. It is no accident as such that Kant has already loomed large in previous approaches to the question of integrity in thinking, whether in Putnam, MacKinnon or Bonhoeffer.[1] But each of these, while sensing the importance and indispensability of what Kant has to say to these questions, has either misconstrued (Putnam) or dealt incompletely (MacKinnon, Bonhoeffer) with key aspects of what Kant himself is proposing in full, or perhaps they have not appreciated sufficiently what Kant himself insists is the essentially 'revolutionary' character of his overall enterprise.

For all the myriad of ways that the *Critique of Pure Reason* is capable of being misunderstood when not read with proper attentiveness,[2] no one could dispute that what it at least *aspires* to be is a project of *restoring the full integrity of reason in philosophical enquiry*. Kant also describes this as the project of restoring integrity to 'metaphysics', as implied in the title of what might be called the *Critique*'s 'user guide', *Prolegomena to Any Future*

---

1. In fact, even Thomas Nagel's *View from Nowhere* (Oxford: Oxford University Press, 1986), despite its essentially Cartesian commitments and at times open hostility to Kantian epistemology, can be seen fundamentally as a protracted endeavour to overcome at least one aspect of what is often referred to as the 'Kantian challenge'. For it is fundamentally the overcoming of the ineluctable anthropocentric viewpoint that Nagel has in mind when he states his basic aims as involving the 'gradual liberation of the dormant objective self, trapped initially behind an individual perspective of human experience'. But it must quickly be added that to construe the Kantian challenge as only this one-sided anthropocentric challenge against objectivism, as is frequently done, is to misunderstand it. In fact Kant's philosophy is a challenge, as much to pervasive subjectivism (thoroughgoing anti-realism or internalism) and, as such, to any standard construal of anthropocentrism, as it is to objectivism (metaphysical/atomic realism or externalism). We shall discuss this further below.

2. Kant himself pleads on more than one occasion for a fair hearing, especially after some of the initial misinterpretations of the first edition of the *Critique*. He voiced concerns that the whole enterprise would be misunderstood because it had not been read with the proper diligence and care: 'I fear that the *Critique of Pure Reason* may well fare just as the [Humean] problem itself fared when it was first posed. It will be judged incorrectly, because it is not understood; it will not be understood, because people will be inclined just to skim through the book, but not to think through it . . .'; Immanuel Kant, *Prolegomena to any Future Metaphysics*, Gary Hatfield (ed.) (Cambridge: Cambridge University Press, 1997), p. 11.

Metaphysics.[3] It is true that the term 'metaphysics' is today often met with suspicion or even disdain (not only by post-subject outlooks, but also by certain strains of Anglo-American philosophies that remain staunchly empiricist, in a Humean vein, even in the wake of the failures of logical positivism). But the reader wary of the term need not be put off by the use of it here. For Kant's broader employment of it is so comprehensive and neutral that it would include virtually all of the outlooks we have discussed so far in this book. For example, the *Critique* actually begins with a broad overview or synopsis of precisely the kinds of polarities and conflicts that we have been discussing over the last five chapters, and then goes on to assert that the *whole* 'battlefield of these endless controversies is called *metaphysics*' (original emphasis).[4] In other words, to engage in metaphysical enquiry is not necessarily to commit oneself in any particularly *realist* way on questions about 'the nature of things'. Indeed one could dispute the validity of any such enquiry into an 'underlying nature of things', or one could even claim that the question itself is fundamentally misstated; but precisely by doing so one would be participating in the 'battlefield of endless controversies' that Kant calls metaphysics. (For our own purposes in this chapter, and in the very simplest of terms, we could describe metaphysics initially as basically concerned with questions about whether, and in what way, it is possible to make *general* statements about the world – i.e., not merely general statements about logic, but genuinely general statements, involving elements of necessity and universality, about the real empirical world of human experience and endeavour.)

However, beyond merely defining metaphysics as a field of fundamental philosophical controversy, if there is one most basic way in which Kant will turn out to be different from what has come before, it will be in the way he shifts the focus of metaphysical disagreement away from questions about the *nature of things* to more preliminary questions about the limits and *nature of reason* both as reason enquires into the empirically real world of space and time, and then further, as it seeks to make judgment on putatively 'supra-sensible' levels. Still, what the *Critique* is engaging in as such remains genuinely 'metaphysical' and not just epistemological, because it

---

3. The *Prolegomena* was written after the *Critique* as a kind of guide into it, especially in response to early misinterpretations of the *Critique*.
4. Immanuel Kant, *Critique of Pure Reason*, Paul Guyer and Allen W. Wood (tr. and eds.) (Cambridge: Cambridge University Press, 1998), Aviii.

continues to ask about the demands of necessity and universality in the nature of reason in these endeavours, and not just about the character and status of noetic processes and states. But again, it will be different from other metaphysical projects because the 'nature' into which it will be enquiring is that of 'reason' and not of 'things'. Kant's point is, of course, that before we could even hope successfully to negotiate any such enquiry into the 'nature of things', or before we could properly understand what such an enterprise should even mean or how it should proceed, we would first need to look into the nature and proper functioning of reason itself, by which any such enquiry must be undertaken. Moreover, once we do proceed in this way, via an antecedent critique of the capacity (reason) by which any (metaphysical) enquiry must be undertaken, certain fundamental flaws in the whole process of engaging in metaphysics in the first place as an enquiry 'into things' will become evident. This is why Kant describes the *Critique* as a 'metaphysics of metaphysics'.[5]

Kant laments that metaphysical enquiry, precisely as the enquiry 'into things', had in his own day reached a particularly onerous state of stagnancy and as such had come to be viewed with 'scorn and contempt'. Whereas real progress was visible and ongoing in all the other sciences, or disciplines of knowledge (*Wissenschaften*), metaphysics, which for Kant rightly deserved the title of 'queen of all the sciences' (at least in terms of its aspirations, or 'if the will be taken for the deed'), remained locked in its age-old perpetual polarities. Kant declares his aim to revolutionize philosophy, via a rigorous pursuit of rational integrity, and as such to restore metaphysics to what he considered to be its proper place of esteem and respect.

The overlap with our own concerns here is already clear, and because his 'revolutionary' contribution to our own theological endeavour will be considerable, I propose now to embark on a discussion of Kant that is somewhat more extensive than our other engagements until now. To that end I will divide the present chapter into four main sections. First I will try to set the *Critique* into an orienting perspective in a broadly 'negative' sense. That is, I will explore its contention about the 'stagnancy' of traditional philosophy as well as the many ways the *Critique* itself has been misunderstood in its endeavour to break out of that stagnancy. Secondly, I will address positively the essentially 'revolutionary' character of the *Critique*,

---

5. Immanuel Kant, *Kant: Philosophical Correspondence 1759–99*, Arnulf Zweig (tr. and ed.) (Chicago: University of Chicago Press, 1967), p. 95.

which Kant himself describes as seeking to undertake a 'complete reform or rather rebirth of metaphysics'[6] or a 'Copernican' inversion of 'all previous philosophy'. This will prove to be not just another inversion from externalism to internalism or vice versa, but a revolution of a fundamentally new and different sort. Sections 3 and 4 will then seek to defend and explicate the claim in a more detailed way that the *Critique* is most fundamentally a project of restoring the full integrity of reason in philosophical enquiry.

1   Standard misconstruals of the *Critique of Pure Reason*

In its opening pages, Kant sets up the *Critique of Pure Reason* as a project essentially designed to overcome the two perennial and recurring opposing philosophical 'stagnancies' – 'dogmatism' and 'scepticism' – to which traditional metaphysical enquiries 'into things' (that is, into things as they are 'in themselves') have invariably given rise throughout the history of philosophy.[7] By far the more prevalent focus throughout the *Critique*, or by far the more primary antagonist, is dogmatism. Indeed, dogmatism is precisely the self-enclosed metaphysical '*project* of pure reason' that the *Critique of Pure Reason* is undertaking to *critique*. Or one could also say that dogmatism is the project of 'purest objectivity', in which reason seeks to fashion for itself or to give itself its own 'object' – an object 'in itself' – which has been freed from all the contingencies, uncertainties and vicissitudes of empirical sense, and which as such allows reason to operate within an empirically sanitized and pristinely conceptual region of pure reason. Catherine Pickstock has aptly described this project of purest objectivity as involving the search for the 'perfectly inert, controllable and present

6. Kant, *Prolegomena to any Future Metaphysics*, p. 7.
7. Kant's own descriptions of the relation between dogmatism and scepticism are often colourful and asserted with a certain dry wit. For example, speaking at the opening of the *Critique*, specifically about metaphysics as the traditional enquiry 'into things', Kant observes that 'in the beginning, under the administration of the *dogmatists*, her rule was *despotic*. Yet because her legislation still contained traces of ancient barbarism, this rule gradually degenerated through internal wars into complete anarchy; and the *sceptics*, a kind of nomads who abhor all permanent cultivation of the soil, shattered civil unity from time to time. But since there were fortunately only a few of them, they could not prevent the dogmatists from continually attempting to rebuild, though never according to a plan unanimously accepted among themselves.' He then suggests that 'once in recent times' (i.e., in the philosophy of John Locke) 'it even seemed as though an end would be put to all these controversies'. Nevertheless, for a variety of reasons, both within and outside of Locke's philosophy, 'metaphysics fell back into the same old worm-eaten dogmatism, and thus into the same position of contempt out of which the science was to have been extricated' (Kant, *Critique of Pure Reason*, Aviii–x, emphasis slightly altered).

object'.[8] Kant condemns any such dogmatic enterprise as precisely the illegitimate exercise of 'pure reason *without an antecedent critique of its own capacity*'.[9] Or, stated conversely, Kant asserts that, whenever reason *does* assume its proper disposition, and begins from self-critique (the heart of Kant's critical philosophy), it will inevitably discover that any presumptions it *might* have entertained that it could 'give itself its own object', or that it could 'cull a real object out of … mere logic',[10] come to be exposed as nothing but 'sweet dogmatic dreams' and 'castles in the sky'.[11] He maintains that in whatever manifestation they are found, whether in Wolff[12] or in Mendelssohn or Spinoza[13] or even in Plato,[14] dogmatist tendencies are always reflective of a kind of 'philosophical zealotry' that leads to error.[15] Now Kant actually sees a culmination of sorts for dogmatism within certain strains of continental rationalism, especially as this had come to expression in his contemporary Christian Wolff, whom he called 'the greatest among all dogmatic philosophers'. But as we shall see, dogmatism for Kant also comes strongly to expression in a new if somewhat more subtle way later on, in what came to be known as 'post-Kantian' German idealism (e.g. in Fichte or Hegel). In short, to borrow Bonhoeffer's terminology, any philosophical enquiry in which thinking or reason (act) makes illegitimate claims over being, or in which reason, without proper justification, claims being as its possession or as falling under its jurisdiction, or declares itself 'lord' over being, is a form of dogmatism.

Scepticism is a secondary, if equally unwelcome outcome at the opposite extreme of dogmatism, which inevitably comes about when the philosophical enquiry 'into things' seeks to avoid the errors of dogmatism. This will be explained more fully as we proceed, but for now we can say in a preliminary way that, whereas dogmatism 'despotically' enforces the rule of pure reason over empirical reality and thus establishes the authority of

8. Catherine Pickstock, *After Writing: On the Liturgical Consummation of Philosophy* (Oxford: Blackwell, 1997), see chapter 3; cited in John Milbank, 'The Theological Critique of Philosophy in Hamann and Jacobi', in John Milbank, Catherine Pickstock and Graham Ward (eds.), *Radical Orthodoxy* (London: Routledge, 1999), pp. 21–37, p. 32.
9. Kant, *Critique of Pure Reason*, Bxxxv, emphasis added.
10. Kant, *Philosophical Correspondence*, p. 253.
11. Kant, *Critique of Pure Reason*, A758/B786; *Dreams of a Spirit-Seer Elucidated by Dreams of Metaphysics*, in David Walford in collaboration with Ralf Meerbote (tr. and eds.), *Theoretical Philosophy 1755–1770* (Cambridge: Cambridge University Press, 1992), pp. 301–59; p. 329.
12. Kant, *Critique of Pure Reason*, Bxxxvi.
13. Immanuel Kant, 'What is Orientation in Thinking?', in H. S. Reiss (ed.), *Kant: Political Writings* (second edition) (Cambridge: Cambridge University Press, 1991), p. 246.
14. Kant, *Critique of Pure Reason*, A5/B8, A312/B369–A319/B376.
15. Kant, 'What is Orientation in Thinking?', p. 242.

metaphysics in a coercive and ultimately unjustifiable way, scepticism for Kant denotes a sweeping *rejection of metaphysics* of any sort – that is, a rejection of any suggestion that our knowledge of the world reflects or depends on principles that are genuinely *universal* or in any way *necessary*, and as such knowable a priori. Most of the British empiricisms,[16] for example, are thus forms of scepticism in the anti-metaphysical sense of rejecting the governance of universal and necessary principles pertaining to our knowledge of the world. Berkeley's empirical idealism fits this description especially well and will serve as an important antithesis to Kant's own empirical realism. But even Hume's empiricism, while by no means idealist (indeed, as we shall see, Hume can be seen as an empirical realist of sorts), remains especially anti-metaphysical in the sense of rejecting any claims to universality and necessity within the world of sense experience. It is precisely on this issue that Kant will part ways with Hume as we shall see, even though Hume remains pivotal in supplying a basic impetus for the *Critique*'s genesis.[17]

1.1 The *Critique of Pure Reason* misconstrued as the thoroughgoing *defence* of pure reason

It is generally acknowledged by current scholarship that Kant interpretation has struggled through a particularly unfortunate and misrepresentative period in twentieth-century Anglo-American philosophy,[18] and that

---

16. Prominently excepting Locke who was at least as much a rationalist as an empiricist.

17. Having said all of this, however, it is important to note that Kant distinguishes – within both dogmatism and scepticism – between these seen as *methods* and seen as *destinations*. As philosophical methods or procedures, both are praiseworthy; as destinations, both are condemnable. As a philosophical procedure, the dogmatic method is praised for its spirit of thoroughness and for its purity in the science of a priori reasoning. But when it contends that it can give itself real truth apart from what is given empirically in sense experience, or when (what is the same thing) it does not proceed from an antecedent critique of its own capacity, it is to be denounced. Similarly, Kant is not criticizing the sceptical method in a basic Cartesian vein, which is necessary for avoiding error, mirage or sophistry. It is not scepticism as a method but scepticism as a destination or an outcome that he rejects. Scepticism as a destination is for Kant the 'principle of artful and scientific ignorance that undermines the foundations of all cognition, in order, if possible, to leave no reliability or certainty anywhere' (Kant, *Critique of Pure Reason*, Bxxxvi, A424/B452).

18. Parts of this paragraph, along with three other paragraphs in this chapter, are basically a restatement of similar points I have made in another essay in a narrower context (see 'Radical Orthodoxy and the New Culture of Obscurantism', in *Modern Theology* (Oxford: Blackwell, 2004). By the kind of 'scholarly consensus' I speak of here, I mean established Kant scholars who have written extensively on his thought in ways that, whether agreeing or disagreeing, are concerned with giving clarity and coherence to Kant's work per se and only thereafter seeking application to current projects or issues. I do not as such mean the majority of Kant conversants who engage with him essentially to serve or buttress a particular perspective. I have rather in mind scholars such as Alan W. Wood, Paul Guyer,

especially in the latter half of the century this has been a reflection to a considerable degree of the massive influence of P. F. Strawson's broadly polemical reading of Kant, centring around Kant's doctrine of noumena or his transcendental idealism.[19] The point here is not to go into the details of Strawson's position or to negate its value on many levels, but only to say that, even though the errors of that position are so obvious that virtually no Kant scholar today any longer holds to it,[20] nevertheless it often still remains the background or default view in many Anglo-American discussions of Kant. Thankfully, after a generation or more in which the Strawsonian misunderstanding had become almost standardized, many of the most trusted authorities today are once again alerting our attention to the errors of that 'received view' and how this view deviates from Kant's own stated intentions and impoverishes his potential contribution to current concerns in both philosophy and theology.[21] Thus, the scholarly consensus would agree today that something similar could be claimed for Kant as has been for Hegel: namely, that although current scholarship 'has cleared him of some false charges, he has in the past been the victim of more various misinterpretation than any other philosopher, and of more shamelessly ill-informed criticism'.[22]

There are two basic and fundamentally opposing ways that the *Critique of Pure Reason* has been standardly – and devastatingly – misconstrued. The first is when its essential character as a *critique* is *ignored* and it is made into a thoroughgoing *defence* of 'pure' reason. The second is when its essential character as a *critique* is *radicalized* and it is made into an all out *assault* on metaphysics per se. Again, these mistakes have been made so prevalently that they have in many discussions become virtually standardized.

Henry E. Allison, Karl Ameriks, Gary Hatfield, Manfred Kuehn, Robert Paul Wolff, Onora O'Neill, J. Michael Young or Donald MacKinnon among others.

19. One of the clearest, most decisively documented and defended expressions of this can be found in Henry Allison's *Kant's Transcendental Idealism* (New Haven: Yale University Press, 1983). Strawson's own definitive position on Kant is given in *The Bounds of Sense* (London: Methuen, 1966).

20. It remains something of a mystery, Kant's ambivalence on certain key issues notwithstanding, as to how Strawson could come to advocate a position that is at fundamental points so obviously at odds with what Kant actually says. One explanation is that Strawson seems to rely almost entirely on Kemp-Smith's translation, which despite its lucidity in some ways is today acknowledged to be seriously flawed in key respects. Another is the basic prejudicial environment vis-à-vis Kant out of which Strawson wrote and from which he did not completely escape: a rather strange mix of late nineteenth-century neo-Kantianism with other anti-psychologistic preoccupations. See, e.g., Howard Caygill, *A Kant Dictionary* (Oxford: Blackwell, 1995), p. 407.

21. See footnotes 18 and 19 above.

22. G. R. G. Mure, *The Philosophy of Hegel* (London: Oxford University Press, 1965), p. viii.

Indeed Kant is not infrequently interpreted in *both* these ways by the same writers, even though they are contradictory positions. Peter Strawson is again the most prominent example in recent Anglo-American philosophy who manages to do just this, and so it is little wonder that he speaks of Kant's project in the *Critique of Pure Reason* as 'disastrous' and 'perverse' and of Kant as 'needing rescuing from himself'.[23] But the double, conflicting mistakes continue to be made prevalently today as well, and in theology as much as anywhere else.

It is Strawson's interpretation of the *Critique* in the former sense, however – that is, as a thoroughgoing *defence* of the project of pure reason – that has had the greatest impact on many recent Anglo-American interpretations of Kant. I will come to some particular aspects of Strawson's own account below but at this juncture I focus on John Milbank's theological project (which shows clear, if inadvertent, signs of the Strawsonian influence) because it exemplifies so well the point I am trying to make. Milbank makes the first of these two mistakes in a particularly obvious way when he depicts Kant's *critical* philosophy as, in his words, the '*attitude* of pure reason itself',[24] that is as the *defence par excellence* or the quintessentially positive case *for* the *sufficiency* of pure reason in the *Critique*'s putative quest for 'purest objectivity'. But Milbank does not stop here. For he then goes on to compound this error by engaging in what has become the prevalent mistake of installing Kant as both the culmination of continental rationalism and as the prototype of German metaphysical idealism. Milbank sets Kant in both of these contexts by making him the purest expression of Wolffian dogmatism and of the 'Spinozistic void', on the rationalist side, and by making him responsible for the subsequent rationalist excesses in different ways in the philosophies of Hegel, Fichte and Schelling, on the idealist side.[25] But when we let Kant speak for himself we quickly see the obvious falsity of such associations, despite the prevalence with which they are made.

Let us look then, to begin with, at Milbank's contention that Kant represents the culmination of the rationalisms of Wolff and Spinoza in order to see how these kinds of charges and associations stand up when we let

23. Cf., e.g., Peter Strawson, *The Bounds of Sense* (London: Methuen, 1966), p. 21, and Henry Allison, *Kant's Transcendental Idealism* (New Haven: Yale University Press, 1983), pp. 4–6.
24. See, e.g., John Milbank, 'The Theological Critique of Philosophy in Hamann and Jacobi', in John Milbank, Catherine Pickstock and Graham Ward (eds.), *Radical Orthodoxy* (London: Routledge, 1999), pp. 21–37.
25. See Milbank, 'The Theological Critique of Philosophy', pp. 22, 26.

Kant speak for himself. We have already seen that Christian Wolff's rationalism was held by Kant to represent the apex of the dogmatism of his day and that it represented for Kant precisely the epitome of the self-assured 'project of pure reason' in metaphysics against which the *Critique* is primarily focused. This is not to say that Kant was not in many ways deeply respectful of Wolff, who was arguably the most important philosopher of the mid-eighteenth century. (Kant especially admired the 'spirit of thoroughness' in Wolff's dogmatic philosophy). Nevertheless, it is Wolff who for Kant remains at least the prime representative of the 'dogmatic mentality of his age',[26] and who as such bears Kant's criticism of the dogmatism within continental rationalism most directly. But Wolff is by no means the only focus of Kant's denouncements here. Kant also clearly identifies Spinoza as a dogmatic philosopher and strongly distances himself from Spinozism in this regard.[27] Kant goes as far as to describe an important essay, 'What is Orientation in Thinking?', as written primarily out of a determination 'to cleanse myself from the suspicion of Spinozism',[28] which in Kant's view 'is so dogmatic... that it rivals even mathematics in the rigour of its demonstrations' and 'leads directly to zealotry'.[29] In fact, as we have discussed above, the *Critique* actually opens with a scathing polemic against the dogmatism of the 'old metaphysics' and contextualizes itself against this. To make this point absolutely clear: the search for the 'perfectly inert, controllable and present object', with which the construal of the *Critique of Pure Reason* as the thoroughgoing *defence* of pure reason wants to saddle Kant, is precisely at the heart of what Kant himself rejects as the 'despotic' tactics resorted to by 'the old worm-eaten dogmatism'[30] which arrogates to itself 'the proud name of an ontology'.[31]

It might be added, in order to put this idea decisively to rest, that the misconstrual of the *Critique of Pure Reason* as 'the *attitude* of pure reason itself' rather than the *critique* of it is not itself anything new or unique. In fact it is virtually identical to one of the first misinterpretations that had

26. Kant, *Critique of Pure Reason*, Bxxxvii.
27. See, e.g., Kant, *Philosophical Correspondence*, p. 158; 'What is Orientation in Thinking?', p. 246.
28. Kant, *Philosophical Correspondence*, p. 158.
29. Kant, *Political Writings*, p. 246. More fully, Kant says: 'It is almost impossible to understand how the above-mentioned scholars [i.e., Mendelssohn and Jacobi] were able to find support for Spinozism in the *Critique of Pure Reason*. The *Critique* clips the wings of dogmatism completely... and Spinozism is so dogmatic... that it rivals even mathematics in the rigour of its demonstrations.'
30. Kant, *Critique of Pure Reason*, Aix–x.
31. Kant, *Critique of Pure Reason*, A247.

emerged immediately following the publication of the first edition of the *Critique* in 1781. That erroneous interpretation arose out of what was to become famous as a notoriously misdirected initial review of the *Critique* by Christian Garve. (Actually, it turned out to be not so much the review itself by Garve that was misguided but rather the massive editing of Garve's piece by J. G. H. Feder. Garve himself was apologetic for the outcome – which was vilified and devastatingly refuted by Kant, as expressing the exact inversion of what he had actually said – and sought to pacify Kant by publishing the original and much friendlier version a year later.)[32] At any rate, Kant himself, on several occasions after that initial misconstrual, fully rejects any idea that what he is advocating is anything like a project of 'purest objectivity', or some sort of 'higher idealism' or 'supra-sensible reality' with which he was then being charged, and which any construal of the *Critique of Pure Reason* as a thoroughgoing *defence* of pure reason wants to lumber him with again.[33]

The other standard mistake in this same '*defence* of pure reason' vein, beyond interpreting Kant as the culmination of continental rationalism, is to install him as the prototype of the subsequent German idealisms of Fichte, Hegel and Schelling. But now let us ask again: What does Kant himself have to say about this association (i.e., even beyond the basic programme of the *Critique*, which, as we shall see, is already clear enough in this regard)? What does Kant himself have to say about the German idealism that (it is claimed) was the *inevitable* product of Kantian critical philosophy and for which he must thus be held responsible? There can of course be little doubt that Kantian philosophy served as the springboard for subsequent German idealism, with its renewed search on even 'purer' levels for the perfectly inert, rational object. But the truth is that Kant himself categorically rejected this 'post-Kantian' move as retrograde. By this I mean that post-Kantian German idealism represented for Kant a slide backwards into a dogmatism of a new sort: an *idealist* dogmatism (e.g. in Fichte) rather then the traditional *realist* dogmatism (e.g. in Wolff) against which the *Critique* had been initially directed. Or in more current language, the inadmissible excesses of *metaphysical realism* are simply traded in for a new set

---

32. See Frederick C. Beiser, *The Fate of Reason, German Philosophy from Kant to Fichte* (Cambridge, MA: Harvard University Press, 1987), pp. 172–77; Johann Schulz, *Exposition of Kant's Critique of Pure Reason*, James C. Morrison (tr.), (Ottawa: University of Ottawa Press, 1995), pp. 171–77; Kant, *Philosophical Correspondence* pp. 15–16, 98–108.

33. See, e.g., Kant, *Prolegomena to any Future Metaphysics*, pp. 5–23, 126–37; Kant, *Critique of Pure Reason*, Bxxxviii–xliv, A ix–x; Kant, *Philosophical Correspondence*, pp. 98–108; Kant, 'What is Orientation in Thinking?', pp. 237–49.

of the same kinds of excesses in *metaphysical idealism*. Accordingly, Kant's repudiation of this new kind of post-Kantian idealism (which he witnessed in his lifetime) is much more outspoken than his critique of either Cartesian 'sceptical' idealism or his rejection of Berkeley's 'visionary' idealism.

The point is that, far from heralding the *completion* of Kant's critical philosophy (as Fichte had claimed to be doing), post-Kantian German idealism was rather, in Kant's own eyes, a fundamental *betrayal* of his own critical principles (and as such, again, an engagement in a new kind of dogmatism).[34] This is clear from several of Kant's later writings but nowhere more decisively than in his 'Open Letter' to Fichte from 1799. Kant begins by declaring his regard for Fichte's *Wissenschaftslehre* as 'a totally indefensible system'. He berates its 'attempt to cull a real object out of logic as a vain effort and therefore a thing that no one has ever done'. Note that it is *this* step, the identification of the *real* with the *logically necessary* or the self-necessitating, *causa sui*, that for Kant is the real heart of the new idealist dogmatism. Kant goes on to say that he is 'so opposed to Fichtean metaphysics . . . that I have advised him, in a letter, to turn his fine literary gifts to the problem of applying the *Critique of Pure Reason* rather than squander them in cultivating fruitless sophistries'. Accordingly, he rejects any claim by 'the Fichtean philosophy to be a genuine critical philosophy' and goes on to 'renounce any connection with that philosophy'.[35]

In sum, to connect the character or spirit of Kantian critical philosophy with that of the German idealism that followed, or to read him as the *original* 'metaphysical idealist', responsible for its emergence and its excesses, is as utterly unwarranted, on any moderately attentive reading of Kant himself, as is making him the culmination of the rationalist dogmatism that preceded him, and which the *Critique* is explicitly trying to overturn.

1.2 The *Critique of Pure Reason* misconstrued as an *assault* on metaphysics per se

But the *Critique* has also been (and continues to be) misconstrued in completely the opposite direction (and again not infrequently by the same

---

34. It is ironic that Kant sees in Fichte a new kind of dogmatism, for it was precisely the rejection of dogmatism – understood as the affirmation of a more ultimate reality, or a world 'out there' impervious to human sensibilities and values – that was the driving impetus behind Fichte's idealism.

35. Kant, 'Open Letter on Fichte's *Wissenschaftslehre*, August 7, 1799', in *Philosophical Correspondence*, pp. 253–4.

people who commit the first offence), as proposing something radically anti-metaphysical: that is, as a radical assault, in a way that surpasses even Hume, on any universal or necessary principles whatsoever governing human enquiry into the world. Stephen Palmquist gives a helpful brief survey of some who have held and continue to hold this view.[36] From this side, the *Critique of Pure Reason* has been described as 'the most thorough and devastating of all anti-metaphysical writings'.[37] Kant's (highly esteemed) contemporary Moses Mendelssohn himself called Kant's critical philosophy the 'all destroyer'; and Heinrich Heine followed him in this assessment, accusing Kant of advocating 'destructive, world-annihilating thoughts' and referring to him as 'the arch-destroyer in the realm of thought'.[38] Etienne Gilson speaks even more broadly in this regard of Kant's thorough 'rejection of metaphysics' or of his having 'no metaphysical interests of his own'.[39] Palmquist has J. N. Findlay summing up this tendency as follows: 'It is usual nowadays [1974] to think of Kant as some sort of incipient positivist, always verging towards a belief in the total non-significance of ideas lacking all empirical illustration.'[40] Indeed we could add Strawson to this list, who does precisely what Findlay says in his virtual identification of Kant with Berkeley's empirical idealism.[41] Strawson thus manages to construe Kant as both a dogmatist metaphysician *and* as an anti-metaphysician, and it is thus again no wonder that he sees him as needing 'rescuing from himself'.

But like their counterparts at the other extreme who want to portray Kant as the climax of dogmatist metaphysics, these kinds of approaches do not read Kant carefully enough, or do not allow his own assertions unequivocally to the contrary to carry the kind of weight that he himself gives them.[42] For example, it is difficult to argue with Kant's own statement that what he was proposing in the *Critique* was not a destruction of metaphysics

36. Stephen Palmquist, 'Kant's Theocentric Metaphysics', *Analele Universitatii Din Timisoara* 4 (1992), pp. 55–70. All of the following quotations in this paragraph are given in Palmquist's essay.

37. W. H. Walsh, *Metaphysics* (London: Hutchinson University Library, 1963), p. 38.

38. Heinrich Heine, *Zur Geschichte der Religion und Philosophie in Deutschland* (Stuttgart: Reclam, 1997 (1834)); (tr.) J. Snodgrass as *Religion and Philosophy in Germany* (Boston: Beacon Press, 1959 (1882)), p. 109.

39. Etienne Gilson, *The Unity of Philosophical Experience* (New York: Scribner's, 1950), pp. 229, 310.

40. J. N. Findlay, 'Kant Today', in P. Laberge et al. (eds.), *Proceedings of the Ottawa Congress on Kant in the Anglo-American and Continental Traditions Held October 10–14, 1974* (Ottawa: University of Ottawa Press, 1976), pp. 3–16, p. 3.

41. Strawson, *Bounds of Sense*, p. 22.

42. See footnote 2 in this chapter.

but a 'complete rebirth and reform of metaphysics',[43] or his desire to re-store metaphysics to its rightful position as 'queen of the sciences',[44] or his description of the *Critique* as a 'metaphysics of metaphysics'.[45] In short, to interpret the *Critique* either as a thoroughgoing *defence* of pure reason or as an all-out *assault* on metaphysics per se (understood as the possibility of necessary and universal cognition with respect to the real world) is to con-strue it as either dogmatism (i.e., 'thing-in-itself metaphysics') or as scep-ticism (anti-metaphysics) and as such to make it into a pursuit of precisely the polar 'stagnancies' that the *Critique* from its very first page onward declares itself determined to overcome.

2   Kant's 'Copernican revolution': the inversion of anti-realism (idealism) *and* realism

It is here, in the face of these standard errors, that my initial proposal of seeing the *Critique* as most essentially a project of restoring the full integrity of reason in philosophical enquiry proves to be especially ac-curate and helpful. For when we do this, several things come into view. First, it allows us to bring Kant's own position on dogmatism and scep-ticism vis-à-vis traditional metaphysics into a proper focus. The specific twofold point I wish to make here is that, on the one hand, Kant sees both dogmatism and scepticism as *exercises in reason which lack proper in-tegrity*, or which forfeit integrity in diverging ways; *and yet*, on the other hand, he maintains that they have historically been the *inevitable* destina-tions of traditional metaphysics, that is, metaphysics pursued as an en-quiry 'into things'. Now it is important to note in this light that all the polarities we have been discussing thus far in the book – *aisthesis/noiesis*, idealism/realism, empiricism/rationalism, internalism/externalism, anti-realism/realism, even act and being, although in a somewhat different way – are polarities that arise precisely out of the traditional metaphys-ical enquiry 'into things'. *Aisthesis* enquires 'into things' by giving pri-ority to the senses, *noiesis* by giving priority to the intellect. Idealism (anti-realism) enquires 'into things' based on mind-dependence, realism based on mind-independence, and so on. So now, configuring this in an

43. Kant, *Prolegomena to any Future Metaphysics*, p. 7.
44. Kant, *Critique of Pure Reason*, Aviii–x.
45. Kant, *Philosophical Correspondence*, p. 95; indeed, as we shall see below, the entire *Critique of Pure Reason* can be seen as a protracted response to the question: In light of Hume's devastating critique of traditional metaphysics, how is metaphysics possible anyway?

admittedly oversimplified way (not everything will fit perfectly here, but roughly), we can say basically, along with Kant, (a) that scepticism is the fate of all philosophical enquiries 'into things' that give priority to the senses, and (b) that, likewise, dogmatism is the fate of all philosophical enquiries 'into things' that give priority to the intellect.

However, what begins to come clear, secondly, when we view the *Critique of Pure Reason* in this way as essentially the enquiry into full rational integrity, is that the real culprit in all of this is not dogmatism per se or scepticism per se, since these are simply the inevitable responses of reason trying to come to terms with the internalist or externalist perspectives from which a philosophical enquiry 'into things' demands to be engaged. The real culprit responsible for the perpetual polarizations and stagnancy is instead found in the fact that philosophical endeavour is pursued in the first place as an enquiry 'into things'. In this light, Kant then goes on to present what has since come to be well known as his advocacy of a 'Copernican revolution' in philosophy. He suggests that, in view of the failure of metaphysics, engaged in as an enquiry 'into things', the philosopher might instead follow the more successful scientific example and 'do just what Copernicus did in attempting to explain the celestial movements. When he found that he could make no progress by assuming that all the heavenly bodies revolved round the spectator, he reversed the process, and tried the experiment of assuming that the spectator revolved, while the stars remained at rest. A similar experiment can be tried in metaphysics . . .'[46] The basic point is that if metaphysics is to be viewed as a science (or indeed if it is to attain to its rightful position as 'queen of the sciences'), and given that the metaphysical method employed hitherto has not been able to explain what it has attempted to explain, then, as with any other science, the failed method should be replaced by some other method. And it is at this juncture that the Copernican analogy is invoked: as with Copernicus, who, in observing the same non-explanatory nature in the *physical* theory of his day, inverted that theory with success, the same may now be attempted in *meta*physics.

But we now come up against one of the biggest hindrances, especially currently, for properly understanding Kant's Copernican revolution. The problem is that this Copernican shift can be viewed so easily as just another form of 'internalism', along the approximate lines of present-day anti-realism or idealism. If Kant's Copernican revolution *is* interpreted

46. Kant, *Critique of Pure Reason*, Bxvi.

merely as *this* kind of shift, from an object-centred view of the world to a human-centred view of the world, then it is seriously misunderstood. Or likewise, if what is often spoken of as the 'Kantian challenge' in philosophy is treated *merely* as an 'anthropocentric' challenge – that is, if it is interpreted merely as Kant's emphasis on the way the perceptive capacities of the knower contribute to what kind of world is 'found' and thus, that these capacities require examination as much as does the world being examined – then this, too, is much too simplistic a view and misses the deeper character of what Kant is really attempting to do. (Indeed, several thinkers prior to Kant, including Descartes, Locke and Hume had already addressed this anthropocentric character of knowledge in one way or another.[47]) But beyond this anthropocentric challenge, it is seldom if ever noted just how literally, rigorously and broadly Kant actually applies his Copernican shift at virtually *every* level of the *Critique of Pure Reason*. In other words, this shift is not observed merely as a general anthropocentric rule of thumb, or loosely as an internalist philosophical inclination or temperament, but it is actually applied over and over again in specific ways, and always as a direct inversion of what the old metaphysics, or the traditional philosophical enquiry 'into things', had been advocating hitherto.[48] I want for our purposes to point out just two fundamental and related levels on which this Copernican shift occurs.

2.1 From 'things' to 'appearances'

First, and most generally, it is against this backdrop of a 'metaphysics of things', and the epistemological polarization and stagnancy to which it leads, that Kant now turns the tables and takes as his own starting point not the *reality* of a world *in itself*, a world of pure essences abstracted of all fallible empirical appearances (whether that is understood as some sort of 'substratum' or as something supra-sensible). Rather, the starting point is

47. See Gary Hatfield's 'The Cognitive Faculties', in *Cambridge History of Seventeenth Century Philosophy* (Cambridge: Cambridge University Press, 1998).
48. There is also another way that Kant's Copernican revolution is misjudged, and this is simply to ignore the essential revolutionary nature of Kant's philosophy altogether. In fact, it is here that we see what is perhaps the main explanation underlying Strawson's basic contradictory misinterpretation of Kant. The point is that the only way that Kantian philosophy can be deemed 'disastrous' or 'perverse' or 'incoherent' or 'nonsensical' or 'nihilistic' is if it is interpreted *sans* 'revolution'. For to ignore the essentially revolutionary heart of Kant's philosophy would make him the supreme purveyor of the very dogmatism that the *Critique of Pure Reason* condemns most forcefully and that it describes as 'worm-eaten', 'proud' and 'despotic'. On that reading the *Critique* does indeed turn out to be contradictory, but the contradiction thus also springs from a fundamental *mis*reading of the *Critique*.

now the *reality* of our *experience itself* of the world – that is, not the reality of 'things as they are in themselves' but the reality of 'things as
they appear'. In short, what he will essentially go on to develop in this
Copernican or revolutionary vein, in contrast to a metaphysics 'of things',
is what might be called a 'metaphysics of appearance', or even better, a
metaphysics of *what appears*. The fuller significance of 'metaphysics' with
regard to each of these phrases will become clearer as we proceed, but
what we can say now, to clarify this somewhat, is that a 'metaphysics
of things' asks fundamentally about the *essences of things*, that is, their
ostensibly 'true' natures, which are thought somehow to exist beyond appearances or underlie them. A 'metaphysics of appearances' (or of what
appears) by contrast will ask about the *conditions for the possibility of appearances*, for by definition it can no longer ask about essences. I qualify appearance as 'what appears' here because it conveys more accurately
the sense of the German term *Erscheinung*. In English, the terms phenomenon, appearance and representation tend to be roughly synony-
mous. Kant, however, as we shall discover more fully in the next section,
distinguishes sharply between empirical appearance (*Erscheinung*) and
mental phenomenon, for *Erscheinung* precisely and uniquely carries the
connotation of 'something' that appears, without this being in any way
separable from the appearance or implying any further 'supra-apparent'
essence. This will already give an indication of how Kant's philosophy of
appearance as *what appears* will not be a return to mere internalism and
back into the polemics of polarization. Indeed, when we look at the foregoing movement – that is, from the reality of things as they are in themselves (in the old metaphysics) to the reality of things as they appear –
we can already see this working on two levels. In the movement *from*
things 'as they are in themselves' *to* things 'as they appear' we see an inversion of externalism or traditional realism. But we also see another inversion at work. In the movement from the *mere perception* of 'things as
they appear' to the *reality* of 'things as they appear' we see an inversion
also of internalism or traditional idealism (anti-realism). In other words,
to make this fully clear, what we are speaking of in Kant's Copernican
revolution is not merely another inversion from externalism to internalism, or vice versa, but rather the inversion of *both* of these (i.e., both idealism and realism, both internalism and externalism). Kant's Copernican inversion as such will turn out to be an inversion of a completely
different sort than any of those taking place *within* philosophy's perpetual
polarities.

And this brings us directly to the second fundamental feature of the Copernican revolution – and really the heart of it, even though it often goes unnoticed. The Copernican shift, which underlies the *Critique*'s whole focus as an enquiry into full rational integrity, is most essentially an inversion of *both sides* of the perennial idealism/realism debate, or an inversion of *both sides* of philosophy's perpetual polarities. The exact nature of what I am speaking of here can be most clearly seen by returning to what I referred to in chapter 3 as the most basic, or the 'classical', formulation of philosophy's perpetual polarities in the idealism/realism dispute: viz. the conflict between empirical idealism and metaphysical realism. The point is that, although these are essentially already opposed to *each other*, Kant will turn both of them fully on their heads in different ways. 'Empirical *idealism*' in the Kantian ('Copernican') revolution will become what Kant calls 'empirical *realism*', which, as we shall see, is both the origin and the goal of what I am calling the project of full rational integrity in the *Critique*. Likewise, metaphysical *realism* – or what Kant calls 'transcendental *realism*' – will become 'transcendental *idealism*'.[49] Moreover, as we come to look more closely at this double inversion, we will discover that something unique has occurred. The way that Kant has set this up means that the 'revolutionary' *inversion* of each of these 'classical' philosophical polarities (i.e., empirical idealism and metaphysical realism) will in fact yield results that are no longer opposites but *corollaries*. In other words, the 'empirical reality' of an object will turn out to *mean* also its 'transcendental ideality'. Or transcendental idealism turns out to be a product of empirical realism. But we must now give a preliminary explanation of what this means.

2.2 'Empirical reality' *means* 'transcendental ideality'

Kant distinguishes between two fundamental sources of cognition or knowledge (*Erkenntnis*): the essentially *receptive* faculty of sensibility which affords us intuitions, and the intrinsically *active* or spontaneous faculty of the understanding or intellect which operates by means of concepts. Although sensibility and intellect are *always actually* united in cognition (i.e., in order for genuine cognition to occur the content or 'aboutness' of a thought or concept will always be found to have been provided in some

---

49. What Kant wants to designate by the term 'transcendental realism' is, as we shall see, virtually identical to what we mean today by 'metaphysical realism'. However, the inversion of this to 'metaphysical idealism' is confusing and does not convey what Kant wants to designate by 'transcendental idealism'. But the important point is that transcendental idealism will still turn out to be a genuine *inversion* of metaphysical realism.

way or other by intuition or sensibility), nevertheless they are logically distinct.[50] Kantian intuition is so closely bound up with human sensibility that for our purposes we may use them interchangeably, even though they are not strictly equivalent. (We could perhaps say that what concepts are to the human understanding or intellect, intuitions are to human sensibility.) Human sensibility in turn refers most obviously to the empirical senses but it is not exhausted by them. For beyond what Kant calls the 'outer sense' (comprising basically the five empirical senses), whose receptivity is attuned to external objects and events, there is also an 'inner sense' pertaining to psychological and affective states.

In view of this, and in order properly to understand Kant's claim that the empirical reality of an object *means* its transcendental ideality, it is important to be reminded about what exactly is being claimed by the qualification 'transcendent' within the term 'transcendental ideality' and also within the more particular and related Kantian terms 'transcendental objects', 'noumena', 'things-in-themselves'.[51] Kant's characterization of all of these entities as 'transcendental' is often misunderstood to mean that they are somehow ultimately 'real' *supra-rational* entities, transcending the grasp of the intellect. This is false.[52] Kant never makes this claim. Noumena, things-in-themselves or transcendental objects are rather *supra-sensible* 'objects' inasmuch as what they 'transcend' is not in the first place reason but sense. This is why Kant calls them purely 'ideal' (i.e., purely *mental*) entities which are in fact *posited by* the understanding and which as such have *no* 'mind-independent being' at all. As *mere ideas*, they are, in other words, quite literally and straightforwardly *ontologically nothing*. Accordingly, Kant also describes noumena as mere 'conceptual problems' or as merely the 'conceptual correlates' of empirical objects,[53] and we can illustrate what he means by this or we can bring to light the relationship, as such, between empirical reality and transcendental ideality in the following simple way.

---

50. By 'logically distinct' we mean, very roughly, that one can be accounted for fundamentally without any appeal to the other. I will discuss this more fully below.
51. These three terms, noumena, things-in-themselves, transcendental objects are overlapping but not quite equivalent in Kant, noumena being a broader designation than the other two. But for the present study we can treat them as roughly equivalent in that all three qualify as versions of transcendental ideality.
52. In a way, this misconstrual is understandable since in other contexts, especially theological ones, 'transcendental' is indeed used in this sense, as in when we say that God cannot be grasped by the human intellect or reason (or any other human capacity), but that he is beyond it, transcends it.
53. See, e.g., Kant, *Critique of Pure Reason*, A255/B311.

If I pick out a particular empirical object, say a certain book resting on a bookshelf in my study, and, with a view to arriving at the putative thing-in-itself beyond 'mere appearances', undertake by a theoretical process of mental abstraction to remove, bit by bit, every appearance or empirical manifestation of the book, every variant of colour, every bit of shape, the aroma, solidity, the smoothness and roughness, every component of the empirical materiality or the *manifestedness* of the thing, every possible way that the book could *be* an object of experience, what I am left with in the end is not some bare substratum or raw matter, but rather only something like a sheer, empty idea of the original empirical object. Furthermore, it would be hard to see how such an idea could be describable as anything more than a mere conceptual *problem*, or a conceptually problematic space, since there would be no way of expressing or even identifying what that sheer idea might be apart from reinstating something of the empirical, sensible spatio-temporal content that we have just abstracted. And this is why the 'empirical reality' of the object (the book) *means* also its 'transcendental ideality': that is, since after all appearances have been taken away (by an experiment of the mind), there is nothing that remains of the original empirical thing except some utterly abstract, indefinable, even inexpressible sheer *idea* of it which *by definition* 'transcends' the possibility of experience. Now it is *this* 'pure idea of the understanding', this transcendental ideality, which *just is* also the 'transcendent' (i.e., *supra-sensory*) thing-in-itself or noumenon. In short, Kant's thing-in-itself is never a *real thing* in-itself (Kant rejects any such notion as 'sheer illusion') but always only the *pure idea* of the thing-in-itself. This is indispensable to a proper understanding of Kant's doctrine of noumena or his transcendental idealism. Kant himself could not be more explicit about it. The noumenon, he asserts, is 'no real object or given thing' but merely a 'problematic concept' 'in relation to which appearances have a [conceptual] unity'.[54] (Besides, if noumena *were* supposed to be real, this would yield a transcendental realism and not Kant's transcendental idealism.)

Let us explore this 'merely problematic' feature of noumena or transcendental ideas somewhat further. Most formally or generally, noumena or things-in-themselves are defined by Kant as problematic concepts because they are *thinkable* and yet they are *unknowable*. More fully, noumena are thinkable inasmuch as the thought of them does not involve a logical

---

54. See Kant, *Critique of Pure Reason*, A255–257/B310–312; Kant, *Reflexionen* 5554, quoted in Caygill, *A Kant Dictionary*; *Critique of Pure Reason*, A289/B345.

contradiction. Yet the thought of them can never be raised to the level of cognition or knowledge (*Erkenntnis*) because, by their definition as 'transcendental objects', no meaningful content (referentiality or aboutness) can possibly be assigned to them, as illustrated above. At first glance this unknowability feature might seem to contradict the important point just made – that the transcendental object signifies in the first place not transcendence of the intellect but of sensibility. But there is no real contradiction here. It is of course true, in what may initially seem somewhat odd, that despite their purely *conceptual* status these noumena or transcendental objects are nevertheless 'unknowable' (i.e., they are not knowable or cognizable even though they are conceivable). However, the *reason* they are unknowable is not because they transcend the understanding or intellect (indeed they are *posited* by it), but rather because, as *pure* ideas of the intellect, they can have no possible content. For any possible content of cognition must, as we have seen in the above illustration, be at bottom furnished by human empirical sensibility or intuition. And there is by definition nothing *in* such supra-sensible ideas that could provide the referent that is necessary for knowledge – *even though* as a mere conceptually problematic correlate of the empirical object it can be thought without contradiction. Kant explains this further, clarifying the basic difference he intends between mere thinking and cognition as follows:

> [E]ven if we cannot *cognize* these . . . objects as things-in-themselves, we must at least be able to *think* them as things-in-themselves . . . To *cognize* an object it is required that I be able to prove its possibility (whether by the testimony of experience from its actuality or a priori through reason[55]). But I can think whatever I like as long as I do not contradict myself, i.e., as long as my concept is a possible thought, even if I cannot give any assurance whether or not there is a corresponding object somewhere within the sum total of all possibilities.[56]

A noumenon or thing-in-itself, then, is precisely such a 'problematic concept . . . that contains no contradiction but that is also [a concept] . . . the objective reality of which can in no way be cognized'.[57] In short, noumena are entirely 'empty' ideas (hence 'pure ideas of the understanding'), devoid of any possible content in reference to which a cognition could be formed, and this is why the only even quasi-positive signification that can be given to them is that of conceptual *problemata*. This leads us in

---

55. I will explain in section 4 what is meant by this distinction.
56. Kant, *Critique of Pure Reason*, Bxxvi; cf. also B310, original emphasis.
57. Kant, *Critique of Pure Reason*, B310.

turn to the following crucial and summary outcome: noumena are solely *epistemically problematic correlates* of empirical objects (appearances) and in no way *ontological essences* of them.

We must however add an appendix to this result, especially for those readers who might still be unwilling to give up the old standard idea that things-in-themselves are somehow supposed to be *real* things-in-themselves, or that Kant wants noumena to be ontologically something. The point is that on a cursory reading there can appear to be a sort of concessionary stance occasionally adopted by Kant with respect to the purely conceptual or problematic (non-ontological) status of noumena. Consider, for example, the following quotation.

> [T]he concept of a noumenon is problematic, i.e., the presentation of a thing of which we can say neither that it is possible nor that it is impossible, *since we are acquainted* with no sort of intuition *other than our own sensible one* and no other sort of concepts other than the categories [of the understanding], neither of which . . . is suitable to an extrasensible object.[58]

Taken in isolation, this quotation might seem to suggest that the *reason* noumena cannot be cognized is only because of certain limitations of human understanding, and that some *other* kind of consciousness and sensibility might indeed be able to cognize and have further positive 'insight' into noumena, which, it would then be implied, exist mind independently or real-ly. In the same prima facie concessionary tone, Kant occasionally inserts a 'for us' qualification, such as in the following passage: 'In the end, however, we have no insight into the possibility of such noumena, and the domain outside the sphere of appearances is empty (for us)' (Kant's parentheses).[59] But it would be a serious misreading to take such qualifications as 'for us' or 'for our understanding' to be suggesting that, apart from our admittedly limited sensibility, there is *after all* something 'more' to these noumena – something mind-independently real, something *ontological* – than the merely problematic intellectual space that Kant continues to insist they remain. For Kant immediately goes on to explain what he means by this 'empty (for us)' qualification: '*that is*', he says, 'we have an understanding that extends farther than sensibility *problematically*, but no intuition, indeed not even the concept of a possible intuition, through

---

58. Kant, *Critique of Pure Reason*, A287, emphasis added.
59. Kant, *Critique of Pure Reason*, A255.

which objects outside the field of sensibility *could* be given'. More clearly still:

> A *noumenon* . . . is not a special *intelligible object* for our understanding; rather *an understanding to which it would belong is itself a problem*, namely, that of cognizing its object not discursively through categories but intuitively in a non-sensible intuition, the possibility of which we cannot in the least represent.[60]

In other words, far from suggesting that for some other intuition and sensibility noumena might be ontologically real *after all*, these 'for us' and 'for our understanding' insertions are intended to do exactly the opposite. They simply broaden the problematic space even further by making, in Kant's own words, *any* sort of 'understanding to which [such a positive understanding of noumena] would belong . . . *itself a problem*'. In order to make this fully clear: it is not only the noumenal object that is purely 'conceptually problematic', but so is any conception of an intellect that could formulate the idea of a noumenon as anything more than this. If one studies this move more carefully, it becomes evident that in it Kant has managed to formulate a logical guarantee of the thoroughly conceptual and problematic (and hence non-ontological) status of noumena.

3   *Empirical* realism

We will return to the discussion of noumena presently and discover a powerful feature that they convey epistemologically, despite their mere problematic status or 'nothingness' ontologically. But with the foregoing as a basic backdrop, we must first refocus our attention on empirical realism, which will turn out, in the last chapter, to make an extremely important contribution to the completion of own theological endeavour. Specifically, we must now ask more critically about these Kantian appearances or *Erscheinungen* which are at the heart of his empirical realism. How is a 'metaphysics of *appearance*' intelligible to begin with? How can we speak meaningfully about the *reality* of things as they *appear*? How can the basic rational requirements of universality and necessity in synthetic cognition be sustained with respect to 'what appears'? But perhaps the most obvious question to be asked initially is this: Why should it be insisted that philosophical enquiry begin from the empirical in the first place? Kant's answer here would be straightforward: Because that is the only place we *can*

---

60. Kant, *Critique of Pure Reason*, A255–256/B311–312, emphasis slightly altered.

begin without argumentation, defence or problematization. Kant's point, in other words, is that there can be a kind of 'givenness' to the empirical – a givenness that is deeply intertwined with the basic *receptive* character of human sensibility or intuition as briefly discussed above – an empirical givenness that at its most basic level remains strictly unproblematized,[61] in a way that even the most self-evident logical axiom cannot be. I am aware that any such discussion of a 'given' is currently viewed broadly with suspicion. But let me assure the reader that the Kantian sense of 'given' is something quite different than what is being attacked by adherents of Sellars' 'myth of the given' or Derrida's 'myth of presence'. In fact we had better get these objections out of the way before coming to a positive development of the Kantian doctrine of appearances as the 'empirical given'. I will proceed with this whole discussion along three basic thematic lines: (i) the Kantian empirical given versus the critiques of mediacy, immediacy and presence; (ii) the Kantian empirical given just *is* 'appearance'; (iii) Kantian appearance and the problem of illusion.

3.1   Demythologizing the myth of the given: Kant's 'empirical given' versus the critiques of mediacy, immediacy and presence

Any talk of 'givenness' today in philosophical discussion is often rejected out of hand because it is understood as some sort of claim to 'immediacy' or unmediated awareness. The basic objection here is that any such claim to immediacy involves a contradiction because awareness of any kind implies some sort of *capacity* for perceiving or 'taking in', and so awareness is by definition inherently mediated, since it comes via a capacity in the aware subject. This claim to immediacy is basically Wilfrid Sellars' interpretation of what is being demanded by the term 'givenness', and thus his rejection of the given as a 'myth' is understandable.[62] But the Kantian *empirical* 'given' is *not* the *immediate* and so it cannot be as easily mythologized, either along Sellarsian lines of the 'myth of the given' or Derridean lines of the 'myth of presence'. The point here is not to argue that these critiques of givenness are faulty but simply to say that they do not touch the Kantian

---

61. However, this does not imply 'unmediated'. There are important differences between sensory 'mediation' and intellectual 'problematization', as we shall see, differences having to do, again, with the essentially receptive character of the one and the active, dynamic character of the other.

62. Wilfrid Sellars, *Empiricism and the Philosophy of Mind* (Cambridge, MA: Harvard University Press, 1997 (1956)). See especially pp. 13–17, 56–7.

'given'. Indeed, in its qualification specifically as the *empirical* given – that is, that which is given in (or to) human *intuition* or *sensibility* – the Kantian given overtly acknowledges its intrinsic mediatedness. In contrast, then, to the versions of givenness that Sellars or Derrida criticize – givenness as immediacy or directness or (slightly differently) presence – one might say that the Kantian empirical given is characterized by two fundamental features, or necessary conditions.

For something to qualify as 'given' in the Kantian sense means for it to be both (a) empirically ineluctable and (b) intellectually unproblematized. These two features are not easily separable because they involve each other. We may illustrate this by recalling MacKinnon's examples of the explosive properties of natural gas or the gradients of hills. The present point is that no amount of conceptual deconstruction will mitigate the authority of the gradient of a particular section of the Saint Bernhard pass if my brakes happen to fail on a holiday trip to Italy. The *reason* for this, moreover, is that there is no conceptual hermeneutic or interpretive framework that the mind brings *to* the empirical 'given' in such a case, the deconstruction of which could diminish, much less negate, the ineluctability of the purely empirical authority of this 'given'. In other words, the authority encountered in the empirical given is, quite literally, *unquestionable*. It is 'unquestionable', moreover, *not* because reason has come to the end of its rope, still less because this authority can be demonstrated as necessary or universal. No, the authority is, in the most straightforward sense of the term, *literally* 'unquestionable' – that is, conceptually unproblematizable – because the finality of what is real-ly encountered here is not the least bit conceptually constituted in the first place. So we come back to the point that, although the Kantian empirical given is of course 'mediated' by the senses, nevertheless the authority or reality of this given remains undiminished and indeed immune from any amount of conceptual problemsolving or reduction or deconstruction. And it remains so, moreover, not *despite* the mediacy of the experience through the senses, but precisely *because* of the *ineluctability* of that mediacy in the light of the essentially *receptive* character of human sensibility.[63]

---

63. A certain similarity may be noted here to the 'proper basicality' of the reformed epistemologists, in which certain empirical beliefs are deemed to be properly basic if they are not held on the basis of any other beliefs (i.e., they are *basic* beliefs), and yet can somehow be shown to be legitimate or justifiable beliefs (i.e., they are *properly* held beliefs). But Kant's empirical given is at bottom different than this. The difference is that the empirical given is not in any way basic or fundamental *for* the understanding, but is simply *given* to it in virtue of the basic receptivity of human sensibility. Proper basicality, by comparison, while it claims

3.2   Appearance (*Erscheinung*) *just is* the 'empirically given'

This can help us understand the really central claim of Kant's empirical realism. The question here is: How can the Kantian doctrine of empirical realism qualify as genuine 'realism', if all that it wants to affirm is the 'reality' of objects merely *as they appear*? To begin with, Kant would contest my use of 'merely' and would maintain to the contrary that it is precisely 'the world as it appears' which *just is* the *real* world.[64] To state the whole matter in a kind of syllogistic form: The real world is the world we live in – the world of experience, the world we breathe, eat, move, sleep, speak and think in. But the world we live in is also necessarily the world as it appears to us. Therefore the real world is the world as it appears. This is not merely a rearranging of words in order to demystify a doctrine that on the face of things might seem perplexing. It is rather to identify a highly unique character of 'appearance' in the *Critique*. To state this as concisely as possible, because Kantian appearance is not just the 'given' but the *empirical* given, therefore, in its very definition as such, it involves elements of both *givenness* (in its designation as 'given') and the possibility of *receptivity* (in its designation as 'empirical'). So we must look more closely at this term 'appearance' in the double-faceted sense of both givenness and receptivity.

To begin with then, Kantian appearances, in virtue of their givenness, are not, to return to MacKinnon's terms, simply subjective constructions or 'inventions'. Furthermore, insofar as they could be deemed to be 'discoveries', they are this in a decidedly different way, even from MacKinnon's highly 'Kantian' view. For the decisive point here is that *what* we 'discover' when we seek to understand the empirical given is always *the world as it appears* and not the world in itself. Indeed, this could not be

to escape the demands of inference, is nonetheless deemed to exert a kind of justificatory authority for rationality, or over it. And the point here is that, even if a belief succeeds in being truly basic (i.e., not inferred from some other belief), nevertheless in its specification not just as basic, but as *properly* basic (i.e., justifiably basic, even if somehow non-inferentially so), it is essentially already 'problematized' (i.e., in the claim to *noetic* justification) and as such claims the kind of conceptual or noetic 'presence' or authority that Sellars or Derrida want to expose as a myth or a ruse. (Proper basicality thus has certain similarities to Putnam's bedrock which wants to claim epistemological authority without itself being subject to it; i.e., there are arguably traces of positivism here.) The empirical given, by contrast, has no such justificatory component or aspirations whatsoever. It is not only not inferred, it is also entirely unproblematized and as such its 'authority' is not in any sense a (rationally) justificatory authority. Rather, its authority is entirely empirical and, accordingly, there is no conceptual 'presence' in the empirical given that could be declared a myth and debunked as such.

64. It is true that Kant sometimes uses the term *bloß* in qualifying appearances. But the German term is just as easily (and much more coherently to the context of the *Critique*) translated as 'purely' or 'sheerly' rather than 'merely', which at times distorts Kant's obvious intentions in using it.

otherwise and on one level is virtually axiomatic since, as Kant so aptly puts it, 'that which is not an appearance cannot be an object of experience'. To speak of 'objects in themselves' – that is, objects that have somehow been purified of all empirical appearances or of all 'extensive magnitudes' (i.e., space and time) and which as such exist in a sort of pristine and splendid supra-sensible isolation – is not only meaningless but is contrary to anything we want to affirm when we speak of 'reality'. To attempt to purge the world of its appearances would be tantamount to purging it of its spatio-temporality. For the 'extensive magnitudes', of which space and time are the pure forms,[65] are, by their very definition as *extensive* magnitudes, inherently *manifested* magnitudes; and *as* inherently manifested magnitudes they can never be magnitudes 'in themselves'. To attempt to purge the world of its appearances, as such, would be to purge it of its reality. Kant makes this same point even more explicitly elsewhere. 'The objects of experience', he states, 'are *never* given *in themselves*, but only in experience, and they do not exist at all outside it' (original emphasis).[66] Now once again, if not read carefully, or if we ignore what I have just stated about the basic extended (and as such empirical) nature of space and time, then this last quotation can look after all to be perilously close to a Berkeleyan kind of empirical idealism, or 'constitutive mentalism', or one of the more current forms of anti-realism. But again, when we look at this closely we will see that Kant is by no means leaning in that direction.

First, it is clearly specified that we are dealing with *objects* of experience: and the German word used here is not *Objekt* but *Gegenstand*. What this distinction means more fully is that the object of experience is not a determinate mental object or a merely intentional object or phenomenon (*Objekt*). Rather, it is *Gegenstand*: that which really – that is, empirically – stands-over-against. It is this empirical object that is 'given' to human sensibility *as* an appearance. There is thus a fundamental objectivity to the Kantian appearance by virtue of its empirical character; and to appreciate the robustness of the reality that Kant means to attribute to this empirical objectivity we need only to think back to our discussion above, that 'empirical reality' *means* 'transcendental ideality'. The point is that, in speaking of the empirical object as empirically real *and therefore* also as transcendentally ideal (i.e., as a sheer contentless idea, and not a reality, when

---

65. I.e., space and time are what extension *is*.
66. Kant, *Critique of Pure Reason*, A493.

considered as a thing-in-itself apart from the possibility of experience), Kant is not denying the full reality – even the *objective* reality – of the empirical object. He is only claiming that *what* is objective in this sense is the *empirical* object, extended in space and time, and not some (quite literally) unimaginable, supra-sensible object-in-itself, transcending the possibility of empirical experience and accessible purely through the intellect. Thus, rather than a diminishment of the reality of the empirical object, Kant's assertion that its empirical reality *just is* its transcendental ideality actually achieves the opposite result. For it robustly affirms the *empirical* reality of the object and then actually reinforces the radically empirical character of this claim by saying that, when we take away this empirical component – when we try to depict the empirical object as transcending sensibility – we are left not with anything resembling an independent reality of the object at all (as a thing-in-itself), but with something more like the mere contentless 'idea' of the object, which is itself inexpressible, conceptually, except as a sheer problem (since no content can be given to it).

But now what about the final part of the foregoing quotation, which seemed to be leaning in a Berkeleyan direction – that is, that objects of experience 'do not exist at all outside' experience? It is statements like this, when removed from their original contexts to serve certain preconceptions of Kant, that can prompt such clearly false assessments as Strawson's, that Kant here is espousing a 'theory of the mind making Nature' and that his empirical realism as such is 'as superfluous to the essential structure of reasoning, as an extra wheel, zealously but idly turning'.[67] To the contrary, a careful and unbiased reading will show that Kant goes on immediately to clarify and qualify this statement in the following way:

> That there could be inhabitants of the moon, even though no human being has ever perceived them, must of course be admitted; but this means only that *in the possible progress of experience* we *could* encounter them; for everything is actual that stands in one context with a perception *in accordance with the laws of empirical progression*. Thus they are real when they stand in empirical connection with my real consciousness, although they are not therefore real in themselves. i.e., outside this progress of experience ... To call an appearance a real thing prior to perception means either that *in the continuation of experience* we must encounter such a perception, or it has no meaning at all.[68]

67. Strawson, *The Bounds of Sense*, p. 257.
68. Kant, *Critique of Pure Reason*, A493, emphasis added.

All of this brings us to a crucially defining point about Kantian appearance, a point that will clearly differentiate it from 'appearance' in any standard idealist or internalist sense. A Kantian appearance is not necessarily an object of *actual* experience or perception, but rather an object of *possible* experience. We have already seen that Kantian appearance is not '*mind* dependent', that is, inasmuch as it is given to human *sensibility* which, as discussed, is logically distinct from intellectual comprehension. (I will explain the logical character of this distinction more fully in the next section.) But we now see that the appearance, or the empirical object, is not, strictly speaking, even *perceiver* dependent either – even though the perceptive faculties play an essential part in what is perceived – for the Kantian doctrine does not make the reality of appearances dependent on the *actual* perception of them but only on the *possible* perception of them. The point is only that we *could* encounter an appearance 'in the possible progress of experience', or 'in accordance with the laws of empirical progression', or 'in the continuation of experience', or else 'it has no meaning at all'. In other words, the Kantian appearance is not just an (ideal) *phenomenal* object but a (real) *empirical* object. It is astonishing the degree to which this distinction between empirical and phenomenal objectivity, that is, the distinction between appearance and phenomenon, although consistently clear in Kant himself, is overlooked or misinterpreted even by some of the most exemplary Kant scholars. Robert Paul Wolff, for example, inexplicably speaks of the 'empirical object' in Kant as a 'phenomenal substance'. He goes on in the same chapter to speak misleadingly of the '*phenomenal* object [a]s a mere *appearance* and therefore a mind-dependent entity. As the product of the synthetic activity of the imagination, it cannot exist independently of the subject who knows it.'[69] It is confusing accounts such as this one, which tacitly obliterate certain fundamental distinctions insisted on by Kant, that make it easy to misinterpret him as a mere internalist. Yet when we allow Kant to speak for himself on these matters, as the foregoing quotations show, we often get a very different outcome than the standard construals. The point once again, in the present case, is that *appearances* in the Kantian sense are *real* whether or not they become objects of *actual* experience or perception – as long as they fall within what Kant calls the laws of empirical progression or, in other words, that in the *possible progress* of experience we *could* encounter them. In short, the Kantian empirical given

---

69. Robert Paul Wolff, *Kant's Theory of Mental Activity* (Cambridge, MA: Harvard University Press, 1963), p. 263, emphasis added.

does not entail that it must be perceived via human sensibility or intuition, but only that it *can* be.

We might at this point venture a rather risky summary of this section so far (risky because it is still somewhat premature and thus susceptible to misinterpretation) and say that for Kant the real world *just is* the empirical world, full stop. But we would immediately have to add two crucial caveats to this, in addition to the foregoing discussions. First, because Kantian intuition or sensibility is not simply limited to the 'outer sense' of the five senses, but also includes the 'inner sense', whether psychologistic or affective, therefore empirical 'objects' are not to be understood as exclusively material or physical objects, but as denoting *any* possible 'object' of experience. Secondly, if we say that for Kant 'the real world is the empirical world, full stop', and that the empirical world *just is* the world of real appearances, then we must have some way of distinguishing between genuine appearance and illusion.

3.3 Appearance and illusion

We have seen that an essential part of what Kant is trying to do in empirical realism is to raise appearance from its usual status as that which is *opposed* to reality (mere appearance) to that which is in some real way *constitutive* of it (real appearance). In this light then, what we require, in order to complete this stage of the enquiry into empirical realism, is some mechanism for judging between that which is *merely* apparent and that which is *really* apparent, or more broadly for judging between illusion and appearance. It is not surprising as such to find that the analysis of illusion is a prominent and recurring theme not only throughout the *Critique of Pure Reason*, but also elsewhere in Kant's writings. There are several ways that Kant distinguishes between appearance and illusion, but I will focus on just one here.

Appearance and illusion are to be distinguished inasmuch as illusion springs essentially from an activity of human *judgement* (specifically, an *error* of human judgement), whereas appearance, in its definition as the 'empirical given' or as the *'undetermined* object of empirical intuition', is entirely absent of any such element of judgement, even in the minimal sense of thematization. It is of course true that in most cases perception is simultaneously thematized and thus in some sense evaluated. (Again, for Kant, genuine cognition or knowledge is *always* 'synthetic', involving an intellectual consideration of what is given to the understanding through sensible intuition.) But this connection is by no means *logically* necessary, as we shall see, or even actually automatic in normal experience. It is a common occurrence, when travelling for example, suddenly to 'come to' oneself without any cognizance or memory of one's visual perceptions over the preceding several minutes even though all the time one has been gazing intently out of the railway carriage or car window. The same can be said for other episodes of preoccupation as when one is told one 'hasn't been listening' even though one has strictly speaking 'heard' every word. One's mind, it is explained, has been somewhere else. But these are just incidental examples from empirical experience to give a kind of bearing on the plausibility of what is to be claimed here in general.

The real point is that the separation between rational and sensory faculties that pervades Kantian philosophy is a *logical* one. The *logical* nature of this separation must be strongly emphasized. For Kant is of course not saying that in actual human psychology, or even in epistemology, we operate according to such a separation (although perhaps occasionally we can, as suggested above). Indeed Kant's well-known insistence that *all* genuine cognition or knowledge is *synthetic* is precisely the insistence that knowledge *always actually* involves a union in some way, or a synthesis of sensible intuition and intellect. But despite this, their *logical* separation remains intact; and by logical separation we mean simply that when we enquire into the nature of human empirical sensibility (or sensory experience) we find that understanding and judgement do not show up as necessary conditions for the possibility of sensory experience. How the inverted form of this plays out (i.e., whether sensory experience is a necessary condition for understanding) is much more complex and opens up into the problem of the possibility of a priori synthetic (i.e., metaphysical) knowledge. We shall discuss this in the next section.

At any rate, it is along these logical lines that Kant wants to insist that 'in the senses there is no judgment [i.e., no exercise of the understanding] at all, neither a true nor a false one'.[70] And this in turn leads to the real key issue with respect to the distinction between appearance and illusion, to which this whole discussion of the logical separation of intuition and intellect has been pointing. The point is that when we speak of truth or illusion we are not speaking about *empirical perception* per se, which occurs via human sensibility (intuition), but rather about a *judgement of the intellect* on what is sensorily perceived. Appearances by contrast contain no such element of judgement, but consist entirely in what is given to human

70. Kant, *Critique of Pure Reason*, A294.

sensibility. Accordingly, in Kant's own words, we may not 'take appearance and illusion for one and the same. For truth and illusion are not in the object insofar as it is intuited [i.e., empirically through sensation], but in the judgment about it insofar as it is thought. Thus it is correctly said that the senses do not err; yet not because they always judge correctly, but because they do not judge at all. Hence truth, as much as error, and thus also illusion as leading to the latter, are to be found only in judgments, i.e., only in the relation of the object to our understanding.'[71] In sum, appearance consists entirely in the real givenness of the empirical object to human sensibility or intuition and has nothing to do with intellectual thematizations or determinations or judgements about it. Illusion, by contrast is *entirely* a matter of (false) intellectual judgement about empirical reality.

But in order to bring this to a completion, we must now show how these logical distinctions between sense and intellect come relevantly to bear on matters of actual cognition or knowledge, in which for Kant they are always united. In a word, what the logical distinction between sense and intellect is going to alert us to, most importantly, will have something to do with the jurisdiction of the categories of the understanding over what is 'given' in empirical reality. Let me explain this briefly. Kant of course would not deny, despite their logical separation as just described, that the way we come to recognize and get closer to the truth about the empirical sensible object is precisely by subjecting it to the rigours of intellectual scrutiny. Still – and now here is the pertinent point – this capacity and authority of reason to get us closer to the truth about the empirical object does not mean that the intellect claims ultimate jurisdiction over the empirical, or that it expects empirical 'extensive magnitudes' to comply *tout court* with more 'pure' or more certain rational demands. Indeed, it is precisely such a demand of the intellect that can be illusory, and we can illustrate this as follows.

To demand that the understanding be allowed to have its way over the empirical object or to enforce its terms on it fully is for Kant to engage in the fallacy of 'subreption'. This fallacy is committed when matters of sense and intuition (empirical objects) are expected to behave in the same way or conform to the same principles as matters of understanding (conceptual objects). In fact, any such application will yield contradictions. For

---

71. Kant, *Critique of Pure Reason*, B350/A294, emphasis added.

example, when the understanding seeks to transfer the perfectly sound principle of continuity and infinite divisibility as it applies to conceptual objects (concepts) onto material objects, it encounters the contradiction of the infinite divisibility of a composed substance. The contradiction here is that the understanding cannot recognize 'simples' but continues to see them as divisible ad infinitum. This makes the object's composition a logical impossibility, even though as a *material* object it is by nature composed. A similar example is found in Zeno's paradox that when an object moves in space and time towards a certain destination, it should never actually reach that destination because as it moves forward it continually halves the distance between itself and its destination and this halving process is infinite. Yet the moving material object meets, and even surpasses, its destination nonetheless. Kant's contention is that none of these kinds of contradictions or paradoxes are genuine but are rather the results of spurious reasoning, something akin to a category mistake: that is, importing the demands of the understanding onto empirical objects in space and time and expecting them, as inherently *extensive* magnitudes, simply to conform fully to the abstract (non-extensive) principles of logic.

Now this in turn brings us to a very interesting and perhaps unexpected result. To aspire to understand the empirical object as something 'in itself' is precisely for the intellect to aspire to have full jurisdiction over the empirical object or the empirical world (i.e., the real world); and as such it is not to preserve the empirical object's external integrity at all as it claims to be doing, but merely to make it mind-dependent in a different manner or on a different level. Or, to state this in another way, although it may seem as if we are preserving the genuine otherness of the empirical object by claiming an 'in itself' status for it, in fact we are doing just the opposite. We are violating its *integral* nature or its over-againstness *as* appearance – or as 'what appears' in the extensive magnitudes of space and time – by claiming in effect that its spatio temporality be understood apart from its *manifestedness* as such. For the 'in itself' aspiration is precisely the aspiration to purest objectivity, that is, to an object of pure reason that has been purified of all empirical uncertainties and imperfections, and which is thus somehow 'open' to rational scrutiny and jurisdiction beyond the contingencies of sense. *This* for Kant is the 'proud ontology' at the root of dogmatism. To make the 'in itself' claim is precisely to engage in the fallacy of subreption, as just discussed, in which the demands of the intellect claim full jurisdiction over the empirical. It is here, too, that for Kant we reach the real nature of illusion. Illusion in the Kantian scheme of things is thus something that goes far beyond the issue of mere *empirical deception* and is more ominously rooted in *illusory axioms and principles* 'which deceive the understanding and which have disastrously permeated the whole of metaphysics'.[72]

All of this to the contrary then, it is only when the empirical object is permitted to be what it *is* – that is, the object as it appears, or the object *that* appears – that its empirical integrity is allowed to remain intact and its genuine otherness or over-againstness is preserved. In short, and paradoxically, the thing-*in-itself* claim turns out to be the mind-dependent claim (on a new level, since it is a response to a purely intellectual demand) whereas the thing-*as-it-appears* claim, within Kant's doctrine of the empirical 'given' or empirical realism, although initially seeming to be more internalistic, actually preserves the integrity of the empirical object in indefeasible ways. But again, this of course is *not* to say that the understanding does not bring us closer to the truth, epistemologically, about empirical objects, but only that it cannot do this purely on its own terms (i.e., by claiming that it is getting closer to the truth about the object 'in itself', apart from its manifestedness). It must rather do this on the terms presented *by* the empirical given, and the empirical given demands to be interpreted *as* its *manifestedness*. It is here that we come to the heart of what Kant means by the claim that '*understanding* and *sensibility* can determine an object *only in combination*. If we separate them, then we have intuitions without concepts, or concepts without intuitions, but in either case presentations (*Vorstellungen*) that we cannot relate to any determinate object'.[73] The point of this is that through critical intellectual scrutiny we do indeed get closer to the truth about empirical objects or closer to the truth about the world, but the truth about these objects or about the world that we are getting closer *to* is, in Kant's own words, the truth about 'how they must be presented as objects of experience, *in the thoroughgoing connection of appearances*, and not how they might be outside of the relation to possible experience and consequently to sense in general, thus as objects of pure understanding'.[74] It is in this stipulation of coming closer to the truth about an object of experience, in the thoroughgoing connection (*Zusammenhang* or

72. Kant, *On the Form and Principles of the Sensible and Intelligible World* ['Inaugural Dissertation'], in David Walford in collaboration with Ralf Meerbote (tr. and eds.), *Theoretical Philosophy 1755–1770* (Cambridge: Cambridge University Press, 1992), pp. 373–416, par. 24.
73. Kant, *Critique of Pure Reason*, A258/B314, original emphasis.
74. Kant, *Critique of Pure Reason*, A258/B314, original emphasis.

'held-togetherness') of all appearances pertaining to that object of experience, that the way opens up also for the possibility of a comprehensive theory of identity for empirical objects as appearances.

4 Rational integrity and Kant's doctrine of noumena

We must now bring this whole discussion of empirical realism back to focus on our own primary concern of rational integrity; and as we do so, we immediately make an important discovery. Reason at full integrity is not necessarily going to mean reason at full autonomy. In other words, the question of integrity is not most fundamentally the question of self-sufficiency, but something else. It is of course true that reason retains a genuine autonomy or self-sufficiency in an extremely important sense when it enquires *purely* into itself (i.e., when it remains genuinely *pure* reason). For here it remains entirely within the domain of the axiomatic or, somewhat more broadly, the analytic. Here it legitimately makes claims, in a fully autonomous and self-sufficient way, based fundamentally – and even solely, as Kant shows – on the law of non-contradiction, in which reason's primary logical requirements of *necessity* and *universality* remain fully intact and unassailable. (To challenge the law of non-contradiction is to make an end to the possibility of thought or discourse, language or genuine exchange of any kind.) Indeed if reason would not operate in this fashion, in claiming necessary and universal status for its axiomatic and analytic pronouncements in a fully self-sufficient or autonomous way, it would precisely become untrue to itself, and as such abandon integrity.

But this story changes dramatically when reason turns its focus outside of itself to the *real* world of human experience and endeavour (i.e., the empirical, spatio-temporal world), where it now tries to make truth claims that are no longer analytic but genuinely synthetic, and that are no longer 'trivial' or tautological but genuinely ampliative. The question that confronts us here is really the new question of metaphysics after Kant. We have seen that reason functions properly in thinking about the world only when it preserves the empirical integrity of the world, and that when it does not do this it forfeits integrity (or trueness to itself) by becoming *dogmatism*. But now *given* this, given the empirical reality over which reason cannot unilaterally claim jurisdiction (without sacrificing integrity), how then can reason remain true to itself or preserve its own integrity in the analytical sense – that is, without sacrificing its own rightful claims analytically to necessity and universality, when it enquires (synthetically) into the empirical world? In short, how can reason ('act') retain integrity by not inadmissibly claiming jurisdiction over empirical integrity ('being') and yet retain its rightful claims to necessity and universality, without which it could not – analytically or by definition – even *be* reason? What I have just stated is in effect the Kantian question of the possibility of synthetic a priori cognition, which now becomes the new question of metaphysics. As already intimated above, in the most general terms, Kant will seek to answer this question by enquiring no longer into 'essences' of things-in-themselves (since in empirical realism these are unavailable), but into the conditions for the possibility of things as they appear. But we must now give some consideration to what this means.

4.1 The *Critique* as answer to the 'Humean problem'

What I have been articulating over the last two paragraphs is a somewhat different expression of what Kant was referring to when he spoke of the 'Humean problem' for metaphysics, which was to become a primary impetus for the whole project that the *Critique* seeks to undertake. Indeed, Kant himself described the *Critique of Pure Reason* specifically and without further qualification as 'the *elaboration* of the Humean problem in its greatest possible amplification'.[75] Kant realized that in Hume we encounter a decisive movement within empiricism, a movement that set him apart from any of his British predecessors or contemporaries. What is this Humean problem, or this decisive movement within empiricism that he represents for Kant? The two aspects of Hume's thought, generally speaking, which were most crucial for the *Critique*'s point of departure were (a) that it was so thoroughly empirical – that is, it was entirely purged of any of the residual rationalist dogmatism still evident in Locke;[76] and yet (b) it managed to retain this radically empirical nature without succumbing on the other hand

75. Kant, *Prolegomena to any Future Metaphysics*, p. 11, original emphasis.
76. Actually, despite attributing the real impetus for his whole way of thinking here to Hume, Kant aligns himself in important respects to Locke as well, Hume's massively influential empiricist predecessor who, in his famous thesis of the mind as a blank slate or *tabula rasa*, had likewise placed limits on the understanding, claiming that all knowledge is grounded in ideas arising from individual experience. But Locke had then 'proceeded inconsistently' (on Kant's reading of him) by daring, despite this initial limitation, 'to make attempts at cognitions that go far beyond the boundary of all experience' (Kant, *Critique of Pure Reason*, B127). It was left to Hume (through his powerful critique against the a priori necessity of causation and his subsequent disposal of metaphysics altogether) to lay these residual dogmatic tendencies within empiricism to final rest – i.e., the lingering vestiges of a purely rationalist metaphysics, or the claim that certain structures of reality can be known from reason alone, apart from sensible experience. But Kant consistently holds Locke in extremely high esteem.

to a kind of Berkeleyan idealism. In other words, for Kant, Hume is something like an original or prototypical 'empirical realist'. This is not to deny Hume's scepticism. It is merely to say that the focus of his scepticism is traditional rationalist metaphysics and not empirical objects as it had been in Berkeley. Indeed, any philosophy that is genuinely empiricist will, as a matter of course, and as we have seen above, naturally tend towards scepticism. In this general light then, Hume's position can for current purposes be situated more specifically historically in the following way.

On the one hand, Locke's empiricism (on the Kantian view, as just described) was not thorough or consistent enough to drive him into the scepticism about metaphysics that naturally accompanies empiricism. On the other hand, Berkeley's empiricism had been so pervasive and radical that it had drawn him into empirical idealism – doubting even the reality of material objects. By contrast, part of what was new and brilliant about Hume, in Kant's estimation, was his ability to be sceptical about traditional rationalist metaphysics in a way that Locke was not, without losing the reality of the material world in the way that Berkeley did. Kant laments the widespread misconstrual of Hume by Hume's own contemporaries in this regard, likening it to the initial misinterpretations of his own *Critique of Pure Reason* in its first edition.

> But fate, ever ill-disposed toward metaphysics would have it that
> Hume was understood by no one. One cannot, without feeling a certain
> pain, behold how utterly his opponents, Reid, Oswald, Beattie and
> Priestley, missed the point of his problem, and misjudged his hints for
> improvement – constantly taking for granted just what he doubted,
> and, conversely, proving with vehemence and, more often than not,
> with great insolence exactly what it had never entered his mind to
> doubt – so that everything remained in its old condition, as if nothing
> had happened. The question was not whether the concept of cause was
> right, useful, and, with respect to all cognition of nature,
> indispensable, for this Hume had never put in doubt; it was rather
> whether it is thought through reason a priori, and in this way has inner
> truth independent of all experience . . . The discussion was only about
> the origin of this concept, not about its indispensability in use.[77]

However far from extinguishing the possibility of genuine metaphysics with these insights, as he thought he had done, Hume had, in Kant's view, instead provided the point of departure for a 'complete reform or rather

77. Kant, *Prolegomena to any Future Metaphysics*, pp. 8–9.

rebirth of metaphysics'. Hume himself had 'brought no light to this kind of knowledge, but he had certainly struck a spark from which a light could well have been kindled, if it had hit on some welcoming tinder whose glow was carefully kept going and made to grow'. Kant then casts himself in the role of this nourisher and bringer of light to Hume's initial insights, and it is from this perspective that he describes the *Critique of Pure Reason* as 'the elaboration of the Humean problem in its greatest possible amplification'.[78]

So then, we can sum all of this up as follows. After Hume's devastating critique of traditional metaphysics, a critique that Kant's own empirical realism seeks to rearticulate in a way that does not undermine the integrity of reason in empirical cognition as Hume had, in this new intellectual environment, the question of metaphysics – if metaphysics is to be preserved at all – is going to have to be asked in a fundamentally new way. I have already said most generally that the shift here was going to be away from the enquiry into essences of things and towards the enquiry into conditions for the possibility of what appears. But now, more narrowly with respect to our own concerns about the integrity of reason, the question is: '*Given*' the thoroughly *empirical* (and hence *contingent*) character of reality (i.e., *given* empirical realism), *how then is necessary and universal knowledge possible anyway?* Or conversely, how can reason retain its intrinsic claims to necessity and universality (i.e., in its analytic demand) without forfeiting its integrity in dogmatism (i.e., in its synthetic demand)?

4.2 Noumena as regulative entities

It is in Kant's response to this challenge that we come to a distinction that opens up to the real heart of what is arguably most decisive and original in his project of reforming metaphysics. Unfortunately, it is also a distinction that in both of its aspects has with few exceptions been turned on its head by the better part of almost a generation of Anglo-American philosophy. The distinction, in the simplest of terms, is that although noumena are indeed 'ontologically nothing', nevertheless they are most emphatically *not* 'epistemologically nothing'.[79] For even though noumena are indeed

78. Kant, *Prolegomena to any Future Metaphysics*, pp. 7, 11.
79. The inverse reading of noumena as *both* 'ontologically something' – i.e., as somehow *real* 'mind-independent' entities populating a transcendental noumenal 'realm' – *and* as 'epistemologically nothing', not only goes against everything that Kant himself says on the matter but is also blatantly contradictory. This, once again, is the reading that enables Strawson or Pritchard and their followers to label the entire Kantian programme 'perverse' and 'disastrous'. Although this view is now slowly being corrected, as intimated above, its

'mere beings of reason',[80] we now find that they are nonetheless posited *by* reason for the epistemologically *regulative* purpose of holding reason 'fully accountable for its own proceedings'.[81] In other words, it is in their function not as 'constitutive' or ontological entities, but as *regulative* concepts that noumena or things-in-themselves become the veritable backbone of the philosophical defence of empirical realism. As *regulative* concepts they are the normative linchpin, the epistemological *sine qua non* and the *operative* heart (empirical realism remains the 'substantive' source and focus) of the entire *Critique of Pure Reason*, albeit now not as independent ontological beings but rather as entities that reason *itself* posits in order to ensure 'the proper use of reason'. This is aptly and concisely formulated, and now with a clear absence of any Strawsonian residue, in the introductory essay to the new Cambridge edition of the *Critique of Pure Reason*: In their regulative capacity, noumena or things-in-themselves are not 'metaphysical beings or entities whose reality is supposed to be demonstrable, but rather goals and directions of enquiry that mark out ways in which our knowledge is to be sought for and organized'.[82] We can state this function of noumena somewhat more precisely, albeit very provisionally for now, as follows: The non-constitutive yet regulative function of noumena will be found in the way they preserve and *maximize the unity of reason* (i.e., the integrity of reason) by *always directing reason back to its empirical use*. In this same provisional light, we may now complete a thought that was begun in the opening sentences of the present chapter section. In the doctrine of noumena, the question of rational integrity for metaphysics gets reconfigured from a question of autonomy or *self-sufficiency* to a question of *self-orientation*. Let us look at all of this more closely.

In characteristic rigour, Kant is unwilling to allow himself merely to project these pure ideas of reason or noumena speculatively as hypotheticals, to see how they might unify reason. Rather he insists right from the outset on bringing forward a proof or deduction of them.[83] However, this

---

effect is still pervasive. See, for example, again, Milbank, 'The Theological Critique of Philosophy'.

80. See section 2.2 above for the discussion of noumena as problematic concepts.

81. Kant, *Prolegomena to any Future Metaphysics*, p. 103.

82. Paul Guyer and Alan Wood, 'Introduction', in Kant, *Critique of Pure Reason*, p. 18.

83. By 'right at the outset', I do not mean at the outset of the *Critique*, but at the outset of the introduction of noumena in their regulative capacity. In fact, this regulative function of noumena, and their epistemological indispensability for the empirical use of reason (i.e., the 'critical' use of reason) is dealt with relatively briefly in the *Critique of Pure Reason* itself (at the very conclusion, as a kind of culmination) and will be taken up again in Kant's third and final 'Critique', the *Critique of Judgment* published some nine years later, where it is the main focus.

will not be an objective proof or an objective deduction yielding a constitutive or objective (i.e., ontological) principle, which is somehow 'out there' in some supra-sensory domain (indeed we do not even want this, for it would then be constitutive, or ontological, dogmatic). The proof will not come by way of the deduction of an *objective principle* but by way of the transcendental deduction of a *subjective maxim*.

In Kant's own words, 'One cannot avail oneself of a concept a priori with any security unless one has brought about a transcendental deduction of it. The [pure] ideas of reason, of course, do not permit any deduction of the same kind as the categories; but if they are to have the least objective validity,[84] even if it is only an indeterminate one... then a deduction of them must definitely be possible.' What Kant is referring to here in comparing the 'ideas of reason' (*Vernunft*) with the 'categories of the understanding' (*Verstand*) is that the deduction of the *ideas of pure reason* or noumena is a deduction of a very special sort, even within the intricate Kantian scheme of things, and is something entirely separate from Kant's much more frequently discussed deduction of the *categories of the understanding*. The fundamental difference between the 'categorial concepts' and the 'pure ideas' is that the former are formulated based on classification of what is given in sense experience, whereas the ideas of pure reason or noumena are by definition entirely supra-sensible, that is, purified of any sensible component whatsoever as we have seen. Thus their deductions or proofs will also differ from one another.[85] Kant continues:

> It makes a big difference whether something is given to my reason as an object absolutely [i.e., as an empirical object through the senses] or is given only as an object in the idea. In the first place my concepts go as far as determining the object; but in the second, there is really only a schema for which no object is given, not even hypothetically.[86]

---

84. A subjective maxim will have 'objective validity' in virtue of its universal applicability.
85. The deduction or proof of the *categories* appears near the centre of the *Critique* whereas the deduction of the *pure ideas* (noumena) appears near the very conclusion of the *Critique*, as a culmination of sorts, or in Kant's words, in order to bring about 'the completion of the critical business of pure reason'. My intention here is neither to defend nor to criticize Kant's deduction of the categories of the understanding but rather only to point out the importance of distinguishing this from the deduction of noumena, which is also precisely what Kant is doing in this passage. Many thinkers, including Hegel and Nietzsche, have taken issue with Kant's deduction of the categories, especially with what they have interpreted as Kant's contention that the a priori categories of the understanding are universal or that all people at all times share the same conceptual categories. Whether or not Kant is actually arguing this, and indeed whether or not it is so, will have no real bearing in any case on Kant's line of reasoning in the deduction of noumena, which is our own present concern – as long as there is basic agreement that reason functions intrinsically to unify and to organize.
86. Kant, *Critique of Pure Reason*, A670/B698.

The point is that, for empirical objects, I have at my disposal[87] conceptual categories by which the object can be recognized and rendered intelligible (place-able within mental classification), whereas the pure ideas of reason (noumena) by definition are absent of any such determinable object. Kant goes on to offer a helpful illustration of what this means. For example,

> the concept of a highest intelligence is a mere idea, i.e., its objective reality is not to consist in the fact that it relates straightway to an object... rather, it is only a schema ordered in accordance with the conditions of the greatest unity of reason, for the concept of a thing in general which serves only to preserve the *greatest systematic unity in the empirical use of our reason*... In such a way the idea is only a heuristic and not an ostensive concept; and it shows *not* how an object [i.e., the noumenal object or the idea of pure reason] is constituted [i.e., ontologically] but *how, under the guidance of that concept, we ought to seek after the constitution and connection of objects of experience in general.*[88]

In other words, even though the idea of a highest intelligence remains a *pure* idea – that is, there is no conceptual category or determination, not even a hypothetical one, that could 'represent' the idea of a highest intelligence, since there is no real object that correlates to it – nevertheless it is not only *not* impossible to think such an idea (because it is not contradictory), but such an idea seems clearly to be meaningful in some way. And we now see that it *is* meaningful inasmuch as it gives us guidance in how 'we ought to seek after the constitution and connection of objects of experience in general'.

As we now approach Kant's transcendental deduction of noumena itself, one further point must be made in advance of it, in order to be completely clear about what it is seeking to achieve. Throughout the *Critique* Kant has spoken of the transcendental ideas (i.e., ideas of pure reason, noumena, things-in-themselves, transcendental objects) as falling into three basic kinds: psychological (ideas about the soul), cosmological (ideas about the world) and theological (ideas about God). In the present treatment we have been limiting ourselves solely to the cosmological; and so, continuing on that level, allow me to expand a bit further on the basic logic underlying Kant's arrival at these three most fundamental transcendental ideas (noumena), which will be pivotal in the transcendental deduction of noumena. In doing so let us return to my example above about a particular

---

87. See the last half of footnote 85, with respect to the claim of having these categories 'at my disposal'.
88. Kant, *Critique of Pure Reason*, A670–1/B698–9, emphasis added.

book resting on a particular bookshelf in my study. As I abstracted all of the sensible empirical components of this object in order to see if I might arrive at the 'thing-in-itself', I found that in the end I was left with nothing ontological but rather with the mere idea of something, and a purely problematic idea at that (since any meaningful content was inevitably empirical). But now recall too that, even though this transcendental 'object' or the purely ideal thing-in-itself was thus undetermined and merely problematic, it nevertheless still functioned as a kind of 'conceptual *correlate*' to the determinate empirical object, 'in relation to which appearances have a unity'.

Now, excusing the oversimplification of all of this, suppose I make not this particular book but all the books in my study the object of conceptual scrutiny, or even the set of all the books on all the bookcases in a particular university, or even further, the set of all the books on earth. Because in each case, even as it expands, the set remains finite, it is still possible for my 'transcendental idea' of this whole set of empirical objects, increasingly complexified as it is, to continue to function as the 'conceptual correlate' to the real determinate empirical appearance or the determinate empirical set of which it seeks to be the pure idea. In each case I begin from a determinate object of some sort and seek (*theoretically*) to arrive at the pure idea of the thing-in-itself, and as I expand the empirical set, the difficulty of representing (or determining) what the transcendental idea correlates *to* also increases. It is clear where this is going. If I take not a determinate object or set of objects, but 'the world', or the totality of all that is given in empirical spatio-temporal reality as my 'object' of scrutiny, I find that there is nothing determinate or determinable, to begin with, to which any suprasensible 'pure idea' of the world could even be a 'correlate'. The reason for this is that the world encompasses all determinations of infinite varieties and descriptions and there is no way, as such, that the world could ever be anything determinate, or itself a possible object of experience. The transcendental idea of the world is thus a *special* transcendental idea because it does not serve as a conceptual correlate to any determinate empirical object or set of objects. It is as such an even 'purer' pure idea which nonetheless, and now actually in more powerful ways than the others, is capable of giving guidance on how 'we ought to seek after the constitution and connection of objects of experience in general'. (It will be clear that the idea of 'the world' in this case is something like the cosmological analogue to Kant's example of the 'highest being' cited above, which is roughly the theological account.) Thus the idea of the world is the broadest possible transcendental idea in cosmology, just as the transcendental ideas of the self and of God can be shown, along related lines, to be the most basic and utterly undeterminable ideas in psychology and theology respectively.

One more thing must be said about these three 'purest' of the pure ideas. Because they are utterly indeterminate, that is, because we can never have a corresponding determinate object nor thus a conceptual category for them, we must in the end speak of all three of these ideas on an 'as if' (*als ob*) basis. With respect to cosmology or the world, then, for Kant we pursue our enquiry into the 'appearances of nature through an investigation that will nowhere be completed, *as if* nature were infinite in itself and without a first or supreme member'. Likewise in psychology we 'connect all appearances, actions, and receptivity of our mind to the guiding thread of inner experience *as if* the mind were a simple substance that (at least in this life) persists in existence with personal identity'. In theology, although we cannot know (cognize) that there is a supreme ground in which spatio-temporal reality has its origin, yet 'we have to consider everything . . . *as if* the sum total of all appearances (the world of sense itself) had a single supreme and all-sufficient ground outside its range, namely an independent, original and creative reason, as it were, in relation to which we direct every empirical use of *our* reason in its greatest extension *as if* the objects themselves have arisen from that original image of all reason'.[89]

With all of this as a basis we now come finally to the heart of Kant's transcendental deduction of the ideas of pure reason, the basic formulation of which turns out to be surprisingly brief:

> Now if one can show that although the three kinds of transcendental ideas (psychological, cosmological and theological) cannot be referred directly to any object corresponding to them and to its determination, and *nevertheless that all rules of the empirical use of reason under the presupposition of such an object in the idea lead to systematic unity, always extending the cognition of experience by never going contrary to experience, then it is a necessary maxim of reason to proceed in accordance with such ideas.* And this is the transcendental deduction of all the ideas of speculative reason, not as constitutive principles for the extension of our reason to more

89. Kant, *Critique of Pure Reason*, A672–3/B700–1. This same principle is found, of course, much more famously in Kant's moral philosophy in his categorical imperative: 'So act as if your maxims were to serve at the same time as a universal law', Immanuel Kant, *Grounding for the Metaphysics of Morals*, tr. James W. Ellington (Indianapolis: Hackett, 1981), p. 43.

> objects than experience can give, but as *regulative principles for the systematic unity of the manifold of empirical cognition in general*, through which this cognition, within its proper boundaries, is cultivated and corrected more than could happen without such ideas . . .[90]

We can try to further clarify what Kant is saying here in the following way. *Given* empirical realism,[91] *if* (a) we can show that these three most basic kinds of transcendental ideas of reason, which are not formed on the basis of any determinate object, nevertheless *never* go against empirical cognition, but actually extend it and strengthen it, while precisely, in so doing, preserving and contributing to the greatest systematic unity in the function of reason as such, *then* (b) – again, *given empirical realism* – it is a *necessary* (and universal) maxim of reason to proceed in accordance with such ideas.

Now several important things are to be emphasized here, especially with regard to the a priori synthetic (metaphysical) status of what Kant is attempting to accomplish. First, note that this deduction is not merely analytic; it is not something that reason gives to itself, or comes to purely through the logical analysis of its own ideas, or its own operations. Rather, *as* pure ideas of the *understanding*, they nevertheless arise in a genuinely *synthetic* way. That is, they arise when reason casts its gaze onto the empirical domain and seeks to understand it. Again, to be absolutely clear about this, the transcendental idea of the world arises not *analytically* through a focus on logic, or as reason focuses on itself or its own operations, but synthetically as reason focuses on empirical reality – *even though* 'the world', *as* such a transcendental idea, is indeterminate and does not have any correlative empirical object.

But secondly, note as such what has just happened here. Because 'the world' has no determinate empirical object, therefore the idea of the world is not formed a posteriori (on the basis of sense experience), nor could it ever be. But although we thus have a genuinely synthetic idea and a '*non-a-posteriori*' idea, this does not *yet* make 'the world' a *synthetic a priori* idea in the genuinely 'metaphysical' sense of necessity and universality. What is required in order to complete this endeavour is a genuinely transcendental (i.e., a priori) *deduction* of the pure idea or noumenon itself. And this has just been provided. For this deduction has shown that noumena or the

90. Kant, *Critique of Pure Reason*, A671/B699.
91. I.e., in the genuine Kantian sense of both 'given' and 'empirical realism' as described at length above.

ideas of pure reason receive their validation or their proof in virtue of their ability both to enlarge and to simplify the field of reasoning *in its empirical use* while at the same time preserving and contributing to the greatest systematic unity of reason as such. As such, we can speak of a unity and integrity of reason *within empirical cognition* (i.e., within reality, *given* empirical realism) which does not 'do violence' to that empirical reality through dogmatism and yet which preserves reason's rightful claims to necessity and universality in the way just stated. This is *synthetic a priori* cognition or *metaphysical* cognition in the new, genuinely Kantian critical mode.

7

Tragedy, empirical history and finality

As the last chapter concluded we saw that in Kant, for the first time, we could speak of engaging in genuinely metaphysical enquiry in a way that preserves and protects both the integrity of the empirical world and the integrity of reason. Our findings with regard to each of these three terms can be briefly summarized as follows. First, the term *metaphysical* is demystified in that it no longer purports to identify any sort of purely rational foundational structures of reality, existing 'out there' somehow beyond the possibility of all experience, or beyond space and time; but rather now, more simply, the possibility of genuine a priori cognition (necessary and universal knowledge) in rational enquiry into the empirical world (i.e., in synthetic reasoning). Secondly, the preservation of *empirical integrity* means essentially an acknowledgement by reason that the empirical world fundamentally reflects 'extensive magnitudes' which do not fall under the jurisdiction of reason, but which stand over against reason as realities that reason cannot at bottom account for, or that reason cannot 'give to itself' but that are given to reason through intuition. (Whenever reason presumes that it *can* do so it engages in dogmatism.) Thirdly, the preservation of *rational integrity* means essentially that, precisely in taking care to protect the empirical integrity of the world in this way, reason's rightful analytical claims to necessity and universality can also be sustained, and reason itself thereby brought to a maximum unity in synthetic enquiry. The overall point is that the intrinsic rational demands of unity, necessity and universality (without which reason could not *be* reason) can be upheld, not only in reason's enquiry into itself or its own ideas (analytically), but also in reason's enquiry into the real empirical world (synthetically), precisely as reason comports itself in appropriate ways vis-à-vis the empirical world; that is, by respecting its integrity as inherently *manifested* reality (i.e., spatio-temporal realty), and not as reality 'in itself'. For reality 'in itself' would, again, be a purely rational kind of reality, or better, a kind of reality responding purely to rational demands and, as such, dogmatism. But, following from this, we also discovered something equally important in the other direction. We found that we were now allowed, without reservation or hesitation, to accept and embrace the *empirical world* fully as the *real world* without fear thereby of relegating reason to the mere a posteriori status of curator or custodian, as Hume had done. Reason retains its full a priori status and thus its integrity, not merely as an organizer 'after the fact', but as a full creative contributor in genuinely predictive ways to philosophical enquiry in reference to empirical reality.

All of this seems to bode well at least in one sense for the theological endeavour, where the central question concerns not how reference to empirical reality is possible but 'how reference to or characterization of the *transcendent* is possible'. For we are looking for a kind of thinking in theology that preserves the genuinely referential integrity (aboutness) of reason while leaving the integrity of that which theological discourse seeks to *be* 'about' also intact, that is, without claiming jurisdiction over it in any way. But it soon becomes evident that, despite its appropriate dispositions in important ways, the Kantian model does not simply map onto the theological endeavour as neatly as one might hope. The problem of course is that transcendence in the Kantian scheme of things is precisely *not real*, as theology demands, but purely ideal or purely mental, posited fundamentally as an orienting or regulative device for the understanding. Thus we found we could get no closer, in Kant, to the kind of real referentiality that theology demands with respect to the transcendent than reference to an *als ob*: that is, reference to an 'as if' whose sole purpose is to give us guidance in how 'we ought to seek after the constitution and connection of objects of experience in general'.[1] The problem then, on the Kantian scheme of things, is not that reason lacks the appropriate noetic disposition for the theological enterprise; the problem is rather that, in order for reason to *come* to that appropriate disposition in the first place, the transcendent *must* be treated as a mere *als ob*,

---

1. I do not wish to minimize Kant's somewhat different discussion of reality on a moral level. But even here, as already noted above, it is often ignored that the categorical imperative itself comes to be expressed in the form of an 'as if': 'So act as if your maxims were to serve at the same time a universal law'; *Grounding for the Metaphysics of Morals*, tr. James W. Ellington (Indianapolis: Hackett, 1981), p. 43.

as a sheerly problematic idea and not as a reality, for as soon as the transcendent could be *regarded* by reason as a *reality* it would by that very fact no longer be transcendent.

And this brings us to a problem of a particularly perplexing sort. How is it possible *at all* to encounter the transcendent as *real* in the way that theology demands, that is, as possessing a kind of authority or finality *of its own*, and not just as a limit that the understanding imposes on itself? Or in other words, how can we possibly make sense of transcendence *demanding* its *own* finality or authority in the first place, since any *encounterable* or recognizable finality as such would by definition be an *immanent* finality or authority? Or again, conversely, in order for a transcendent finality or authority to be genuinely transcendent it would have to be unperceivable and unencounterable as such. But how then could such a claim be intelligible or meaningful at all or, indeed, anything but nonsense?[2] In order to help us get beyond this impasse, or at least to understand it better, I want once again to return to MacKinnon, this time to his treatment of tragedy, and specifically to the idea that in tragedy we encounter a kind of finality or authority that enables us to project our questioning in reference to the transcendent in unique ways.

1 Tragedy and transcendence

MacKinnon addresses this topic from within an array of contexts, but there is one passage that can serve as a particularly apt starting point. 'In tragedy', he says, 'we reach a form of representation that by the very ruthlessness of its interrogation enables us to project as does no available alternative, our ultimate questioning' in reference to the transcendent. Or the same point is made in somewhat different words as follows: 'tragedy, regarded as a form of discourse, itself provide[s] a way of representing the relation of the familiar to the transcendent' like no other form

---

2. This is something arguably that Karl Barth has understood better than almost anyone, and his brilliant exposition rooting the authority of transcendence in the *hiddenness* of God remains one of the quintessential contributions for the preservation of the integrity of transcendence; cf., e.g., Karl Barth, *Church Dogmatics II.i* (Edinburgh: T&T Clark, 1957), pp. 179–204. But Barth too fails to give us a proper indication of how transcendence in this genuinely Christian sense could be encountered as anything *tangibly* final, or *meaningfully* authoritative, and so he must resort to this authority being purely posited in revelation in a way that seems to pre-empt the integrity of reason and by extension also human freedom. The conundrum at bottom in Barth, then, is that the finality or authority of transcendence cannot be recognized apart from the revelation of that transcendence. This problem moreover is self-perpetuating or self-exacerbating for we have no way of knowing even what the act of God in revelation means apart from the act of God in revelation.

of discourse.[3] We must now try to decipher what this means exactly, and I want to engage this task around three different points of focus. First I will speak to an implicit distinction between two senses of tragedy in MacKinnon, the relation between which is crucial for understanding what he is attempting to do in connecting tragedy and transcendence. On this basis I will suggest and explore the claim that in tragedy we are confronted by a new kind of finality or authority, different from anything we have encountered thus far. I will then look thirdly into how all of this can shed light on MacKinnon's injunction that we attend to the tragic in the narrative of Jesus, especially insofar as the tragic here will be held to express especially uniquely the relation of the familiar to the transcendent. The balance of the chapter will then seek to apply these findings, based on Bultmann, Bonhoeffer and Marion – and in a preparatory way for the final chapter – to the problem of theological reference and empirical reality.

1.1 Tragedy-as-discourse and tragedy in empirical history

To begin with then, MacKinnon operates implicitly under two separate senses of tragedy: tragedy as a form of discourse, and real human tragedy in empirical history. The way these relate to one another will be vital for the connection that MacKinnon wants to establish to transcendence, even though he himself seldom if ever distinguishes clearly enough between them. Tragedy in the first sense essentially refers to tragedy as a literary form (e.g., Shakespeare's *King Lear*, Sophocles' *Antigone*, the book of Job). Tragedy in the second sense is defined by MacKinnon as referring to 'the sheerly intractable in human life': an intractability that is borne out most starkly in particular (or in collectively particular) instances of appalling, pointless suffering, or in specific unspeakable instances of evil or oppression, especially as these give way to a descent into inevitable and hopeless human undoing. As such, we would encounter with unmistakable clarity the 'sheer intractability' and the 'ruthlessness of interrogation' of real tragedy not only in Auschwitz, Rwanda or Cambodia, but also in countless individual stories of tragic human demise: for example, in the unhealing woundedness experienced by victims of especially dehumanizing acts of violence and abuse, or in the loss of self-identity in Alzheimer's disease, or in the self-destructive and unstoppable descent into certain

3. Donald MacKinnon, *The Problem of Metaphysics* (Cambridge: Cambridge University Press, 1974), pp. 136, 135.

kinds of addiction. But it is specifically tragedy in the former sense, as a form of discourse, that is spoken of here as being able to provide a way of representing the relation of the familiar to the transcendent (i.e., as 'no other form of discourse' can). Yet before we can make proper sense of how, precisely, MacKinnon wants to make the connection to transcendence, there is one further intermediate step hidden here which must be brought to light. This tacit intermediate claim is that tragedy as a literary form, or tragedy-as-discourse, allows for a kind of articulation and representation of real tragedy in human history or of 'the sheerly intractable in human experience', better than any other form of discourse is able to do – better than the essay, novel, sonnet, elegy or homily, better even than the parable. In other words, tragedy-as-discourse reflects a certain unique kind of disposition which enables it somehow to become a window for apprehending or 'reading' real tragedy in history or the sheerly intractable in human life, and thus, as it were, to speak on behalf of the unspeakable.

What is it then about tragedy-as-discourse, or tragedy as a literary form, that enables it to represent the sheerly intractable in human life in this unique way, or that qualifies it to speak on behalf of the unspeakable, on behalf of the humanity within whom this unutterable undoing is actually taking place? Again, although MacKinnon himself neither specifically asks nor responds to this question, the implicit answer is clearly that tragedy as a literary form allows – indeed *demands* – that its subject matter remain ultimately self-referential and unresolved. In other words, tragedy-as-discourse is capable of giving proper expression to real instances of irresolvable evil and unspeakable suffering precisely because it *aligns itself utterly* with the human undoing being experienced so intractably and because it does so *without ever attempting to bring the unfolding tragedy into any broader system of explanation*, still less, justification or resolution. It does so without ever seeking to draw from the unfolding tragedy any sort of 'moral', or to make 'sense' of it, even to draw a poetic or dramatic 'point' from it in any way that would soften its sheer intractability or seek to blunt the sharpness of the discontinuity. At the root of all of this is a deep and abiding concern to protect the empirical integrity or reality of the sufferer, so to speak, or the ungeneralizable private integrity of the reality of evil in the victim's experience. Such a view would maintain, for example, that the Montgomery County police spokesperson got it right when he said, in his statement to the families of the victims of the random Beltway sniper shootings in 2002, after the apprehension of the killers, that 'we do not know your pain'. The same kind of respect for the (collectively) private reality of tragedy is evident in the reluctance, which one frequently senses among participants of discussion groups in universities or churches, to venture to speak about the ethical or theological ramifications of the organized massacres of Jews in twentieth-century Germany or Russia, without a Jewish person present. There is an implicit recognition here that the collectively private particularity of that specific tragedy does not admit of treating it publicly or formulaically as a general theme that admits of easy forum-style discussion. It is against the backdrop of this kind of unspeakability that tragedy-as-discourse offers the non-participant (in this case, for example, the non-Jew) a language, at least of alignment, if not identification, with those particular instances of tragic evil or suffering or human undoing. The point is that tragedy-as-discourse is capable of accommodating or 'representing' the *fact* that real suffering and evil can exist in such intrusive and discontinuous particularity, or in such 'ruthlessness of interrogation', that in the end it can only be apprehended as calling attention to *itself* irresolvably, confronting us on its own terms with a kind of *sui generis* authority or finality, which is at one and the same time both undeniable and unspeakable. Tragedy-as-discourse can give expression to these discontinuities while protecting them against violation or obliteration in any system of explanation.

1.2 Two finalities

What we encounter in tragedy then – and now it is specifically the *relation* between tragedy-as-discourse and real tragedy in history that fully bears this out – is a kind of authority or finality that is entirely different from any we have seen so far. The kind of finality or authority we naturally strive for in any kind of discourse – indeed, the kind of finality or authority that has served as the basic common denominator between all of the perpetual philosophical polarities discussed thus far – is what I will call a *finality of resolution*. Whether purely rationally or empirically, whether analytically or synthetically, the key feature about what I am calling a finality of resolution is that we propound and advocate certain points of view or theories and hold them to be authoritative, in virtue of how well they are able to assimilate, explain and resolve the often conflicting elements in human experience and cognition. In fact, this kind of finality can become especially pronounced within theology, in the development of apologetic strategies or theodicies; the authority we invest in these is based on how satisfactorily, or how reasonably, they are able to resolve theological conundrums or suggest solutions that harmonize or at least illuminate, in some way, its key paradoxes.

But against all of this, tragedy-as-discourse *by definition* is *irresolvable*. Whether in Sophocles, Shakespeare or Racine, tragedy-as-discourse keeps its integrity *as* tragedy (in part) precisely by remaining a form of expression that never, on any level, seeks to become harmonizable with a grander picture of things or with a higher rationale. That is an essential part of what makes tragedy what it is. If a course of events can be understood as leading to a resolution that somehow 'makes sense' of it, then that course of events is by definition no longer 'tragic'. In other words, the real value of tragedy-as-discourse is that it helps us to see or to give expression to the *fact* that there are aspects of human experience and episodes of human history, for which resolution cannot and may not properly be sought. In an odd way it thus 'legitimizes' for the understanding the utter *absence* of any possible 'legitimacy' or justification for real tragedy in human history, by drawing attention to the unspeakable, irresolvable, yet sheerly intractable empirical *fact* of it. As such we might even say that in tragedy-as-discourse we have a true example of the freedom from end-orientedness that we saw Derrida trying to achieve in chapter 1.

In short, the kind of finality we encounter in instances of tragic suffering and evil is the radical inversion of any finality of resolution sought for in rational and empirical enquiry, or even in any other kind of literary expression. It is instead utterly a *finality of non-resolution*, a sheerly intractable, non-negotiable, empirically and morally indefeasible finality that 'stumps' every conceivable theodicy, rationalization or apologetic strategy. In this light it is worth restating the severe point made earlier by Dietrich Ritschl that 'anyone who wants to say that Auschwitz – as a paradigm of evil and suffering in our time – is willed by God or good, even if we only realize it later, has to shut up, because such statements mark the end of both theology and humanity'.[4] In other words, to suppose that there could be any sort of 'argument from design' (a *human* argument, after all) that could absorb Auschwitz or Rwanda or Cambodia is not in the first place to violate the reality of God; it is rather to violate the reality of the world which is *not* God, yet a world whose integrity *as* that which is *not* God must be preserved, as we shall see later, if the Christian understanding of the reality of God is to be preserved at all. There can be no teleological suspension of the ethical here. The Kierkegaardian picture

4. Dietrich Ritschl, *The Logic of Theology* (Philadelphia: Fortress Press, 1987), p. 38.

of Abraham and Isaac is not 'tragic' in this sense, for tragedy marks the end not only of ethics but even of *telos*. It is when we meet utterly with the end of design, with the end of telos, that we meet truly with the sheer intractability of what I am calling the *finality of non-resolution* experienced in tragedy.

This is the basic backdrop that gives proper meaning to MacKinnon's implicit claim that tragedy-as-discourse gives better expression *at bottom* to what we encounter in the problem of God and evil (i.e., real tragedy in history) than any theodicy or apologetic strategy ever could. Of course this is by no means to belittle Christian apologetics or the important insights that such endeavours can and do provide in dealing with particular difficulties or, even to a certain extent, more general problems. After all, when we claim that the Christian faith is true, this must include a fundamental commitment to the basic *sustainability* of its truth-claims, or else we might as well give up on theology (and indeed on Christianity) altogether. Rather, what is being insisted here is only that any theodicy or apologetic strategy that claims to have 'moved beyond tragedy', to 'the alleged general solution to the problem of evil, the all inclusive answer to the questions elicited by bitter experience of suffering', *this* must be met with the firmest resistance. Here, the book of Job 'remains as a standing protest against the suggestion that undeserved suffering can find through the intellectual virtuosity and consecrated zeal of the apologist a justification which will still in the sufferer the sense of outrage that must remain'.[5] It is clear where this is leading. Orientation to the tragic – to the sheerly discontinuous in human life – allows us to project our questioning to the transcendent like no other form of discourse because it gives us *factual, tangible* examples in *real empirical* human experience, of the finality of non-resolution that we must encounter in the transcendent.

1.3 Attending to the tragic (in the narrative of Jesus)

However, this is not to suppose that tragedy now becomes some sort of model for representing transcendence, for transcendence by definition

---

5. MacKinnon, *The Problem of Metaphysics*, pp. 124–5; Donald MacKinnon, *Explorations in Theology* (London: SCM Press, 1979), p. 21. MacKinnon continues by saying that we find in Job a classical example 'of a man defeated in the attempt existentially to reconcile experience of personal catastrophe with confession of beneficent and just design; an attempt set in hand because the subject of the experience is, by formulation, initially predisposed to subsume the hammer blows that rain upon him under some general law which would enable him to receive such shattering experience as, for example, ultimately remedial'. In the end, however, 'no form of the "argument from design" has ever silenced the cry elicited by tragic experience' (MacKinnon, *Explorations in Theology*, pp. 125–7).

admits of no representative model. It is rather only to suggest that the relation we see between tragedy-as-discourse and real tragedy in history may in some way illuminate the relation of the familiar to the transcendent. Indeed, as soon as we even try to apply tragedy directly to transcendence we immediately see the futility of the endeavour. For we have ample – agonizingly ample – subject matter for a finality of non-resolution with respect to tragedy. But what sort of 'subject matter' do we have for a finality of non-resolution with respect to the transcendent? Indeed, as already explained, how could we possibly make sense of a transcendent *demand* for authority or finality anyway, since the very *recognition* of it *as* a demand would render it an immanent demand?

Yet it is precisely at this sharpened impasse, and still lacking any subject matter for a finality of non-resolution with respect to the transcendent, that continued attention to the tragic can help us forward, and this in a twofold way. In the first place, the tragic, and with it the problem of evil, is the only exemplification we have, in all of human experience, of a *real* finality of non-resolution. All other human endeavours and encounters are treated as being at bottom somehow explainable, resolvable. Even mysterious, inexplicable experiences that some might refer to as 'paranormal' continue to be treated as 'open questions' inasmuch as they are expected ultimately to fall in line with some notion of sufficient reason. There are of course different kinds of intractability that we encounter, for example in mathematics or quantum physics. But these are always either discovered or constructed intractabilities, whether logically derived or projected on the basis of hypotheses tested against axioms or observation; perhaps via proof through a reductio, or perhaps in the way that an intractable puzzle of physical theory remains an 'open question' and is treated as an enigma awaiting further clarification.

The point by contrast is that the tragic reality of Auschwitz – in the way that both MacKinnon and Dietrich Ritschl want to draw our attention to it – is by no means an 'open question', but a hermetically closed one; it is by no means an enigma awaiting further clarification. For to treat it as an open question would be to violate the empirical integrity of the human demise that went on there, precisely by ignoring its inalienable 'onceness' and 'pure pastness' as empirical history. In other words, the reason it demands to be treated as hermetically closed or non-resolvably final or sheerly intractable is because the tragedy that it *remains* cannot be abstracted from its *empirical historicity*, that is, from the onceness of the empirical reality within the particular human experience that it is and remains.

In fact we now see why any 'all inclusive answer to the questions elicited by bitter experience of suffering' *must* fail. The reason that it must fail is that any general solution – by its very definition as 'general' – must *abstract* from the empirical reality within which the real tragedy actually unfolds and treat not the onceness of the experienced reality itself, but rather only a generalized idea of it; and at this point the question not only loses all of its original urgency and burdensomeness, but in effect it has become an entirely different *kind* of question. For the original tragic question ceases to exist apart from its empirical particularity in its origin; or to borrow a phrase that Marion will use later in a very different but related way, it ceases to exist apart from 'the referent in its very advent'. The general question – that is, the abstract question – is thus a question, as Bonhoeffer might say, concerned purely with the good and not with the real. And the point is that in tragedy, the question of the good (i.e., the utter absence of it) cannot be abstracted from the real, that is, the empirically real.

We will discuss this further in the final chapter but for now we may observe that attentiveness to the tragic has at the very least led us this far: The only possible place that the 'subject matter' for a finality of non-resolution of *any* sort *could* be recognized (and this must now include any 'subject matter' for the transcendent, which as yet eludes us), the only possible place that its sheer intractability could be encountered as a demand is in the onceness and particularity of *empirical history*. And it is in connection with this point, in order to fix the still missing 'subject matter' for what I am calling a finality of non-resolution with respect to the transcendent, that we can now turn secondly to MacKinnon's injunction that we 'attend to the tragic in the narrative of Jesus'.

We must try to explain how attention to the tragic in the narrative of Jesus can serve to direct our questioning with regard to the transcendent 'subject matter' that we lack and still seek. In the most straightforward and direct way, of course, the injunction draws us first of all to the Paschal event itself, to the passion and death of Jesus, and with it, to the utter finality of non-resolution of the cross *in empirical history*. But what exactly do we mean by the utter finality of non-resolution of the cross in empirical history? And how might it be that attention to the tragic will help to bear out the transcendent character of this finality in relation to the familiar? We can venture a response to this in the following way. To begin with, when the cross is abstracted from the empirical history of Jesus, that is, when the tragic is not attended to, it becomes essentially a symbol; and then by its very nature *as* a symbol – even though it is indeed here a powerful symbol of redemption and hope – the cross becomes fundamentally the focus of a supreme kind of resolution. But the hope it then proclaims, if the sheer intractability of the empirical history of God-with-us on the cross is forgotten, is no longer the hope of genuine reconciliation (which must remain the response precisely to utter and intractable *non-resolution* if we are speaking about *genuine* reconciliation in the biblical sense), but only the hope of an ultimate kind of holism. And the integrity of transcendence in the Paschal event, its finality of non-resolution, is lost. It has become a finality of resolution.

To help us further with this point, it may be significant that Jesus' cry 'it is finished' appears not in the Synoptic Gospels but only in the more theological Fourth Gospel. Attention to the tragic in this statement confronts us with the unthinkable, the unresolvable, the transcendent, especially against the backdrop of John 1. The unthinkable, the unspeakable, the transcendent here is this: that perhaps, rather than as the victorious expression of a mission successfully completed, this cry is encountered more genuinely, its disturbing contingency (non-necessity) projected more authentically, the hiddenness of the resurrection protected more terrifyingly, in order to break once for all any likeness between holism and genuine reconciliation: when it is understood as the *irrevocable* self-giving, over to the utter finality of death – and now in the most final sense of 'it is finished' – of the one who was from the beginning and by whom all things are made. This is by no means to return to the tired nihilism-cum-idealism of the radical death-of-God (a)theologies from the mid-twentieth century (none of which ever understood this seriously anyway in the *genuinely* 'radical' sense of the *real* participatory death of God in empirical history). It is rather to return to the heart of nothing less than reformation theology, and to the full weight of the Lutheran doctrine of the crucifixion, which came later to be expressed in terms of the *nihil negativum*. No recent theologian has understood better than Dietrich Bonhoeffer the genuinely radical yet thoroughly orthodox nature of what is being claimed in the *nihil negativum* for the relation between crucifixion and resurrection.

> The dead Jesus Christ of Good Friday and the resurrected kurios of Easter Sunday – that is creation out of nothing, creation from the beginning. The fact that Christ was dead did not provide the possibility of his resurrection but its impossibility; it was nothing itself, it was the nihil negativum. There is absolutely no transition, no continuum between the dead Christ and the resurrected Christ but the freedom of God that in the beginning created God's work out of

nothing. Were it possible to intensify the nihil negativum even more, we would have to say here, in connection with the resurrection, that with the death of Christ on the cross the nihil negativum broke its way into God himself – O great desolation! God yes God is dead.[6]

I will return to develop this point more fully in the last chapter. But here we can simply acknowledge that there is something compelling and important about Bonhoeffer's placement of what might be called the 'impossible continuity' between the crucified and risen Christ (or, in my terms, between the familiar and the transcendent), not automatically in God's love, but first and fundamentally in God's freedom. For it is precisely this demand to be encountered via the freedom of God that protects the love of God from portrayal as the supreme authority of resolution, as the grandest, all-embracing holism, as the ultimate coherence theory, as the highest 'necessity'. Attention to the tragic in the narrative of Jesus, and by extension to the empirical history of God-with-us, refers us by way of God's freedom to an encounter with the love of God (and also with the resurrection), which, as MacKinnon says in another context, has been 'purged . . . of every taint of facile optimism'.[7] Yet this is not to descend into morbidity but rather to become open to genuine hope. The focus on the empirical history of Jesus, to which attention to the tragic refers us, causes us to bear full witness to the stark suggestion that what we encounter most fiercely and tragically, in both of Christ's cries from the cross, is not first of all the love of God, but rather the unbridgeable distance and strangeness of the unconditioned freedom of God, without which the love of God would not be the love *of God*.

But we must now also cast this understanding somewhat more broadly. For attention to the tragic in the narrative of Jesus refers us not only to the authority in the empirical history of his passion and death, but also to the authority in the empirical history of his birth, his life and resurrection. The point here is that even though the Christmas and Easter narratives do not have the same thematically tragic content as that of the Paschal journey and the cross, nevertheless it is still attention to the tragic in the Christian narrative of the birth, life, death and resurrection of Jesus

---

6. Dietrich Bonhoeffer, *Schöpfung und Fall*, Martin Rueter and Ilse Tödt (eds.), Dietrich Bonhoeffer Werke, 16 vols. (Munich: Christian Kaiser Verlag, 1988), vol. III, p. 33; Dietrich Bonhoeffer, *Creation and Fall*, ed. John W. de Gruchy, tr. Douglas Stephen Bax (Minneapolis: Fortress Press, 1997). p. 35, translation slightly altered to better reflect the original German. The last part of this passage is a direct quotation from a Lutheran hymn.
7. MacKinnon, *Explorations in Theology*, p. 164.

that *prohibits* any and all of this from remaining *mere narrative*. In other words, attention to the tragic serves to guarantee that the very crux of the Christian faith – 'that Jesus Christ is come in the flesh' – *remains a claim about empirical reality*, about the empirical history of God-with-us.

When we now focus all of this back on our more specific and overarching question of how reference to or characterization of the transcendent is possible, we discover something extremely important. For attention to the tragic has also demonstrated that *the 'referent' we seek for theological discourse* will be found fundamentally nowhere else than in the empirical history of God-with-us, and that accordingly the empirical reality of this referent may not, at any cost, be interpreted away either into pure symbolism or into metaphysical world enigma, or into any other important-sounding abstraction. But even further than this, if we want to be truly consistent, as we must be in holding to this point (otherwise we will inevitably find ourselves falling back into reductionism or positivism which either compromises orthodoxy or makes it indefensible), then we are presented also with the following problem. Even if we are careful to grant, fully and actually, that Jesus Christ has come in the flesh some 2,000 years ago, and then go on to make of this life of flesh and blood and bone an 'ideal actuality' for the possibility of theological reference today, we have already stepped away from orientation to the tragic and, as such, away from the empirical history, the empirical reality, of God-with-us.

2   Theological reference as empirical reference

Here we come to a watershed point. For if this empirical approach is to be consistently sustainable, then there must be some way that *the empirical history of Jesus continues today*, continues in the tangibly present here and now. Now the imperativeness of being able to account for such a genuinely empirical response to the demands of theological reference continues to be recognized by an array of prominent thinkers today, and we will presently discuss one endeavour in that regard in the thought of Jean-Luc Marion. But it was really Rudolf Bultmann, a generation ago, who, for all his faults, got us thinking again along these lines. Despite the unsustainability of his theological programme overall, Bultmann recognized the indispensability for theology of tangible empirical (or, for Bultmann, 'existential') reference, and articulated the problem with a kind of critical urgency unparalleled among his contemporaries. The point is that Bultmann was not advocating demythologization simply for its own sake;[8] rather, the *purpose* of demythologization was to explore ways in which the incarnation and the cross can once again become meaningful *present realities*, which he saw that they must be. But Bultmann then went on to identify revelation so exclusively with proclamation that the content of revelation became 'radically nonfactual', that is radically non-empirical, non-spatio-temporal, thus removing us forever from the real, historical Paschal event itself.[9] The problem as such is that what Bultmann leaves us with is not the *continuing* empirical history of the historically crucified and resurrected one, not a continuing empirical history that passes through the empty tomb (for *that* history, it would be claimed, belongs to the mythical three-tiered universe), but rather a separate and 'new' history – and a fragmented one at that – in the lives of individual believers as a movement towards God in human self-discovery. It is the absence of empirical continuity here that endangers orthodoxy.

Thus, Bultmann's existentialist project in theology, despite its initial intentions, turns out to be a prime example of the neglect of the tragic in the narrative of Jesus, and perhaps this is why central aspects of his broader theological project seem to self destruct. Yet we cannot simply ignore the important issues Bultmann raises, for the basic challenge he set remains. It was Bonhoeffer, again, who in his final years recognized and picked up on this challenge. One of the reasons that we continually find ourselves returning to Bonhoeffer on these kinds of issues is similar to the reason for our inevitable confrontation with Kant on the philosophical level. Bonhoeffer not only invariably takes these impasses as starting points, but he then proceeds to ask questions about them in ways that completely invert our focus. So here again we have Bonhoeffer not initially rejecting Bultmann, but rather insisting that he 'didn't go far enough' with his demythologizing; that is, that virtually *all* religious terminology, and not only that belonging to the three-tiered universe, needs to be demythologized: 'revelation', 'salvation', 'redemption', 'sin', 'incarnation', 'resurrection' and, as Bonhoeffer himself insists, even 'God'.

---

8. And even here he is apt to be misunderstood, since he was not attempting to remove the *skandalon* or the offense from the gospel proclamation; cf. H. W. Bartsch (ed.), *Kerygma and Myth I* (London: SPCK, 1953) and H. W. Bartsch (ed.), *Kerygma and Myth II* (London: SPCK, 1962), especially pp. 181–94.

9. Jean-Luc Marion, *God without Being* (Chicago: University of Chicago Press, 1982), pp. 145, 223.

Now I want to suggest that in Bonhoeffer's assessment of Bultmann we come to something of a crossroads for this whole present discussion of empirical reference in theology. For what Bonhoeffer, I think, implicitly sees here is that the real danger is not mythologization or anachronism or loss of 'relevance' or obsoleteness. No, the real danger is the much broader and deeper, yet more subtle and sinister peril of *abstraction*. For no matter how 'relevant' the subject matter it focuses on, no matter how relevant its terminology, abstraction actually seals the fate of genuine theological thinking because it immediately closes off any possibility of reference to the transcendent, inasmuch as the abstract *just is* the purely conceptual and as such defines the field par excellence in which the authority of *resolution* must have final jurisdiction. Even the least onerous of abstractions in this regard – the understanding of the history of Christ in the time after his flesh in terms of an 'ideal actuality', that is, of allowing that Jesus Christ has indeed come in the flesh 2,000 years ago, and that *that* now becomes the 'ideal' model – even this forecloses on the possibility of progress for the problem of theological discourse, for even an ideal actuality remains, in the end, an abstraction, and hence within the jurisdiction of a finality of resolution. This is not of course to say that there is anything wrong with abstraction per se. All of our thinking occurs within abstraction; indeed, conceptualization means abstraction. The danger I speak of here is concerned only with abstraction with regard to the *referent itself* of theological discourse. Or, in other words, the danger has only to do with the abstractness of that which our theological discourse seeks to be 'about' – no matter how metaphysically important, in virtue of its claims to 'generality', this abstract referent may be made out to be – whether as symbol or world enigma or even as 'ground of being' or 'ultimate reality'.

In light of all of this we might say that the challenge for theology today is to rediscover the real burdensomeness of Bonhoeffer's question 'Who is Jesus Christ for us today?' *as a genuine question of non-resolution,*[10] and accordingly then, by its very nature as such, as a question at one and the same time about empirical reality and about the possibility of reconciliation. In fact, the real anguish and weight of that question is completely lost when it is treated rather glibly, as it frequently is, as a question of the 'relevance' of Jesus Christ for the 'contemporary mindset', or as a question

10. Bonhoeffer himself left this question entirely and conspicuously unanswered, even in outline.

of what the church must do today to make what Jesus stands for meaningful for an outlook that has 'learned to live without God'. When it is taken in this way, merely to reflect an ongoing concern with theological relevance or resolution (and indeed most of these Bonhoefferian stock phrases have themselves become tiresome as they have been made the carriers of all manner of 'relevant' or 'cutting-edge' or 'startling' conversations), the question loses all of the burdensomeness and urgency under which it was originally asked. For the point is that, regardless of how robustly we affirm the historicity in flesh and blood and bone of the life, death and resurrection of Jesus of Nazareth, any such shifting away of the pressing empirical question of the present living Christ to the general innocuous level of ongoing theological 'relevance' is essentially its relegation to the tactical, strategic or holistic, or at best to the level of ideal actuality. The question becomes truly authentic and genuinely burdensome again, in the way that Bonhoeffer himself clearly encountered it, only when it is asked in the genuinely *difficult* sense of the continuing empirical history of Jesus Christ himself today.

The point is that Bonhoeffer's call for a radicalization of Bultmann is not an undisciplined reaction to stodgy traditionalism bordering on heterodoxy. It is rather a particularly uncompromising kind of orthodoxy, an orthodoxy that reflects a relentless and undiminishing determination not to compromise the reality of God-with-us as anything but *the continuing empirical history* of Jesus; for anything else is abstraction, which closes off the promise of the transcendent. To re-emphasize this, when Bonhoeffer claims, along these same lines, that essentially *all* these religious terms have lost their meaning, the point is not so much that they have become too archaic, too mythological – although often they have admittedly become that too – but more fundamentally that they have become *abstract*. The proper theological response here as such is not, as some are suggesting today, to undertake somehow to make these words 'strange' again[11] in order to set them in sharper *conceptual relief* so that they may stand out, or so that we cease to take them for granted, for this is merely to re-enter the circle abstraction on another level and to begin all over again. The answer is rather to make them, as Bonhoeffer himself insisted, *konkret*, or empirical, and thus indeed *familiar* again, but now in a new way. The German terms

---

11. Bonhoeffer's own focus on the *disciplina arcani* aims at something different in that it is a focus not on theological discourse, but on spiritual disciplines. But insofar as it might have application to present concerns, its focus is always on the *Wirklichwerden* – that is, the becoming real – of the Word of Christ among us.

das konkrete and *Konkretion*, which are so pivotal in Bonhoeffer's *Ethics* and later writings, bear none of the unfortunate connotations of hardened-ness, obstinacy and ossification of the misleading English translation 'concrete'. Rather they always and only signify, as does *konkret* always in Kant, the *empirical* given, the *empirically real*; *das Konkrete* as such is always set in direct opposition to *das Abstrakte*.

It is here also that the insistence on the empirically real is shown to be fundamentally what Bonhoeffer meant in his call for 'this-worldliness' in theology. The call to this-worldliness (*Diesseitigkeit*) is by no means a call to the profane over the sacred (as some questionable readings of Bonhoeffer's 'non-religious Christianity' suggest), since for Bonhoeffer all of these kinds of conceptual dualities have been overcome in Christ. Rather it is again the same call to empirical reality, in the full and integrated Kantian sense that I have described above. For it is precisely in drawing attention to the empirically real that 'this-worldliness', far from closing off the promise of meaningful reference to the transcendent, actually reopens the way to it, since empirical history is the only place that a finality of non-resolution can be encountered. In sum, while in one sense it shares a similar concern with Bultmann, this rescuing from *abstraction* by bringing into the *empirically real* is something fundamentally different from Bultmann's project of rescuing from an *anachronism* and bringing into the *existentially relevant*. In the next chapter I want to lay out in broad strokes a way in which this is achievable. Or to state it precisely, I want to explore a way in which theological terms can avoid abstraction by finding their reference in present empirical reality, yet such that the continuity to the original historical actuality is preserved and the integrity of both reason and transcendence remains intact.

But there is one immediate response to this specific set of problems, which should be mentioned here preliminarily, that might seem to provide a 'natural' solution to them, but which, on closer inspection really only defers them to another level. That immediate response is firstly that no question about the continuing empirical history of Jesus can be properly broached apart from a full engagement with the doctrine of the Holy Spirit and the doctrine of the Church; and secondly that the Church and the gift of the Holy Spirit as such fully provide the present 'empirical referent' that theological discourse requires. While the first part of this assertion is of course granted, it does not in the least diminish the fundamental point being made here about the need for continuity with the empirical history of the crucified and risen Christ. For the same questions would then have to be answered on the levels of pneumatology and ecclesiology, since it is only in continuity with the empirical history of the crucified and risen Christ that the orthodoxy of pneumatology and ecclesiology can and must be demonstrated. Thus the urgency of a genuinely empirical response to the demand for theological reference – one that demonstrates Christological continuity – remains. Before coming to what this book seeks to offer in response to that, and as a way of further clarifying what it will seek to achieve, I want to turn to Jean-Luc Marion's highly illuminating treatment of precisely this demand for empirical reality in theological reference in his book *God without Being*.

3   The Eucharist as empirical referent

Marion seeks to situate the empirical referent for theology within the Eucharist, but his explication of the theological need for empirical reference is at least as compelling as his response to it. Let me begin then with a brief account of Marion's own articulation of the theological task. He asks the initial question in this way: 'On what does Christian theology bear? On the event of the death and resurrection of Jesus, the Christ. How does this event, separated from us by the course of time and documentary distance occur to us?' Marion's initial response to this clearly (and consciously) echoes Bultmann: this event 'occurs to us through a word spoken to us by a man, *fides ex auditu* . . . the announcement makes use of a [biblical] text to tell an event'. But here the difficulty already begins to emerge, for the spoken word as such does not purport merely to 'transmit the text, but rather, through the text, the event'. In other words, in the text's very announcement of the event a gap already begins to open up between the text and the event inasmuch as even the text itself is separated from the historical event it announces. In Marion's words, 'the text does not coincide with the event or permit going back to it since it results from it'. He then makes the following pivotal assertion which expresses the severity of the theological demand with a unique kind of clarity and succinctness: 'We cannot lead the biblical text as far back as that at which it nevertheless aims, precisely because no hermeneutic could ever bring to light anything other than its meaning, *whereas we desire the referent in its very advent*.'[12]

Granted, what is being asked for here, in desiring the referent in its very advent, is technically somewhat different from the question of the

---

12. Marion, *God without Being*, pp. 144, 145, 147, emphasis added.

continuing empirical history of Jesus today. In Marion's case the question is how we, today, can have access to the empirical reality of the *original* Paschal event in its historical onceness, whereas the basic question we have been considering until now asks by comparison about the *continuing* empirical history of Jesus, the Christ, today. But whatever significance that difference might otherwise turn out to have, nevertheless the questions are fundamentally alike insofar as both recognize the onceness and the unrepeatability of the original historical event, and both are concerned with the theological demand of a real empirical (non-abstract) encounter with the Christological 'referent' in present reality, in a way that stands in full continuity with the referent in its very advent. What I propose to do over the next few pages is first to follow Marion's account of the particular difficulty faced by theology in its demand for 'the referent in its very advent', and then secondly to show how he finds the Eucharist to be capable uniquely of responding to the problem of theological reference as such.

In a way that is reminiscent of what MacKinnon was attempting to achieve for theological discourse through his focus on tragedy-as-discourse, Marion likewise considers how various other forms of discourse treat their 'referents', in order subsequently to draw attention to the unparalleled difficulty involved in the task of theological reference. Firstly, the novel or fiction 'as regards the referent, either dispenses with it ([Flaubert's] Emma Bovary, [Goethe's] Werther . . . "do not exist") or rediscovers it in each of its readers (Emma Bovary "is me", Werther "is not me," etc.), which amounts to the same thing. In any case literature dispenses with having recourse to an event in order to find its referent in that event.' In other words, the novel, or other forms of fiction, or drama, do not in any way have to concern themselves with the empirical reality of their referent. Secondly, poetry, perhaps uniquely, 'provokes, if not produces, its referent by a pure and simple text: the very emotion that the letter causes in us; immanent, this referent, in a sense, does not constitute one'. Thirdly, history (i.e., not empirical history but history as a form of discourse) 'publishes an abolished text, or rather publishes the text of an abolished referent at which one aims to the very extent that it remains abolished, undone'.[13] All of this now serves as a preamble or as a backdrop to set the theological task in particularly sharp relief. For theology demands not a fictitious referent nor an emerging referent nor an abolished one, but a *real* referent in the full, empirical sense of the term. Moreover, theology then

13. Marion, *God without Being*, pp. 145–6.

radically intensifies the difficulty of its own task by demanding full continuity between the text and the real referent it announces. Thus, in Marion's account, the continuity-relation between text and referent demanded by theology is more radically opposed to the 'post-modern' *annulment* of the distinction between text and referent (as discussed in chapter 2) than anything we have seen so far, including even what the correspondence theories of metaphysical realism or atomic realism seek to achieve. Or one could say that Marion sets the 'correspondence' bar so extremely high for theological discourse, that in the face of it even the staunchest metaphysical realist or atomist would falter. For theological discourse or theological reference cannot be satisfied merely with the 'correspondence' of its statements on a propositional level with 'what is the case' (although this will enter into theological thinking and should not be minimized); but rather it demands a *continuity*, here and now, and even despite the essential *pastness* of the referent, with the *original* historical reality announced by the text: *the referent in its very advent*.

It is of course no accident that all of this appears to be moving towards what I have spoken of above as a finality of non-resolution; and there is indeed now a further and final difficulty, in a more strictly theological sense, that we encounter as we approach the sheer intractability of the theological task. This is that, in addition to its essential *pastness* as empirical history, the referent announced by the text is also *accomplished*, completed, finished definitively at Easter and hence at the origin.[14]

> The Paschal event is accomplished, the Paschal accomplishment has occurred (Luke 24:18 = John 19:28). For the disciples as for us, it no longer belongs to the present. Once things have happened there remain only words: for us, there remains the text of the New Testament, just as for the disciples there remained only the rumour, or already the chronicle, of the putting to death (Luke 24:17).

So the referent desired, given both its pastness and its completeness, is now doubly foreclosed to the demands of theological discourse; and this to the extent that, in Marion's own words, we must consider whether this 'hollowing out the gap between the text and the event, the sign and the referent' does not 'destroy the possibility in general of all authentically theological discourse'.[15]

14. Marion, *God without Being*, p. 158.
15. Marion, *God without Being*, p. 145.

Against this impasse, and now in the face of the failure of all other forms of discourse to provide any direction, 'theology alone remains; it claims to tell the only living one; it therefore must open up access to the referent... in its very advent'. But how can theology accomplish this in a genuinely orthodox way that retains integrity at both levels – that is, in a way that brings access genuinely to *transcendence* (i.e., avoids reductionism) and in a way that opens up genuine *access*, truly *human* access to this referent (i.e., avoids positivism)? Specifically, what theology requires for this task is a hermeneutic, an interpretive context, that will again open up access to this doubly foreclosed referent (and here we may insert as referent whatever it is that the text announces: incarnation, resurrection, salvation, sin, judgement, reconciliation and so on). In response to this, and building around a penetrating exegesis of the Emmaus story of Luke 24, Marion goes on to demonstrate how the Word himself provides this hermeneutic.

> Only the Word can give an authorized interpretation of the words (written or spoken) 'concerning him' ... The referent itself is interpreted in [the text] as referring only to itself: 'and Jesus himself (*autos*) approached and went with them ... and he himself (*autos*) said to them ... beginning with Moses and all the prophets, he carried out the hermeneutic at length, in the Scriptures, of what concerned him' (Luke 24:15, 25–27).

Thus the first principle for the theologian in undertaking the task of theology, Marion maintains, quoting Gregory of Nazianzus, is to imitate 'the theologian superior to him, our Saviour'.[16]

Yet even as the theologian thus imitates the superior theologian, how is it that the Word carries out this hermeneutic here and now in the days after his flesh? Marion's response to this question is: The Eucharist. And it is a circumspect and considered response, one that consciously and wilfully operates within a carefully constructed hermeneutical circle. To begin with, The Eucharist is offered not as the *form* or the framework of the hermeneutic, but, echoing Heidegger, and rather like the way to Emmaus itself, 'the Eucharist offers itself as the *place* for a hermeneutic. Offers itself as place: at the very moment of his recognition by the disciples [in the Emmaus story], the Word in flesh disappears: "for it is to your advantage that I go away" (John 16:7)'. The Eucharist, moreover, is the place where the Word himself 'intervenes in person ... to accomplish in this way

the hermeneutic'; and 'if the Word intervenes in person only in the eucharistic moment, [then] *the hermeneutic (and hence fundamental theology) will
take place, will have its place, only in the Eucharist*' (original emphasis). We thus
see two interlocking and mutually supporting elements at work here: the
Eucharist, as the place of the hermeneutic, and the *Word* who, while himself
visibly absent, 'characterizes the priest as his *person* and assimilates to himself those who assimilate him'. When we now bring to bear on place and
person the further fundamental components of the scriptural text itself,
and then also the community of faith, we have a nexus of elements comprising the 'hermeneutic site of theology' within which, 'thanks to the
liturgical service of the theologian par excellence, the bishop', through
whom the circle is made complete, genuine theological interpretation can
be exercised and theological discourse can take place.[17]

As creatively insightful and valuable, liturgically and otherwise, as
Marion's account doubtless is, perhaps especially in terms of the new
clarity and depth with which it expresses the problem of reference to
the transcendent per se, there are several key reasons why it nonetheless falls short of providing the kind of reference we require for theological discourse. In the first place, although it certainly does not constitute the kind of shortcut we briefly encountered earlier in Bonhoeffer's
hasty 'solution' in the Church, it remains no less enigmatic. The particular hermeneutic involving the eucharistic site, the bishop, the text and
the community of faith, although rich in meaning for the believing participant, nevertheless at bottom only reproduces at the eucharistic site,
or reconfigures in eucharistic terms, the very problem with which we are
seeking to come to terms. Secondly, Marion's account still reflects strong
elements of positivism along Barthian lines. It does not matter, finally,
whether the 'theologian . . . speaks well or poorly' for it is the Word who
'speaks our words'. The theologian must 'abandon . . . his discourse and
every linguistic initiative to the Word, in order to let himself be said by the
Word, as the Word lets himself be said by the Father – him, and in him, us
also.' Only 'the referent itself . . . Jesus himself . . . can aim at the referent
since he assures it'.[18] Only the bishop, who alone is invested by the *persona
Christi* authorizes the referent.

While not detracting from the supreme importance of what Marion
(or Barth) is saying here – and indeed, we will return to the importance

17. Marion, *God without Being*, pp. 151, 150–1, 152, original emphasis.
18. Marion, *God without Being*, pp. 144, 147.

of its focus in the final chapter – I have also written sufficiently above about the need for theology to avoid the kind of positivism toward which this points. Finally, Marion's account seems too specialized, too spatio-temporally particular in its sacramentality to serve properly as a basis for a comprehensive account of Christian thinking. We want fundamental theological discourse, after all, to be meaningfully possible outside of the actual Eucharistic celebration. And if we were to broaden this by suggesting that the Eucharist somehow provides the referent *vicariously* for the rest (the bulk) of our theological speech and writing and thinking, then this would be to make it precisely into the 'ideal actuality', on a new level, that we have been trying to overcome with respect to the original historical event itself, that is, with respect to the referent in its very advent. For these reasons we must look beyond Marion's eucharistic account in our search for the kind of empirical reference demanded by orthodoxy for theological thinking.

8

Penultimacy and Christology

This final chapter introduces and explores a different kind of 'hermeneutic' – the relationality of 'penultimate' and 'ultimate' – in order to address the difficulties still remaining with regard to the problem of theological reference, and accordingly to bring my own broader enquiry into Christian thinking to something of a conclusion. The penultimate/ ultimate formula as I will develop it here, leading into a particular kind of confrontation between epistemology and Christology, aims to provide an interpretive framework that is broader, more transparent and flexible than either the foregoing explorations in tragedy based on MacKinnon or the hermeneutic of the Eucharist in Marion, both of which are pursued and developed for somewhat similar purposes. The point of similarity is that Marion's desire for 'the referent in its very advent' and MacKinnon's insistence, amplified by his focus on tragedy, that the reality of the theological referent must be protected against idealism of any kind, even if this takes the form of an ideal actuality,[1] these two must be understood as expressions of the same fundamental concern, voiced in different ways. This shared concern is, at all costs, to *avoid abstraction* with regard to the theological referent, since an abstract referent is a guarantee of immanence, a logical exclusion of transcendence, in a way that empirical reality is not.[2]

---

1. That is, as explained in the previous chapter, allowing that Jesus Christ has indeed actually come in the flesh 2,000 years ago, and that *that* now becomes an 'ideal' or merely *conceptual* (i.e., abstract) model for theological reference.
2. Abstraction is a guarantee of immanence both because it is *abstract* (i.e., offering only a conceptual or ideal 'other' and thus no real other, since *as* an ideal other this is *my* 'other'), and because it is the quintessential domain of *resolution*, as explained in the previous chapter. The contrasting point here is not, of course, that empirical reality is anything like a 'guarantee' of transcendence, only that it is not a logical exclusion of it, and thus that if the transcendent is to be genuinely *encountered* at all it must be encountered here.

An abstract (non-empirical) referent would thus effectively mark the end of *theo*logy by the reduction of it to some form or other of religious phenomenology.

But there is also a second, related concern (implied in MacKinnon and explicit in Marion), and this is the need to provide a meaningful account of real empirical reference for theology today, in the time after 'the referent in its very advent'. MacKinnon essentially leaves us in negative territory here, even while bringing the problem of theological reference itself to light in important new ways. Marion likewise advances this discussion with depth of insight, with relevance and with economical clarity, especially in his characterization of the problem of reference to the transcendent as, at heart, 'the desire for the referent in its very advent'. Yet the scope here remains too narrow, the 'hermeneutic' of the Eucharist, while deeply important, too specialized; and Marion's whole enterprise still tends towards positivism. It is to this more specially defined task that I now bring, as a different kind of 'hermeneutic', the relationality of penultimacy and ultimacy.

1 Penultimacy

It will be clear, to begin with, that the relation expressed between penultimate and ultimate is not meant to be simply another way of stating our own broader theological-epistemological problem of the relation between the familiar and transcendent. Rather, the whole penultimate-ultimate relation is to be pictured as residing fully at the transcendent 'pole', in hopes of bringing some added texture or movement to the 'sheer intractability' that we encounter in the demand of the transcendent itself. It is important to emphasize, however, that this 'addition' of the penultimate *prior* to the ultimate, or the next-to-lastness of the penultimate *prior* to the lastness of the ultimate (the transcendent), is in no way meant to suggest the possibility of anything like a continuum from the familiar to the transcendent. It is introduced only in order to guide our thinking, in a new and hitherto largely unexplored way, as we seek to approach the transcendent in this new empirical (non-abstract) light. The prospect of such a continuum between the familiar and the transcendent, and the reductionism (or 'natural theology') implied by it, is clearly what Barth fears in his insistence along these lines that 'the ultimate, the eschaton is ... never the continuation ... but to the contrary always the *radical severance of everything penultimate'*.[3] Bonhoeffer's treatment of the relation, which I shall use as a rough basis for my own discussion in this chapter, is importantly different from this, while no less concerned about the dangers of reductionism. The comparison between Barth and Bonhoeffer on this point, for our purposes, can be summarized briefly as follows. Barth sees the penultimate as a kind of pinnacle of the immanent as it reaches for the transcendent, and accordingly as a sort of terminus for what the previous chapter called a finality of *resolution*. Bonhoeffer, by contrast, sees the penultimate as already 'the outer covering of the ultimate', and accordingly as already a finality of *non-resolution*.

One of the reasons that Bonhoeffer's treatment of the penultimate/ultimate relation is a more suitable or promising candidate than Barth's for the kind of broadly applicable hermeneutic we require for theological reference[4] is that he begins straightforwardly from the analytical or formal definitions of these terms themselves. In other words, just as we can know, for example, simply by examining its concept, that all the points on the circumference of a circle are equidistant from its centre, so we can discover certain things about the penultimate-ultimate relation simply by examining its concept. These analytical or formal meanings, moreover, are always universal meanings. The point is that Barth's definition of the ultimate as 'the radical *severance* of everything penultimate' is already a sharp and highly specialized theological departure from the analytical meaning of the relation in which *pen*ultimacy is *defined* in its essential relationality to ultimacy. Bonhoeffer's treatment of penultimate and ultimate, by contrast, builds much more naturally from the analytical meaning of the relation, as we shall see, and is thus a suitable candidate, in a way that Barth's is not, for the broad kind of interpretive framework we need. So it is indeed Bonhoeffer's account that I want to use now as something of a basis for my own discussion here. More specifically, I will build around Bonhoeffer's often puzzling and obscure (partly because unfinished) treatment of the relation between ultimate and penultimate in his *Ethics*; but I will also be especially concerned to show how this applies, importantly and relevantly for our concerns, to his Christology. But I begin with asking about penultimacy simply as an idea, in its analytical relation to ultimacy. In other words, in looking at it purely as an idea, I am not at

3. Karl Barth, *Das Wort Gottes und die Theologie*, Gesammelte Vorträge (Munich: Christian Kaiser Verlag, 1924), p. 67, emphasis added.
4. That is, in order to accommodate the genuineness of theological discourse in the wide array of contexts and circumstances in which it actually occurs.

all trying to impute any 'metaphysical' status to the penultimate as if this signified or reflected some underlying structure of 'the way things are'. I am merely looking at it analytically on a purely conceptual basis and then asking how its relation to the ultimate as a pure idea of the understanding might provide a 'hermeneutic', in Marion's sense, for the theological task of reference to the transcendent.

Purely analytically or formally then (i.e., by definition, before having stipulated any theological 'content' about the ultimate), we can say that the penultimate is most simply that which is next to last, or that which directly precedes the ultimate, that which leads into it. When we begin to try to appropriate this theologically, we find that the definition can be expanded somewhat without transgressing its legitimate formal or analytical parameters. The penultimate can be seen not only as that which precedes the ultimate, but also thereby anything that announces it, or that prepares the way for it. Yet the penultimate by definition as pen-*ultimate* can never claim any independent status apart from the ultimate; or as Bonhoeffer puts it, 'the penultimate is really nothing in itself, such that anything could be justified as penultimate of its own accord'. Rather, the penultimacy of what is next-to-last consists entirely in its 'being regarded as penultimate by the ultimate once the ultimate has been found. By the same token, it is everything which follows the ultimate in order once again to go before it.' In other words, because the penultimate must, so to speak, follow the ultimate wherever it goes in order to precede it or be next to it, therefore it can be seen as something like 'the outer covering of the ultimate' – but again, even here there is no way that this status could be seen as an independent possession of any sort. Instead, what is next to last 'becomes something penultimate only through the ultimate, which is to say, [it becomes a penultimate] in that moment in which it has become incapacitated or has lost its potency as anything in itself. It is not a condition of the ultimate, rather the ultimate conditions the penultimate. The penultimate is not a state of being in itself but is rather a judgment which the ultimate passes on that which has preceded it.'[5]

Still working roughly within what can be seen as the basic intelligibility of these formal or definitional parameters, Bonhoeffer depicts this *unidirectional* dependency as so complete that he insists that 'there can be no "method", no way to the ultimate' from the penultimate. Rather,

---

5. Dietrich Bonhoeffer, *Ethik*, Ilse Tödt, Heinz Eduard Tödt, Ernst Feil and Clifford Green (eds.), Dietrich Bonhoeffer Werke, 16 vols. (Munich: Christian Kaiser Verlag, 1998), vol. VI, pp. 149, 151.

penultimacy can concern itself only with 'preparing the way' (*Wegbereitung*) for the ultimate to come to *it*. The real theological significance of this difference between *preparing* the way *for* the ultimate and *finding* or making a way *to* the ultimate becomes especially clear once it is recognized, as Bonhoeffer says, that this 'way' from ultimate to penultimate is the way of the cross that only Jesus Christ himself can and must go.[6] Or, to make the connection more explicitly in the terminology of chapter 4, the 'preparing' disposition of penultimacy is shown to be something fundamentally different from the 'making' and 'finding' dispositions of idealism and realism. For the penultimate knows that it has no capacity to 'make' or to 'find' a way to the ultimate (i.e., to the incarnation, cross and resurrection of Jesus Christ: the 'referent in its very advent'), but that it can only make preparation for the ultimate to make its own way. Holism is thus indirectly shown to be the full antithesis of the basic disposition of penultimacy here, for holism is serene and confident in its ambitions for ultimate unity, or resolution, whereas penultimacy remains perpetually burdened with the task of preparing the way for the ultimate, which must come as non-resolution.

2   Autonomous and creaturely ways of being human

But aside from these general and more formal considerations, which remain obscure apart from some empirical reference, how can the penultimate now be made tangible for theological purposes? The heart of Bonhoeffer's answer to this question, despite the vital importance of it overall, is addressed only obliquely in his *Ethics* itself, and is left largely undeveloped. After giving several examples of particular actions that are specified as penultimate insofar as they uniquely 'prepare the way' for the ultimate, Bonhoeffer asserts that, beyond all of the above general qualifications, it is *Menschsein* or 'being human' that, for theological purposes, is the real empirical centre of everything penultimate.[7] But again, this remains rather opaque in *Ethics* itself, and much of what I propose to do for the balance of this chapter is to explore the fuller meaning of this claim. Specifically, what does it mean to say that 'being

---

6. Bonhoeffer, *Ethik*, p. 159.
7. Actually, Bonhoeffer asserts specifically that 'Empirically speaking [*Konkret*] . . . two things are addressed as penultimate: being human (*Menschsein*) and being good (*Gutsein*)' (Bonhoeffer, *Ethik*, p. 151). It is *Menschsein*, however, that is the more fundamental of these two as it is the condition for the possibility of the second.

human' can be the most basic penultimate, theologically speaking? And secondly, how can this help us to articulate an appropriate response to the problem of how reference to or characterization of the transcendent is possible?

We can gain some important insight on how Bonhoeffer himself understood this assertion by looking outside of his *Ethics*, to two earlier works in particular. In *Act and Being* and *Creation and Fall* we find that it is not just 'human being' per se that is addressed in *Menschsein* as the most basic penultimate, but rather a certain way of being human, or a certain orientation to human being. At the close of *Act and Being*, Bonhoeffer compares two very different ways of being human: *autonomous human being* and *creaturely human being*. Let me just relay Bonhoeffer's definition of each of these briefly to begin with, without yet asking about his justifications for making the distinction, or about the specific relations involved in it. Autonomous human being is, of course, a self-sufficient way of being human. It is based on a kind of self-understanding that perceives human being as capable of placing itself into the truth about itself, in some basic way, including the truth about the world it inhabits. Such an autonomous way of being human, in Bonhoeffer's words, is ultimately 'imprisoned within itself, it sees only itself . . . it understands itself out of itself, which means at bottom that it does not understand itself at all . . . it thinks itself to be free and is imprisoned; it stands fully empowered but rules only over itself. This is what protestant theology means by the corruption of reason. It is the ontic introversion into oneself, the *cor curvum in se*.'[8]

In direct contraposition to the *cor curvum in se* of autonomous human being, 'creaturely being' is then presented as 'the human being of the believer'.[9] Creaturely being, Bonhoeffer says, is *non*-autonomous human being in true freedom; it is human self-understanding that has 'moved out from under the power of I into the power and authority of Christ and only here recognizes itself in its original freedom as a creature of God'.[10] It is, of course, specifically this *creaturely* way of being human, this creaturely way of *Menschsein*, which is to be understood as that which is spoken of in *Ethics* as 'the most basic penultimate'. But we must again look elsewhere to discover what Bonhoeffer means by this more exactly. The idea begins to come clearly to expression in *Creation and Fall*, in Bonhoeffer's brief but influential account of theological analogy, *analogia*

---

8. Dietrich Bonhoeffer, *Akt und Sein*, Hans-Richard Reuther (ed.), Dietrich Bonhoeffer Werke, 16 vols. (Munich: Christian Kaiser Verlag, 1988), vol. II, p. 39.
9. Bonhoeffer, *Akt und Sein*, p. 150.
10. Bonhoeffer, *Akt und Sein*, p. 149.

relationis. 'The creatureliness of the human being, no less than its freedom, is not a quality, not something locatably "there" (*Vorfindliches*), nor is it any existing thing . . . The "image that is like God" [or] the likeness, the *analogia* of human beings to God is not *analogia entis* but *analogia relationis*.' This means two things fundamentally. First, 'even the *relatio* is not a human capacity, possibility, a structure of human existence; rather it is the ordered relation which comes as a gift and into which humans are placed'. It follows, secondly, that 'this *analogia* may not be understood as though human beings somehow had this likeness as a possession or as a claim; rather, *analogia* or resemblance is to be understood very strictly in the sense that the simulacrum (*das Ähnliche*) has its resemblance *alone* from the original or archetype (*Urbild*), that it always directs us as such only to the archetype and in this directedness *alone* can be said to "resemble".'[11]

Even more straightforwardly, Bonhoeffer speaks elsewhere about the fundamental problem involved in 'interpreting one's human-being as "*one's own*" being'. '"One's own" being, that is, the structural being of creatureliness, is being which derives from God. There is no possibility here of a formal ontology. [Creaturely] being is always *in reference to* being, in other words, *analogia relationis*, not *entis*.' And then comes the really pivotal statement around which this whole connection of creaturely human being to penultimacy comes to its most important expression: 'Because humans have their being from God, they do not understand themselves from out of themselves, but only from God.'[12] In view of all of this, it is now easy to see how this theological definition of creaturely being meets the formal stipulations for penultimacy, as discussed above, and thus qualifies, as Bonhoeffer wants it to do, as 'the most basic penultimate': because creaturely being recognizes that it 'is really nothing in itself such that [it] could be justified of its own accord'; because it recognizes that 'it is not a state of being in itself' but rather that it has its being entirely 'from a judgment that the ultimate passes on it'; and because it recognizes as such that it cannot 'understand itself from out of itself but only from God', that is, from the ultimate: therefore a creaturely way of being human is a penultimate, and indeed the most basic penultimate since, at least instrumentally, it is a condition for the possibility of all other penultimates.

---

11. Dietrich Bonhoeffer, *Schöpfung und Fall*, Martin Rueter and Ilse Tödt (eds.), Dietrich Bonhoeffer Werke, 16 vols. (Munich: Christian Kaiser Verlag, 1989), vol. III, pp. 60f., original emphasis.
12. Dietrich Bonhoeffer, 'Dogmatische Übungen "Theologische Psychologie"', in Carsten Nicolaisen and Ernst-Albert Scharffenorth (eds.), *Berlin, 1932–1933*, Dietrich Bonhoeffer Werke, 16 vols. (Munich: Christian Kaiser Verlag, 1991), vol. XII, p. 184, emphasis slightly altered.

However, all of this has been given really only to set a preliminary framework for the main task that still awaits us, and that task is as follows. Most basically, and by far the most crucially, we must provide some sort of authorizing account or explanation of this ostensible movement from an autonomous or self-enclosed way of being human to a creaturely or penultimate way of being human. In other words, this must somehow be made tangibly meaningful and empirically intelligible to the individual questioner, and not just suggestive or speculative. Secondly, and on this basis, it must be demonstrated how this can provide the kind of empirical reference, in the truly comprehensive way that we require, for the problem of theological thinking. But there is also a third problem here: as chapter 7 showed, this authorizing account itself will not be able to appeal at bottom to a justification based on *resolution*, for that would mean a logical exclusion of transcendence or ultimacy and by extension also of penultimacy. And this leads to the following conundrum. In order for this authorizing account to be genuinely *authoritative*, it must somehow be *recognizable* as authoritative.[13] Yet how is it possible that an authority could be recognizable as *noetically* (or conceptually) authoritative, except on the basis of resolution, since all conceptual or discursive authority is measured and demonstrated on the basis of resolution? This is the problem that confronts us here, and it can be seen as building towards a particular kind of confrontation between the demands of epistemology and the demands of Christology. Or in the language of chapter 7, it builds towards a confrontation between the demands of rational authentication based on *resolution* and the demands of transcendence or the ultimate (the referent in its very advent, the life, death and resurrection of Jesus Christ) based on *non-resolution*. In order to create a framework for exploring this encounter, and in order to demonstrate the intelligibility of Christological authority in confrontation with epistemology, I now bring together aspects of Bonhoeffer's Christology lectures and Kierkegaard's *The Sickness unto Death*.

3   A 'derivation' of penultimacy as creaturely human being

3.1   The human classifying logos and the Logos of God

Bonhoeffer's Christology papers are especially appropriate to our concerns because they begin in exactly the kind of confrontation with epistemology

---

13. Or conversely, anything that declares itself to be an authority, but is recognized by no one as such, is hardly a genuine authority.

that I have just outlined, a confrontation that comes to be framed in terms of an encounter between the human classifying logos (rationality) and the Logos of God, or what Bonhoeffer will call the 'Counter-logos'. Bonhoeffer outlines a progressive sequence of cognitive events on the basis of which this confrontation unfolds. I begin with a somewhat amplified and recontextualized version of that here, for current purposes.

Philosophers often differentiate between two basic ways of knowing, or two different ways of justifying knowledge claims. One kind of knowledge is gained by observing empirical causes and origins, the other by analysing the meanings of terms. Thus, I can make knowledge claims, say, about a medical epidemic, such as the recent global SARS outbreak, by acquainting myself with its causes and origins whether geographically, sociologically or biologically. Knowledge here comes by *explanation* through establishing causal connections. This kind of knowledge or understanding is gained in a different way from my understanding, say, of the terms 'bachelor' or 'quadrangle' or 'quinquagenarian'. Knowledge here comes by *analysis* of the definitions of these terms or by analysing, within a given linguistic frame of reference, what these terms are said to refer to or to mean. This distinction has been a commonplace within traditional philosophy. For example, it corresponds basically to Hume's division of knowledge, as we encountered it in chapter 6, into matters of fact and the relations of ideas. Hume went so far as to maintain that these two species of knowing do not overlap. Kant recognized (roughly) the same division in his distinction between a posteriori and a priori cognition, but claimed that these kinds of knowing (matters of fact and relations of ideas) can indeed overlap in what he called synthetic a priori knowledge. Again, this distinction is also what the logical positivists were speaking about when they claimed that all genuine knowledge claims must be either empirically (causally) verifiable or analytically true (true by definition or by the meanings of terms).

It is true that the authenticity of these kinds of distinctions has recently come into question, perhaps most influentially in Quine's essay 'Two Dogmas of Empiricism'.[14] But that is beside the point for the present line of reasoning. The reason for drawing attention to these different basic kinds of human knowing is to point out that, however they may or may not be connected, all of them are fundamentally concerned with and based on questions of *classification*, or of classificatory ordering. This is what

14. W. V. O. Quine, 'Two Dogmas of Empiricism', in *From a Logical Point of View* (Cambridge, MA: Harvard University Press 1961), pp. 20–46.

Bonhoeffer means when he says that the question of knowledge, whether scientific or philosophical, is most essentially a question of 'How?' or of possibility: that is, the possibility of accounting for any object of scrutiny (material or purely conceptual) within some broader, intelligible classificatory frame of reference. The central question here is always: *How* does any object of scrutiny fit within an existing or given order of things?[15] Note here that it does not matter whether this 'existing order' is understood as 'real' (roughly externalist, metaphysical, atomist, based on correspondence theory) or 'ideal' (roughly internalist, conceptual, phenomenological, based on coherence theory). It must only be a genuine *order*, a classificatory framework, that is, intelligible as having or aspiring towards a certain unity or resolution. So again, the 'object' under scrutiny (whether conceptual or empirical) is identified and understood, and knowledge about that object justified – whether through analysis or explanation, conceptual meaning or causal origin – always on the basis of its 'How?', that is, on the basis of its 'possibility'. The summary point to which all of this is leading is that the final justificatory authority of any human enquiry is the human *classifying logos*, or rationality.[16]

Against this basic backdrop, let us now suppose a scenario in which the human classifying logos encounters a kind of subject matter that refuses to submit to this classifying authority. What happens then? Bonhoeffer himself poses this question directly with a Christological subject matter in mind; and we will come to that presently. But actually we have already seen two instances of this sort of resistance to the claims of reason in the preceding chapters, one in Kant and one in MacKinnon. In Kant, as we will recall, the empirical object was encountered by reason as an inherently *manifested* object; that is, as an object fundamentally reflecting 'extensive (spatio-temporal) magnitudes' which, it was found, reason can never give to itself out of its own purely rational categories, or can never concoct out of its own logical powers, but rather which are 'given' *to* reason through sensory intuition. Moreover, when reason, in the face of these limitations, ignored its own inability to engender or explain, from pure reason alone,

15. Dietrich Bonhoeffer, 'Vorlesung "Christologie"', in Carsten Nicolaisen and Ernst-Albert Scharffenorth (eds.), *Berlin, 1932–1933*, Dietrich Bonhoeffer Werke, 16 vols. (Munich: Christian Kaiser Verlag, 1991), vol. XII, p. 281.
16. This incidentally is true even of the current so-called anti-rational approaches discussed in chapter 2, which invariably opt for different modes of ordering or classification (based on pragmatism, archeo-genealogy, solidarity or even undecidability), and indeed often give these the same predominance as what they repudiate in rational classification as hegemonic and as a 'ruse'.

either the extensive magnitudes of space and time or the empirical reality constituted in (or constituting) these magnitudes; and when reason persisted in demanding answers *on its own terms* with respect to empirical reality, that is, persisted with the purely rational classificatory requirements of 'How?' or of possibility, two kinds of errors occurred. We found that this not only gave rise to explicit contradictions ('subreption', and more broadly the 'antinomies' of pure reason), but also that reason thereby forfeited its own basic integrity by forcibly asserting its authority in areas over which it had no demonstrable jurisdiction.[17]

Our study of tragedy in MacKinnon gave us another example of a subject matter that refuses to submit to the classifying authority of reason. To demand a rational resolution to tragedy, or to allege a general or theoretical solution to the problem of evil, ignores the sheer particularity of tragedy and evil and violates the integrity of the private human undoing within which the tragedy really, empirically unfolds, by treating this theoretically and abstractly. Both empirical reality and the reality of tragedy are thus found to confront reason with a challenge that acts as a kind of limit for what reason can properly claim with respect to objects of experience.

With this in mind then, when we come to Christological subject matter – the referent in its very advent, that is, the incarnation, death and resurrection of Jesus Christ – we face, on the one hand, a similar resistance, and yet, on the other, a completely new kind of challenge to the authority of autonomous reason. On the one similar level, the challenge is indeed a refusal by the transcendent or the ultimate (like the empirical object or tragedy, as just discussed) to submit to the general classifying authority of reason. But Christological subject matter will be shown also to be radically different inasmuch as it mounts a challenge against the very authority of the human logos to be *its own final presupposition*, or to be the *condition of its own possibility*: a challenge, that is, against the very claim of the

---

17. The point is not of course that reason overextends itself simply through the classification of empirical objects. There is a perfectly legitimate synthetic classification of the objects of experience as we enquire into the world. This is what makes scientific enquiry (and indeed, as Kant will claim, all *genuine* 'cognition') possible. The point is only that when reason tries to understand these *essentially extended* objects purely on the basis of its own rational categories (i.e., prior to the synthetic categories that arise when empirical content is imported), then it sacrifices its own integrity by violating the integrity of the empirical object through inadmissibly demanding that the empirical object comply fully with purely rational requirements. Whether one is a 'Kantian' on these issues or not (and I hope the discussion in chapter 6 will have gone some way to providing a convincing defence of the plausibility and current relevance of a Kantian approach), one will at least be able to see the kind of logic underlying that position, which warns against the overextension of reason.

classifying logos to be able to place itself into the truth about itself and the world. It is in this second aspect of the confrontation that the Logos of God now truly reveals itself as 'Counter-logos'. For the Counter-logos – in a way that remains to be more fully explained – will not only negatively challenge the authority of the human classifying logos to be able to *make* this self-authenticating claim, but it will then also positively demand further that this authority belongs to the Counter-logos alone, that is, that the Counter-logos alone is able to place the human logos into the truth about itself and the world.

So then, what happens or how does the human classificatory logos respond when it is addressed and challenged in this way? The first and most natural response will be to construe this challenge once again as a formally rational challenge, that is, as a challenge to reason on its own terms. And accordingly the human logos will repeat its old formal, classificatory question of 'how' such a strange counter-claim could be possible at all. Indeed, as such, it may even succeed in assimilating the Counter-logos, still understood in these formal or abstract terms, into itself,[18] in the way, for example, that Hegel does in his movement of double negation, in which the human logos is in the end reaffirmed in 'higher' and accentuated ways; or as, for example, newer versions of holism do in a similar manner, by progressively broadening the scope of vision so as to include and counterbalance all conflicting elements in order that, at all costs, unity, reflective equilibrium, resolution is achieved.

However, it is at this point, in the face of the unrelenting insistence of autonomous human self-understanding to be permitted to encounter all of its 'subject matter' entirely on its own formally rational (classificatory) terms, it is here that the Christological challenge now finally declares its *own* 'form'. The Counter-logos declares itself in a 'form' that allows for no possibility of 'formal' classificatory assimilation into the human logos, and as such demands to be encountered entirely on *its* own terms. Bonhoeffer describes this particular 'station' in the unfolding Christological-epistemological confrontation in the following way:

> But what happens if the Counter-logos suddenly stakes its claim in a radically new form (*Gestalt*) – not proclaiming itself as an idea or a word which challenges the dominion of rationality; but rather in such a way that the Counter-logos appears somewhere and sometime in history as a human being, and *as* this human being declares itself to be the

18. Bonhoeffer, 'Vorlesung "Christologie"', p. 282.

judgment over the human logos, over rationality, and says: 'I am the truth', I am the death of autonomous human self-understanding, I am the Logos of God, the first and the last? . . . Here there is no longer any possibility of assimilating the incarnate Word into rational classification. Here there is only one question which remains: Who are you?'[19]

We will come to the centrality of this question 'Who are you?' presently. But first, it is important to recognize that this challenge by the Counter-logos is not mounted specifically against the authority or dominion of rationality, as if in Jesus Christ human reason merely encounters an infinitely greater mind, or as if in this encounter 'like meets like' and human rationality is merely quantitatively superseded. For if this were the case, the classifying logos would still be able to assimilate the challenge of the Counter-logos into itself because it would be a challenge still based on resolution. That Christ, as the Counter-logos, is the final challenge to and the 'end' of human rationality means neither the abrogation of the formal nature of rationality nor, as we shall see, the undermining of the proper authority of reason in the natural order. Instead, Christ as the Counter-logos is the challenge to the very 'manner of existence' of rationality, to its own very *ontology*, that is, to its self-understanding as its own final presupposition or precondition. The Counter-logos successfully mounts this challenge by confronting rationality not as the supreme 'formal' idea, nor as the highest in an ontological 'order' or hierarchy of being, but rather as the 'form' (*Gestalt*) of Christ which is his body.[20] In the face of a 'formal' confrontation, human rationality can still respond on its own terms of 'How?' and 'What?', of act and being, of possibility and essence. But in the confrontation with the 'form' (*Gestalt*) of Christ, rationality is silenced. The only proper response here, indeed in one sense the only 'possible' response, is 'Who are you?', because to continue to address this *Gestalt* with 'How?' questions yields impossible answers.

3.2 'Who are you?' as the question of transcendence

The focal point of the confrontation between the human logos (rationality) and the Counter-logos (revelation) then, or between epistemology and Christology, is the question 'Who are you?' And it is around this question that we must now pursue and try to bring to completion our own

19. Bonhoeffer, 'Vorlesung "Christologie"', p. 282.
20. Bonhoeffer, 'Vorlesung "Christologie"', pp. 282, 286; cf. also Bonhoeffer, *Ethik*, p. 84.

enquiry into Christian thinking, an endeavour that until now has been formulated around the question of how reference to or characterization of the transcendent is possible. Now a central axiom of the basic problem of Christian thinking, from which our whole study proceeds, is that there could never be an 'ontology of transcendence'. That is, there could never be a rationally structured account of the 'being' of transcendence, even if only for the purely logical reason that such an account is precisely what transcendence *transcends*. Yet Bonhoeffer, without really explaining himself, now goes on to claim that the question 'Who are you?' is *both* the question of transcendence *and* the question of ontology and *as* both of these, it is the Christological question par excellence. I must try to make this clear.

In the first place, the contention that 'Who are you?' is an ontological question seems straightforward enough since it asks about the being of that which confronts the questioner. But what does it mean to say that 'Who?' is 'the question of transcendence' (in contrast to 'How?' which is 'the question of immanence')? The problem we are facing here is elaborated by Bonhoeffer himself more fully as follows:

> The question 'Who?' expresses the strangeness and the otherness of the one encountered and at the same time it is shown to be the question concerning the very existence of the questioner. He is asking about the being which is strange to his being, about the boundaries of his own existence. Transcendence places his own being in question.[21]

We can gain some preliminary clarity on this enigmatic assertion by approaching it first of all in a more straightforward ethical sense. On an ethical level this can be understood to mean that in the challenge of the Counter-logos I recognize before me a Person, an 'other', who, as *subject*, is beyond objectification and thus transcends all my knowing. There is an essential epistemological aspect even to this 'ethical' construal of transcendence, however, especially with respect to the claim that as *subject* you, my neighbour, are beyond objectification. The reason that your subjectivity transcends all my knowing, in a way that mere objects do not, is of course that your subjective experience of self and world – the conscious, self-aware 'having' of it – remains utterly yours, subjectively and unobjectifiably. As soon as I claim to 'know' or 'share' your experience, I find that all I really 'know' is an *idea* of your subjective experience or perhaps an empathetic approximation of it (which is still an objectification),

21. Bonhoeffer, 'Vorlesung "Christologie"', p. 283; cf. Dietrich Bonhoeffer, *Christ the Center*, tr. Edwin H. Robertson (San Francisco: Harper, 1960), pp. 30–31.

and never really your own 'what-it's-like' subjective reality and self-understanding.

In the same way that I can never 'get behind' myself to view myself as an object, but always find myself already there as the subject that is *doing* the viewing, so now accordingly I recognize you as an *other* 'subject' before me, a subject who is beyond objectification in the same way that I am, and who thus transcends my knowing. Accordingly, you yourself present a boundary or limit to me, as 'an other I', in a way that no object could ever do, and effectively as such you place a constraint on my freedom and by extension on my existence as a subject who knows itself as free. Or as Emmanuel Levinas says, 'to welcome the Other is to put in question my freedom'.[22] What this whole problematic is centrally concerned with is the claims to *possessiveness* that are implicit in all classificatory or rational discourse. And the ethical point here is that to encounter this other as 'Who?' or as an 'other I', as one who transcends my knowing, is tacitly to recognize this 'Who?' as transcending all such claims to possessiveness over it.

But Bonhoeffer's statement that 'Who?' is the question of transcendence is more than just this ethical claim; or it is something like a radicalized version of it. In fact he implies that the question 'Who?' can never be asked genuinely or with full integrity in any merely epistemological or even ethical context. The reason for this, we might say, is that the human logos can never *actually* ask the question 'Who?' in the truly dispossessive way that the question itself demands. We do of course ask it on social and ethical levels, but the contention is that we invariably employ the question itself as just another way of classifying and, as such, objectifying. In other words, the real intent of 'Who are you?' in these contexts still inevitably amounts to something like: 'Tell me how you are, tell me how you think, and I will tell you who you are.' This, Bonhoeffer says, is a 'secularized reduction of the true question, "Who?"', which in its integrity is 'simply *the* religious question . . . posed for every life'.[23]

The real point we can draw here then for our purposes is that only in the challenge of the Counter-logos can the question 'Who?' be asked without any vestiges of 'How?', or of possibility. Or in other words, only in confrontation with the Counter-logos does the question 'Who are you?' become a *genuinely dispossessive* question. And the reason this can be so is

22. Emmanuel Levinas, *Totality and Infinity*, A. Lingis (tr.) (Pittsburgh: Duquesne University Press, 1969), p. 85.
23. Bonhoeffer, 'Vorlesung "Christologie"', p. 283; cf. *Christ the Center*, p. 31.

that the Counter-logos mounts a challenge that is not merely quantitative, but is rather a challenge to the autonomous self's *very manner of existence*, to its own very *ontology* which operates naturally and intrinsically according to these 'possessive' questions and which claims to know itself and the world *by means of* them. The difference then, at bottom, compared to ethics, is that the Christological encounter is a challenge not only as an *'other I'* (which the human logos can always still refashion into something classificatory or quantitative), but rather much more a challenge to the *autonomous self's own* basic self-understanding *as* 'I', to its whole ontology *as* 'I', defined as the kind of self-understanding or ontology that claims self-sufficiency, or that the human logos can place itself into the truth about itself.

Bonhoeffer leaves us basically with this result without much further clarification. However, we need considerably more than this in order to follow through properly with the 'derivation' of creaturely human being from autonomous human being. What more can we say about this question 'Who are you?' other than its characterization as the question of transcendence? To begin with, in light of the fully dispossessive stance or disposition that the human logos now at last assumes in confrontation with the Counter-logos, it might seem initially as if the 'Who are you?' spoken here reflects something like an appropriate disposition of worship and reverence before the transcendent. Or it might seem at least that here the human logos manifests a temperament of humility out of which worship can spring, and that here, in the question 'Who are you?', we have finally located our 'reference' to the transcendent.

But although worship will indeed have to be both the source and ultimate goal of any genuine theological discourse, such an understanding would not only engage in exactly the kind of positivistic shortcut we are trying to avoid, but it would also fundamentally misread the character here of 'Who are you?' For the state of autonomous reason here, even in its dispossessive comportment, is surely not one of quietude and rest, much less one of adoration and reverence. It is rather, at least initially as I want to suggest, reason in a state of profound despair. Bonhoeffer himself seems to point to this when he describes the question 'Who are you?' at this juncture as 'the question of dethroned reason, appalled and languishing'; but to this he then adds, 'and it is also the question of faith'.[24] Here we reach what is arguably the most crucial moment in this whole

24. Bonhoeffer, 'Vorlesung "Christologie"', p. 282.

'derivation' of creaturely human being from autonomous human being. For it will be precisely this unavoidable path through intellectual despair that will be found to guard not only the present 'derivation', but our whole enquiry into Christian thinking against resorting to positivism or succumbing to reductionism. In other words, it is an indispensable moment for the preservation of integrity in theological thinking; and in order to explore in proper depth what is involved in this 'moment', we must turn to Kierkegaard's treatment of despair as developed in *The Sickness unto Death*.

3.3 'Who are you?' as a question of despair

Kierkegaard's whole discussion of despair is set around the definition of the human self as a self-relating relation. We must look briefly at this construal of the self in order to understand the despair that he sees arising from it. 'The human self', says Kierkegaard, 'is a relation that relates itself to itself and in relating itself to itself relates itself to another.'[25] We can best understand this by setting it out in three stages. With respect to just the first half of the definition, to begin with, we can say this: The human self recognizes itself as a psycho-somatic unity, or a mind-body unity, or an I-as-subject/me-as-object unity. The human self, of course, is neither just 'I' nor just 'me'; indeed the human self understands itself as somehow the inseparable relation of these two. But the self is not solely the *relation* of I and me, for that would merely be something negative or abstract.[26] No, the human self knows itself as a *positive* 'third'. It is not just the relation of I and me; it is rather the *relation that relates* the I and the me. It is the 'third' within which the synthesis of the two occurs consciously.

The second point about this definition of the self is straightforward. *As* such a self-relating relation, a self must either have established *itself* (and this would include, we might add here, any 'establishment' by the self's own world of immanent causes and processes) or it must have been established *by another*. And then thirdly, following from this, if the self has indeed been established by another, then this 'other' enters into the self's very understanding of itself as that through which (or in relation to which) the self must come to a proper understanding of itself as a self-relating

25. Søren Kierkegaard, *The Sickness unto Death*, Howard V. Hong and Edna H. Hong (eds. and tr.) (Princeton: Princeton University Press, 1980), pp. 13–14.
26. The simple relation between I and me or mind and body is 'negative' in two senses: first, because it is *neither* 'I' *nor* 'me' but merely a conceptual (abstract) relation between them; and secondly, *as* a purely conceptual or abstract relation between I and me, it is negative also in the sense of 'non-substantial'.

synthesis. And this is indeed a Christian, or a theistic understanding of the human self: 'a relation that relates itself to itself and in relating itself to itself relates itself to another'.

Now it is possible for this self-relating relation, the self, to be in a state of *mis*relation; and Kierkegaard calls this state of misrelation 'despair'. Strictly speaking there can be two forms of despair or misrelation. If the self had established itself, there could only be the one form of despair: 'to will *not* to be oneself', that is, to will not to be the self-relating relation that one is, 'to will to do away with oneself', or most simply, to will to die. But if the self-relating relation is established by another, then there can also be another form of despair in addition to the first. This second form of despair turns out to be formulated as something like an opposite of the first. It is: 'in despair *to will to be* oneself', that is, despite having been established by another, *still* to will to be oneself autonomously and thus to be in an actual state of misrelation with oneself. Kierkegaard then goes on to explain how all despair can ultimately be traced back to this second form of despair, or that this is the most fundamental form of despair.[27] Moreover, the magnitude of this second and most fundamental misrelation is infinite. For because this 'misrelation of despair is not a simple misrelation but a misrelation in a relation that relates itself to itself and has been established by another, [therefore] the misrelation in that relation which is *for itself* also reflects itself infinitely in the relation to the power that established it'. In direct opposition to this is Kierkegaard's formula for the state of the self 'when despair is completely rooted out', which is 'also the formula for faith'. This opposing formula runs as follows: 'in relating itself to itself *and in willing to be itself*, the self rests transparently in the power that established it'.[28]

Now the parallels here to Bonhoeffer's autonomous and creaturely ways of being human are obvious, as is Bonhoeffer's basic indebtedness to Kierkegaard on these points. Bonhoeffer's autonomous human being, which claims to be able to place itself into the truth about itself, is precisely Kierkegaard's self 'for itself' which is the self in misrelation with itself (and with God). Bonhoeffer's creaturely human being, which knows that its being is from God and therefore that it cannot understand itself from out of itself but only from God, is Kierkegaard's self which, in willing

27. As we shall see, part of the logic underlying this will be that to claim to be a self-established self (including establishment by the self's world of immanent causes and processes) *just is* to be in despair but to be ignorant of it.
28. Kierkegaard, *The Sickness unto Death*, pp. 15, 14, 49, emphasis added.

to be itself, rests transparently in the power that established it. I will begin to apply these parallels to my main 'derivation' again presently. But in order to do that successfully, I need to make one further clarification on what can seem to be a puzzling distinction between what Kierkegaard refers to as the *possibility* of despair, which in his words is 'a surpassing excellence', and the *actuality* of despair, which is 'misery and ruination'.

The explanation for this is as follows: To be *actually* in despair is precisely to be *unaware* of being in despair. It is 'despair that is the ignorance of being in despair'.[29] That is, to be *actually* in this state of misrelation in which the self is 'for itself' (in Kierkegaard's terms), or in which the self as autonomous human being claims to 'understand itself out of itself' (in Bonhoeffer's terms), is precisely to be *unconscious* of being *in* that state of misrelation. The reason for this is that the misrelation of despair, which Kierkegaard also calls a 'sickness', is not something that 'happens' to the autonomous self or comes upon it as a normal disease or sickness. It is not the corruption or infection of something that is fundamentally or essentially whole, such that the removal of the corruption or infection would yield the self in its soundness or health. No, in this instance, the sickness or corruption is the misrelation *itself*, such that the removal of the sickness would mean the removal of the self itself. We will return to this again presently, but the point to be made for now is that the *actuality* of despair is 'ruination'. As such, it is essentially what Bonhoeffer, citing Luther, spoke of above as the *cor curvum in se*, the heart (and mind) turned in upon itself, the ontic introversion of the self into itself.

By contrast, the *possibility* of being in despair is a 'surpassing excellence' and 'an infinite advantage'. 'The possibility of this sickness is man's superiority over the animal . . . for it indicates . . . that he is spirit.' Or to explain this more fully in somewhat different words: it is precisely the self's capacity for recognizing that *in willing to be itself* it is capable of being in a state of *mis*relation that marks its first 'glimpse' of *itself* as *non*-autonomous, its first 'glimpse' of the power that established it, and thus its first glimpse of its own eternal nature.

In light of all of this then, we now come to the connection to be made to the question 'Who are you?', which is spoken in the meeting between autonomous human being and the Counter-logos. And the point I wish to make here is that 'Who are you?', in this very first articulation, denotes precisely the ascending from the actuality of despair to the possibility of

29. Kierkegaard, *The Sickness unto Death*, p. 21.

despair. It does not denote an immediate ascendancy into worship or even into faith; yet this move into the possibility of despair is indispensable for faith. For it signals the self's first awareness of the despair that the self really, actually inhabits. The question in its first articulation is thus essentially an expression of what Kierkegaard calls 'despair over oneself'. This means that it is not in the first place despair over the self's relation to the Counter-logos, to the power that establishes it. It is not in the first place concern over this relation. It is rather despair over the self's *own* autonomous human being in the face of its demise. Kierkegaard likens this to the despair of 'the ambitious man whose slogan is "either Caesar or nothing"', who, after he does not get to be Caesar (or in our case, autonomous human being), 'he now cannot bear to be himself'.[30]

And now here is the central point, the heart of the internal conflict of the *cor curvum in se*. For *the self he is and cannot bear to be, is precisely the self that wills to be itself*. This is what Kierkegaard means by the 'sickness unto death'; it is a sickness that is always only *unto* death, and that can never pass over into it because the despairing self that cannot bear to be itself (in the face of the Counter-logos) is the very same self that wills to be itself, and that prohibits this from happening. This utterly unique inability to die, within the self that cannot bear to be itself, is precisely the torment and inner contradiction of despair. 'When death is the greatest danger, we hope for life; but when we learn to know the even greater danger, we hope for death. When the danger is so great that death becomes the hope, then despair is the hopelessness of not being able to die.'[31] This is the impossible conundrum of the state of being in 'despair over oneself' which 'Who are you?' in its first articulation announces.

Yet even as this question 'Who are you?' is spoken initially as no more than an expression of 'despair over oneself', it nevertheless marks an extremely important station on the way from autonomous human being to creaturely human being and to penultimacy. For even though the despair is 'over oneself', nevertheless because it is for the first time *recognized as* despair over oneself *even in willing to be oneself*, or because it is recognized for the first time as the *possibility of a misrelation* within the self *even as the self wills to be itself*, therefore it signals the ascendancy from the actuality of despair (in which the self does not recognize its despair or misrelation) to the recognition of the possibility of despair and as such the recognition of

---

30. Kierkegaard, *The Sickness unto Death*, p. 19.
31. Kierkegaard, *The Sickness unto Death*, p. 18.

the possibility of sin, and thus also the readiness for repentance and faith. 'Who are you?' is thus shown indeed to be *both* 'the question of dethroned reason, appalled and languishing, *and* it is also the question of faith'.[32]

It is here perhaps more than anywhere that Luther's '*Pecca fortiter, sed fortius fide et gaude in Christo*'[33] must be given fullest force. For the bolder this movement from the actuality of despair, in which the self is blind to its sin, into the possibility of despair, in which the self becomes conscious of its sin, the greater the readiness for genuine repentance and the gift of faith by grace alone. The bolder the ascendancy into the possibility of sin from its actuality or into the consciousness of it from blindness to it, the greater the consciousness also that this is *original* sin: that is, in the Kierkegaardian sense that the self alone is the *origin* of it, that this 'original sin' has not come upon the self as a normal sickness from outside the self, such that the self could be absolved of responsibility for it, but that this sin *originates* in the self itself as a misrelation.[34] The distinction I am pointing to here is also expressed by Kierkegaard as the difference between despair *over* and despair *of*.

> We despair *over* that which binds us in despair – over a misfortune, over the earthly, over capital loss, etc. – but we despair *of* that which, rightly understood, releases a person from despair of the eternal, of his salvation etc . . . And the haziness, particularly in all the lower forms of despair, is that he so passionately and clearly sees and knows *over* what he despairs, but *of* what he despairs evades him. The condition for healing is always this repenting *of*.[35]

So then, this brings an important clarity to Luther's declaration cited above. To despair *over* is to sin timidly, whereas to despair *of* is precisely to sin boldly, and thus to prepare the way for repentance.

For in the same way, repenting *of* the misrelation that one *is*, rather than merely repenting *over* the misfortune that this misrelation has wrought, always presupposes such a despairing *of*, presupposes a

---

32. Bonhoeffer, 'Vorlesung "Christologie"', p. 282.
33. 'Sin boldly, but believe and rejoice in Christ more boldly still.'
34. 'Once the misrelation, despair, has come about, does it continue as a matter of course? No, it does not continue as a matter of course; if the misrelation continues, it is not attributable to the misrelation [despair, and later, sin] but to the relation that relates itself to itself. That is, every time the misrelation manifests itself and every moment it exists, it must be traced back to the relation . . . Every actual moment of despair is traceable to possibility; every moment he is in despair he is bringing it upon himself. It is always in the present tense' (Kierkegaard, *The Sickness unto Death*, pp. 16–17).
35. Kierkegaard, *Papirer*, VIII B, p. 156, cited in *The Sickness unto Death*, p. 153, within the supplement 'Entries from Kierkegaard's Journals and Papers', pp. 139–65.

pecca fortiter in the most robust Lutheran sense of the term. Repentance *over* aspires to a state of resolution, existential quietude, becoming whole, holism. Repentance *of*, by contrast, must leave the self utterly at the mercy of the reconciliation of God, in the face of the intractable non-resolution of which the self is now conscious in its own being *as* a misrelation. Holism is powerless here. No matter how broad it reaches, it cannot encompass the non-resolution that the despairing self is. Indeed, pervasive holism itself can be seen as precisely the quintessential activity of this very misrelating self, seeking at all costs to understand itself autonomously as a resolution, or out of itself. What is required by contrast is nothing less than the reconciliation of the still-despairing self, which *cannot bear to be the self it wills to be*, to the power that established it.

One might say as such that asking 'Who are you?', in this 'bold' sense of despairing *of* the misrelation that the self is, places the questioner into a state of ontological risk that puts the old autonomous self-understanding in jeopardy. Yet this very *despairing of*, this very *pecca fortiter* actually prepares the way (and now already in a genuinely penultimate sense of that term) to a new kind of self-understanding through the resulting readiness for a genuine repentance *of*. The new kind of self-understanding is this: that I have my being from God, and that if I have my being from God and not from myself, therefore I cannot understand myself from out of myself but only from God. And what occurs here is the inception of a genuinely new existence, a whole new manner of being, which has moved ontologically, yet with full empirical continuity (i.e., *really*), from an autonomous way of being human to a creaturely way of being human. It is important to recognize that this movement from the actuality of despair to the possibility of despair, from despairing *over* to despairing *of*, and from repenting *over* to repenting *of*, does not occur merely as an abstract, 'possible', timeless 'existential' movement in which all is now theoretically well and one can be ushered into a kind of sublimity of faith and worship. The movement demands rather a real transformation or reorientation[36] ethically

---

36. I borrow this term from Daniel W. Hardy, whose deployment of it in the context of worship has strong affinities with what I am trying to do here in the reorientation to creaturely being. Worship can be seen as the supreme penultimate act; that which is worshipped is the ultimate. 'Worship itself is the recognition of ontological position and movement of that which is worshipped, and it entails the proportioning of human knowledge and behaviour to the being and activity of that which is recognized . . . In directed openness to this divine dynamic order there also occurs an ontological movement in those who recognize it, whose existence is totally oriented to that which is recognized, in a total alteration of affection which brings about a habit of life . . . So it is that in worship, cognition

and ontologically, yet in the full empirical continuity of space and time, from an autonomous way of being human to a creaturely way of being human, that is, from self-enclosedness to penultimacy, and the movement or reorientation is impossible apart from the passage through despair.

4 Penultimacy and Christian thinking

We must now ask where all of this brings us with respect to our broader concerns about Christian thinking. In order to address this, let me offer a brief synopsis in two or three paragraphs of the basic ground we have covered, before drawing some conclusions. We are asking about how theological discourse can be genuine, or in other words, how it could be possible at all to gain genuine reference to God who is transcendent, incomprehensible and hidden. If this is to be genuine reference – and it must be if theology is to keep its integrity as *theo*logy – it will have to avoid three basic pitfalls. First, it cannot be reductionist, for this loses transcendence.[37] Secondly, it cannot be positivist, for this loses meaningful reference and rational integrity.[38] Thirdly, it cannot treat transcendence as a hypothetical 'as if', for this loses both genuine transcendence and real reference.[39] We have further determined that abstraction is a guarantee of immanence, a *logical* exclusion of transcendence, in a way that empirical reality is not, and so our attention must unavoidably be turned to empirical reality in the consideration of the question of reference to the transcendent. Again, we have not thereby shown how the real appearance or revelation of transcendence in history is *possible* (indeed there seems prima facie to be something of a contradiction here). We have merely said that only in empirical history could transcendence be encountered by humans as *real* and not abstract (if it is encounterable at all). And indeed, we find along these lines that the heart of the Christian gospel, the heart of orthodoxy, is that the Christian God is always God-for-me, God-with-us in empirical history, the referent

and ethics find *their* dynamic order.' Daniel W. Hardy, *God's Ways with the World: Thinking and Practising Christian Faith* (Edinburgh: T&T Clark, 1996), p. 14, original emphasis.
37. That is, transcendence must remain *genuine* transcendence, and may not be reconfigured as something merely about human consciousness or a world mystery.
38. That is, Christian thinking may not simply 'posit' God sheerly arbitrarily as a 'real' referent of theological discourse, in a way that entirely overrides questions of rational authority and responsibility, and declares itself utterly free of its scrutiny, while fundamentally appealing to rational authority in other ways.
39. That is, this is not the real transcendence that theology claims to be able speak of but merely an ideal, abstract 'transcendence' posited in order to give guidance to the understanding in other endeavours.

in its very *advent*, and not God in his self-existent unconditioned aseity. If the revelation of the transcendent God is truly to be the *revelation* of God to God's creation in any meaningful sense of this term, then it has to be the revelation of the transcendent God-with-us.[40]

But now what about reference to *this* transcendent 'in its very advent'? How can we speak about genuine reference to, or encounter with, the referent in its very advent without engaging in the very same reductionisms, positivisms, as 'if' projections, or other forms of abstraction that we faced in the original formulation of the question? Or in other words, how has the placement of the transcendence of God within history, in the life, death and resurrection of Jesus Christ, as demanded by Christian orthodoxy, helped this particular problem of Christian thinking at all, especially given that, as Marion reminds us, the transcendent (as the referent in its very advent) is both past (in its required empirical historicity) and completed (in the resurrection)? However, as we have scrutinized this whole method of enquiry more critically we have found that it reflects essentially a kind of questioning based on an autonomous way of being human, and thus the question itself is asked falsely. The question of reference to the transcendent can never be asked by autonomous human being because autonomous human being will by its very nature demand to encounter the transcendent as non-transcendent (even while perhaps giving an appearance of attempting to preserve transcendence), that is, as that which is classifiable within, or referenceable according to, some system of ordering. Or in other words, autonomous human being will always ask about the transcendent on its own terms and accordingly will not be searching for genuine transcendence at all. This is part of its despair.

Thus, an ontological transformation is required in the questioner's very self in order for genuine *theo*logical questioning to occur, an ontological reorientation involving a movement from an autonomous way of being human to a creaturely way of being human. This is a process in which the self learns, by a stirring of God's grace within it and through an emerging consciousness of intellectual and existential despair, to move from the intrinsically possessive questions of 'How?', of possibility, of immanence, to the one genuinely dispossessive and thus the only permissible transcendent question 'Who are you?' Here the self begins to recognize

---

40. Or as Barth puts this: 'God does not wish to know Himself without Himself giving us a part in this event in the grace of his revelation'; Karl Barth, *Church Dogmatics II.i* (Edinburgh: T&T Clark, 1957), p. 204.

truly that, because it has its being from God, therefore it can understand itself only from God.[41] And at this point something remarkable begins to occur.

For as I recognize, in a creaturely way of being human, which rests transparently in the power that established it, that what the question 'Who?' desires and searches for can never be expressed or contained in the intrinsically possessive answers that 'How?' and 'What?' kinds of questioning are capable of yielding; or, more specifically, as I recognize that the question 'Who is Jesus Christ for us today?' can never be answered by the question 'How is Jesus Christ real-ly present before me now in the least of these, the destitute, the sick, the dying?', or 'how is Jesus Christ really present where two or three are gathered in his name?', or 'how is Jesus Christ really present in the Eucharist?'; and as I thus ensure that my desire for the 'referent in its very advent' is never *anything* but a desire dispossessively for the 'Who?', and does not degenerate into questions of how this referent, which is both past (in empirical history) and completed (in the resurrection), can possibly be a real non-abstract referent today; in other words, as I recognize that I must indeed *ask* for the 'Who?' of dispossession but precisely thereby can never 'have' the 'Who?' (for I would always 'have' it only as a 'How?' or a 'What?' of possession); or as I recognize that I do and indeed must *desire* the referent in its very advent, but that I can never 'have' this referent in any sense that I could grasp as a *resolution* to or satisfaction of the questions of 'How' and 'What?'; as I recognize all of this, something remarkable and genuinely new begins to occur within my understanding of self and world, that is, within my very manner of existence or ontology.

The whole real world of human habitation, endeavour and possible experience now opens up as a penultimate, as the world of creaturely being, as that which has its being from God and therefore can be understood only from God, that is, only from the 'Who?' Or in other words, the whole empirical world, as manifest to my experience in the extensive magnitudes of space and time – this whole real world in which God himself became

---

41. This is not of course to contend that every instance of worship, prayer, participation in the sacrament, or a child's own genuinely childlike faith always includes or requires this actual process within Christian self-understanding. (Indeed that would be rare.) But we are speaking here about Christian thinking and our expectation that, when these Christian activities and ways of being are looked at more closely, they manifest an integrity that shows that they are not merely of human making, not merely reflective of secret, hidden ways of the world (world enigma), and that they must as such be able to demonstrate that integrity in a way that is recognizable and intelligible.

flesh – is suddenly set free and opened up *as the 'subject matter' within which and in relation to which this question 'Who are you?' must be asked*. Indeed, this new question of reference to the transcendent, 'Who are you?', can be asked *only* in the real empirical world and not in abstraction, because it is in empirical history and only in empirical history that God himself in Jesus Christ becomes incarnate and enters into the reality of the world. All of this brings a new and proper clarity to Bonhoeffer's controversial assertion that 'just as in Christ the reality of God entered into the reality of the world, so now too, what is Christian is to be found only in the worldly, the "supernatural" only in the natural, the holy only in the profane, the revelational only in the rational'.[42] What is most emphatically *not* being claimed here is that what is Christian is to be sought in 'cosmology', nor the supernatural in 'naturalism', nor the holy in 'secularism', nor the revelational in 'rationalism', still less that the supernatural just is the natural, or that the holy just is the worldly.

No, it is rather only as the worldly, the natural, the secular and the rational are participated in and lived *in a certain way* – in creaturely directedness towards Christ, the referent in its very advent, centred around the question 'Who are you?' – that the supernatural is given in the natural, the revelational in the rational[43] and so on. Understood as such, however, the real *penultimate* force of Bonhoeffer's point should not be lost, that 'what is Christian is [indeed] to be found *only* in the worldly, the "supernatural" *only* in the natural, the holy *only* in the profane, the revelational *only* in the rational'. For what we most manifestly do *not* 'have' is the revelational, we do *not* 'have' the holy, we do *not* 'have' the supernatural or the divine. Rather, the 'extreme limit' of what we do 'have' is always *only* the penultimate, and this penultimate is never anything but the lived, empirical, creaturely directedness and orientation of *all* that we do 'have' – secular, natural, rational, worldly – towards Christ, centred around the one true question of transcendence 'Who are you?'

There are two vitally important caveats, however, that must be re-emphasized as we apply all of this to Christian thinking in terms of penultimacy. The first is that orthodox Christology actually demands the kind

---

42. Bonhoeffer, *Ethik*, p. 44.
43. Kant's point about the necessary directedness of reason back to its *empirical use* should not be forgotten here. Yet his dictum 'all cognition of things out of mere pure understanding or pure reason is nothing but sheer illusion and there is truth only in experience' does not mean a demotion of logic or mathematics as we saw in chapter 6. I address this somewhat further in the following paragraph.

of empirical realism along roughly Kantian lines as I developed this in chapter 6.[44] The reason for this is that any other kind of view, whether based roughly on 'externalist' realisms or on 'internalist' idealisms (anti-realisms), will, as we have seen, lead ultimately either to some form of dogmatism or scepticism. Both dogmatism and scepticism in turn undermine the integrity of empirical reality: dogmatism by alleging a 'truer' reality of supra-empirical or supra-spatio-temporal metaphysical 'essences' beyond the contingencies of sense experience; scepticism by doubting the reality or genuineness of the world of human experience because of the same fallibility of the empirical senses. What this means theologically is that both dogmatism and scepticism (including the externalisms-realisms and internalisms-idealisms from which they spring) will lead unavoidably to Christological heresies along Docetic lines,[45] because in either case the empirical world of spatio-temporal human history and experience, in which God became flesh, is demoted to some level or other of mere seeming.

The further, positive aspect of this is that the kind of Christian thinking I am advocating here in terms of penultimacy not only meets this Christological demand of empirical realism, but it does so with a breadth of scope and depth of texture that captures and reflects the whole world of possible human experience and real endeavour in all of its multi-faceted temporal and spatial richness. For the penultimate precisely does not permit a view of empirical historical reality as that which is 'merely' apparent, or a restriction of reality merely to the five senses, as if the empirical world of real human experience, the empirical world of human striving and endeavour, in the fullest social, ethical, political, aesthetic, intellectual and even religious senses of this, the empirical world of human acts of kindness and goodness, the empirical world of human tragedy, suffering and death, as if this were all *merely* apparent, and the true reality of things were to be found by somehow dispensing with the empirical or by getting beyond it, or even by not treating it as central. No, Christian thinking guided by penultimacy demands that the empirical world of possible experience *just is* the *real-ly* apparent world: it is the *inherently manifested*

---

44. It is absolutely vital, once again, to recognize that 'empirical reality' here is *not* a restriction of reality to the limits of the five senses. Empirical realism is not 'mere empiricism' leading either to positivistic materialisms or sceptical idealisms, but exactly the inversion of both of these. Empirical realism must be understood in the fully integrated and multifaceted Kantian sense as discussed at length in chapter 6.

45. That is, the view that the body of Christ was not real but merely apparent or 'seeming'.

world in which God himself, the ultimate, is made *really* manifest, *really* apparent, takes on *real* bodily form in Jesus Christ, 'in the likeness of sinful flesh' (Romans 8:3).[46]

Secondly, it is crucially important to understand that this penultimate way of viewing or thinking is not just another 'worldview', not just another anthropological or philosophical perspective like realism, idealism, anti-realism, pragmatism, existentialism and so on. In fact – and this must be maintained conscientiously and in full earnestness – penultimacy is at bottom not a view of the world at all but the search for God. Yet precisely *as* this search for God, the real, spatio-temporal world of possible empirical experience is propelled sharply and unrelentingly into the foreground. Precisely as I set my mind on things above (Colossians 3:2), I find that I am brought inexorably back to the things of this earth ('as you did it to one of the least of these, you did it to me', Matthew 25:40). And this is exactly why penultimacy neither seeks to add anything to empirical reality in order to make it 'ready' or 'enfranchised' for religious or theological awareness, nor does penultimacy try to abstract anything from empirical reality in order to render it 'purified' or suitable for religious participation or theological handling. The empirical world of space and time, the inherently manifested world of possible experience and of human habitation, *this* is the real world into which the reality of God has come in Jesus Christ in the flesh, in *his own* empirical history, and therefore also in mine.

But note now what this means. It means that the believing questioner must not seek to become detached from this world or the things of the world, either its joys or its cares, but must rather and in a true sense become much more deeply, passionately (empirically) and properly attached to it *as* a penultimate. This is no licence for carnality. It is instead a reassertion of the biblical and orthodox teaching that the real detachment that must occur here is precisely the detachment from the false self, that is, from the despairing way of being human, from the autonomous way of being human, and the movement towards a creaturely way of being human.

> You have taken off your old self with its practices and put on the
> new self, which is being renewed in knowledge in the image of its
> Creator (Colossians 3: 9–10).

---

46. In Jesus Christ God himself took on real 'human form', became real 'sinful flesh', and 'lived among us', not in timelessness as a sublime unifying principle or symbol, but 'for awhile' (in *time*) so that we might be 'reconciled by Christ's physical body through death' (Philippians 2:7; Romans 8:3; John 1:14; Colossians 1:22).

> You were taught, with regard to your former way of life, to put off your old self . . . to be made new in the attitude of your minds; and to put on the new self, created to be like God in true righteousness and holiness (Ephesians 4:22–24).

Indeed, a *creaturely* way of being human, essentially *means* the attachment to God's creation as a penultimate. Thomas Merton makes exactly this point in his advice to those who might be tempted to seek the 'contemplative way' in abstraction:

> Detachment from things does not mean setting up a contradiction between 'things' and 'God' as if God were another 'thing' and as if His creatures were His rivals. We do not detach ourselves from things in order to attach ourselves to God, but rather we become detached from our [false] selves in order to see and use all things for God.[47]

This can be stated even more strongly in its positive aspect. The believing questioner must seek to 'desire' the world, must seek truly and passionately to love his or her given creaturely life, with the same kind of intensity and depth of attachment that is manifest in Gethsemane by the very Creator himself become flesh: the deep extent of the Creator's love of his own creaturely human life and creaturely world is manifest here when he asks if it is possible that the cup of his human death be taken away from him. Again Bonhoeffer's words are especially apt:

> It is only when one understands the unutterability of the name of God that one may come to speak the name of Jesus Christ; it is only when one loves this life and the earth so deeply that without them everything seems to be lost and at an end that one may believe in the resurrection of the dead and in a new world; it is only when one submits to the law of God that one may indeed come to speak of grace . . . One cannot and must not speak the last word before the penultimate word. We live in the penultimate and believe in the ultimate.[48]

This focus on the penultimate allows us to address certain problematical areas in theology in new ways. First, Christian thinking in terms of penultimacy enables a new kind of confidence and straightforward openness for theology in embracing the full integrity and authority of

---

47. Thomas Merton, *New Seeds of Contemplation* (New York: New Directions, 1972), p. 21; actually, all of chapters 1, 4 and 5 in this volume resonate strongly with what I am saying here about penultimacy.

48. Dietrich Bonhoeffer, *Widerstand und Ergebung*, Christian Gremmels, Eberhard Bethge and Renate Bethge in collaboration with Ilse Tödt (eds.), Dietrich Bonhoeffer Werke, 16 vols. (Munich: Christian Kaiser Verlag, 1998), vol. VIII, p. 226, emphasis added.

nature and reason[49] without fear of jeopardizing the *mystery* of Christ that must remain the heart of the gospel. For the mystery of Christ is not hidden in secret esoteric depth which requires special aptitudes for apprehending it. Empirical reality is not just a 'front' for some deeper supra-sensible reality in which the mystery of Christ is 'really' hidden as something 'subterranean' within immanence. No, the mystery of Christ is hidden in empirical history *as* empirical reality, 'in the likeness of sinful flesh' (Romans 8:3). In other words, empirical reality – in its very spatio-temporal manifestedness as a penultimate – is *itself* 'the dawn and approach of the mystery as such'.[50] This now means further, for example, that the penultimate emphasis on the empirically historical in no way undermines the reality of the Church or the sacrament as the mystical body of Christ in the world. It rather reinforces its reality by assuring that the mystical body is never mistaken for a merely metaphysical superstition or cosmic principle, but is rather the real, tangible presence of God in the Church and the sacrament in empirical history as a penultimate. Nor does this undercut the reality and important place of mystical contemplation or the *disciplina arcani*; for these now become precisely special and penetratingly meaningful ways of asking the question 'Who are you?' Nor does it subvert the place of the more charismatic gifts in the life of the community of faith. Indeed it not only reinforces these, in their genuine manifestations, as not mere religious or paranormal phenomena, but it also suggests new ways of articulating the kind of non-constricting normative centre that a genuinely authoritative 'charismatic theology' would seem to require and which is today still lacking. Likewise, symbolism, metaphor, imagery, iconography are opened up to a new freedom, as now they can turn their attention away, somewhat, from the often excessive preoccupation with the problem of how these ways of speaking could ever be successful with regard to the transcendent. All of this allows us to espouse orthodoxy with a greater dynamic authority and confidence, and in genuinely integrated ways, without resorting to isolationism or decreeing a kind of scholarly supremacy for theology over all other disciplines in which orthodoxy remains immune from attack, but thereby also from correction, thus undermining its own integrity.

49. Including reason's rightful demands of universality and necessity in its empirical use, as explained in chapter 6.
50. Karl Rahner, 'The Hermeneutics of Eschatological Assertions', in K. Smith (tr.), *Theological Investigations Volume 4, More Recent Writings* (London: DLT, 1966), pp. 323–46.

But everything depends on the centring of all Christian thinking and theological questioning around the one true question of 'reference' to the transcendent: 'Who are you?' This is not only a theological requirement but an empirical fact. The searching questioner need only pursue these difficulties for a time apart from that centredness in order to experience the re-emergence of despair within his or her own empirical awareness, and the renewed need to reach for reductionist and positivistic 'resolutions'. By contrast, Christian thinking in terms of penultimacy centred around the question 'Who are you?' expresses a relationality that, precisely in its empirically real focus,[51] is always directed more deeply and engagingly to the Christological heart of the gospel, always more positively and passionately to the search for God in the world, and yet for that very reason always more earnestly to the kind of ontological dispossession in which all questions of act and being, possibility and essence, 'How?' and 'What?' fall away, and in the face of the Counter-logos only one question redemptively remains: 'Who are you?', which is the question of repentance, of rational silence, of transcendence and of worship.

---

51. And again, this must always be understood in the fully textured and integrated sense as presented in chapter 6.

Bibliography

Allison, Henry, *Kant's Transcendental Idealism* (New Haven: Yale University Press, 1983).

Barth, Karl, *Church Dogmatics II.i* (Edinburgh: T&T Clark, 1957).

Das Wort Gottes und die Theologie, Gesammelte Vorträge (Munich: Christian Kaiser Verlag, 1924).

Bartsch, H. W. (ed.), *Kerygma and Myth I* (London: SPCK, 1953).

Kerygma and Myth II (London: SPCK, 1962).

Bonhoeffer, Dietrich, *Akt und Sein*, Hans-Richard Reuther (ed.), Dietrich Bonhoeffer Werke, 16 vols. (Munich: Christian Kaiser Verlag, 1988), vol. II.

Barcelona, Berlin, Amerika 1928–1931, Reinhart Staats, Hans Christoph von Hase in collaboration with Holger Roggelin and Matthias Wünsche (eds.), Dietrich Bonhoeffer Werke, 16 vols. (Munich: Christian Kaiser Verlag, 1991), vol. X.

Ethik, Ilse Tödt, Heinz Eduard Tödt, Ernst Feil and Clifford Green (eds.), Dietrich Bonhoeffer Werke, 16 vols. (Munich: Christian Kaiser Verlag, 1998), vol. VI.

Nachfolge, Martin Kuske and Ilse Tödt (eds.), Dietrich Bonhoeffer Werke, 16 vols. (Munich: Christian Kaiser Verlag, 1994), vol. IV.

Schöpfung und Fall, Martin Rueter and Ilse Tödt (eds.), Dietrich Bonhoeffer Werke, 16 vols. (Munich: Christian Kaiser Verlag, 1989), vol. III.

'Vorlesung "Christologie"', in Carsten Nicolaisen and Ernst-Albert Scharffenorth (eds.), *Berlin, 1932–1933*, Dietrich Bonhoeffer Werke, 16 vols. (Munich: Christian Kaiser Verlag, 1991), vol. XII.

Widerstand und Ergebung, Christian Gremmels, Eberhard Bethge and Renate Bethge in collaboration with Ilse Tödt (eds.), Dietrich Bonhoeffer Werke, 16 vols. (Munich: Christian Kaiser Verlag, 1998), vol. VIII.

Brunner, Emil, *Reason and Revelation*, Olive Wyon (tr.) (Philadelphia: Westminster Press, 1946).

Caygill, Howard, *A Kant Dictionary* (Oxford: Blackwell, 1995).

Clifford, James, and George E. Marcus (eds.), *Writing Culture: The Poetics and Politics of Ethnography* (Berkeley: University of California Press, 1986).

Craig, Edward (ed.), *Routledge Encyclopedia of Philosophy*, 10 vols. (London: Routledge, 1998).

Davidson, Donald, *Inquiries into Truth and Interpretation* (Oxford: Oxford University Press, 1984).

Subjective, Intersubjective, Objective (Oxford: Oxford University Press, 2002).

Derrida, Jacques, 'A "Madness" Must Watch Over Thinking', *Points...Interviews* (Palo Alto: Stanford University Press, 1995), pp. 339–43.

Derrida, Jacques, 'The Principle of Reason: The University in the Eyes of its Pupils', *Diacritics* 19 (spring 1983), pp. 3–20.

Descombes, Vincent, *The Mind's Provisions* (Princeton: Princeton University Press, 2001). *Modern French Philosophy* (Cambridge: Cambridge University Press, 1980).

Dews, Peter, *Logics of Disintegration: Post-structuralist Thought and the Claims of Critical Theory* (London: Verso, 1987).

Ferry, Luc, *Man Made God* (Chicago: University of Chicago Press, 2002). *The New Ecological Order* (Chicago: University of Chicago Press, 1992).

Ferry, Luc, and Alain Renaut, tr. Mary H. S. Cattani, *French Philosophy of the Sixties* (Amherst: University of Massachusetts Press, 1985).

Findlay, J. N., 'Kant Today', in P. Laberge et al. (eds.), *Proceedings of the Ottawa Congress on Kant in the Anglo-American and Continental Traditions Held October 10–14, 1974* (Ottawa: University of Ottawa Press, 1976), pp. 3–16.

Ford, David, *Self and Salvation: Being Transformed* (Cambridge: Cambridge University Press, 1999).

Foucault, Michel, *The Order of Things* (New York: Random House, 1970).

Gilson, Etienne, *The Unity of Philosophical Experience* (New York: Scribner's, 1950).

Guttenplan, Samuel (ed.), *A Companion to the Philosophy of Mind* (Oxford: Blackwell, 1995).

Hacking, Ian, 'Is the End in Sight for Epistemology?', *The Journal of Philosophy* 77. 10 (October 1980), pp. 579–88.

Hardy, Daniel W., *God's Ways with the World: Thinking and Practising Christian Faith* (Edinburgh: T&T Clark, 1996).

Hatfield, Gary, 'The Cognitive Faculties', in *Cambridge History of Seventeenth Century Philosophy* (Cambridge: Cambridge University Press, 1998), Vol. II, ch. 28.

Heine, Heinrich, *Zur Geschichte der Religion und Philosophie in Deutschland* (Stuttgart: Reclam, 1977 (1834)); tr. J. Snodgrass as *Religion and Philosophy in Germany* (Boston: Beacon Press, 1959 (1882)).

Janz, Paul, 'Radical Orthodoxy and the New Culture of Obscurantic', in *Modern Theology* (Oxford: Blackwell, 2004).

Kant, Immanuel, *Critique of Pure Reason*, Paul Guyer and Allen W. Wood (tr. and eds.) (Cambridge: Cambridge University Press, 1998).

Dreams of a Spirit-Seer Elucidated by Dreams of Metaphysics, in David Walford in collaboration with Ralf Meerbote (tr. and eds.), *Theoretical Philosophy 1755–1770* (Cambridge: Cambridge University Press, 1992), pp. 301–59.

Grounding for the Metaphysics of Morals, tr. James W. Ellington (Indianapolis: Hackett, 1981).

Kant: Philosophical Correspondence 1759–99, Arnulf Zweig (tr. and ed.) (Chicago: University of Chicago Press, 1967).

Kant: Political Writings (second edition), H. S. Reiss ed., (Cambridge: Cambridge University Press, 1991).

Prolegomena to any Future Metaphysics, Gary Hatfield (ed.) (Cambridge: Cambridge University Press, 1997).

'What is Orientation in Thinking?', in H. S. Reiss (ed.), *Kant: Political Writings* (second edition) (Cambridge: Cambridge University Press, 1991), pp. 237–49.

Kierkegaard, Søren, *The Sickness unto Death*, Howard V. Hong and Edna H. Hong (tr. and eds.) (Princeton: Princeton University Press, 1980).

Kuhn, Thomas, *The Structure of Scientific Revolutions* (Chicago: University of Chicago Press, 1962).

Kulp, Christopher, *The End of Epistemology: Dewey and his Current Allies on the Spectator Theory of Knowledge* (London: Greenwood Press, 1992).

Realism/Antirealism and Epistemology (Oxford: Rowman and Littlefield, 1997).

Levinas, Emmanuel, *Totality and Infinity*, A. Lingis (tr.) (Pittsburgh: Duquesne University Press, 1969).

Lyotard, Jean-Francois, *The Postmodern Condition: A Report on Knowledge*, Geoff Bennington and Brian Massumi (tr.) (Manchester: Manchester University Press, 1984).

MacKinnon, Donald, *Explorations in Theology* (London: SCM Press, 1979).

The Problem of Metaphysics (Cambridge: Cambridge University Press, 1974).

Marcus, George E., and Michael M. J. Fischer, *Anthropology as Cultural Critique: An Experimental Moment in the Human Sciences* (Chicago: University of Chicago Press, 1986).

Margolis, Joseph, *Pragmatism without Foundations: Reconciling Realism with Relativism* (Oxford: Blackwell, 1986).

Marion, Jean-Luc, *God without Being* (Chicago: University of Chicago Press, 1982).

Milbank, John, 'The Theological Critique of Philosophy in Hamann and Jacobi', in John Milbank, Catherine Pickstock and Graham Ward (eds.), *Radical Orthodoxy* (London: Routledge, 1999), pp. 21–37.

Mure, G. R. G., *The Philosophy of Hegel* (London: Oxford University Press, 1965).

Nagel, Thomas, *The Last Word* (Oxford: Oxford University Press, 1997).

The View from Nowhere (Oxford: Oxford University Press, 1986).

Norris, Christopher, *Derrida* (London: Fontana, 1987).

New Idols of the Cave: On the Limits of Anti-realism (Manchester: Manchester University Press, 1997).

Palmquist, Stephen, 'Kant's Theocentric Metaphysics', *Analele Universitatii Din Timisoara* 4 (1992), pp. 55–70.

Papineau, David, 'Does the Sociology of Science Discredit Science?', in Robert Nola (ed.), *Relativism and Realism in Science* (Dordrecht: Kluwer Academic Publishers, 1988), pp. 37–57.

Pavel, Thomas, 'The Present Debate: News from France', *Diacritics* 19. 1 (spring 1989), pp. 17–32.

Pickstock, Catherine, *After Writing: On the Liturgical Consummation of Philosophy* (Oxford: Blackwell, 1997).

Polkinghorne, John, *Science and Theology, an Introduction* (London: SPCK/Fortress, 1998).

Putnam, Hilary, 'Comments and Replies', in Peter Clark and Bob Hale (eds.), *Reading Putnam* (Oxford: Blackwell, 1994), pp. 242–95.

'The Meaning of "Meaning"', in *Language, Mind and Knowledge*, Minnesota Studies in the Philosophy of Science Vol. VII (Minneapolis: University of Minnesota Press, 1975).

Realism and Reason, Philosophical Papers (Cambridge: Cambridge University Press, 1983).

Realism with a Human Face (London: Harvard University Press, 1990).

Reason, Truth, and History (Cambridge: Cambridge University Press, 1981).

Representation and Reality (Cambridge, MA: MIT Press, 1988).

Quine, W. V. O., 'Two Dogmas of Empiricism', in *From a Logical Point of View* (Cambridge, MA: Harvard University Press, 1961), pp. 20–46.

Rahner, Karl, 'The Hermeneutics of Eschatological Assertions', in K. Smith (tr.), *Theological Investigations Volume 4, More Recent Writings* (London: DLT, 1966), pp. 323–46.

Ritschl, Dietrich, *The Logic of Theology* (Philadelphia: Fortress Press, 1987).

Rorty, Richard, *Consequences of Pragmatism* (Minneapolis: University of Minnesota Press, 1982).

'Realism, Anti-realism, and Pragmatism', in Christopher Kulp (ed.), *Realism/Antirealism and Epistemology* (Oxford: Rowman and Littlefield, 1997), pp. 149–71.

Philosophy and the Mirror of Nature (Oxford: Blackwell, 1980).

Saussure, Ferdinand de, *Course in General Linguistics*, tr. Wade Baskin (New York: McGraw Hill, 1966).

Searle, John, *The Construction of Social Reality* (London: Penguin, 1996).

Sellars, Wilfrid, *Empiricism and the Philosophy of Mind* (Cambridge, MA: Harvard University Press, 1997 (1956)).

Smith, Ronald (ed.), *World Come of Age* (London: Collins, 1967).

Strawson, Peter, *The Bounds of Sense* (London: Methuen, 1966).

Taylor, Charles, 'Understanding in Human Science', *Review of Metaphysics* 34 (1980), pp. 25–38.

Tracy, David, 'The Post-Modern Re-Naming of God as Incomprehensible and Hidden', *Cross Currents* (spring–summer 2000), pp. 1–7.

Walsh, W. H., *Metaphysics* (London: Hutchinson University Library, 1963).

Wolff, Robert Paul, *Kant's Theory of Mental Activity* (Cambridge, MA: Harvard University Press, 1963).

Zelgin, Catherine, 'Epistemology's End', in *Considered Judgment* (Princeton: Princeton University Press, 1996), pp. 3–20.

Index